Contents

Assessment of Performance

Science in Schools

Department of

y of London.

Her Majesty's Stationery Office

© *Crown copyright 1982*
First published 1982

The monitoring teams

Much of the work described in this report is the product of planning and development in which all members of the teams and the Steering Group on Science have had a part. The teams are based at two centres, at Chelsea College, University of London and at the University of Leeds. The work of monitoring at three ages (11, 13, 15) in science is divided between these centres so that the responsibility for monitoring at the lower two age groups rests with Chelsea and the responsibility for monitoring at age 15 and for the data processing and analysis rests with Leeds.

Chelsea team: Paul Black, director
Brenda Denvir (Jan to Aug 1981)
Wynne Harlen, deputy director
Cynthia Millband (1980–1981)
Patricia Murphy
Tony Orgee (from Feb 1981)
David Palacio (from 1980)
Terry Russell (from Sept 1981)
Beta Schofield
Ardrie VanderWaal (1979–1980)

Leeds team: David Layton, director
Rosalind Driver, deputy director
Roger Hartley, deputy director
Richard Gott (from 1980)
Jennifer Head (from 1981) (statistician)
Sandra Johnson (statistician)
Brian Maher (from 1979) (programmer)
Christopher Worsley
Fiona Wylie (from 1979)

ISBN 0 11 270388 7

Tables

Figures

Preface

This first report by the Assessment of Performance Unit on the performance of thirteen year olds in science covers a survey of pupils in England conducted in June 1980 by the monitoring team at Chelsea College.

The approach to science monitoring adopted by the APU Science Steering Group and developed by the monitoring teams at Chelsea College, University of London and the University of Leeds contains some novel features — notably the innovatory system of separating the variety of activities contributing to scientific performance into categories for separate assessment and the emphasis on the processes of scientific thinking.

The report describes how a national sample of thirteen year olds, drawn from all levels of ability and from different school backgrounds, coped with a wide range of questions covering scientific processes and knowledge. It also contains information about the curricular organisation and the physical, financial and human resources for science activities in the schools surveyed. The authors invite discussion on the interpretation of the survey results, but at this stage do not themselves draw conclusions from the results. We hope that those to whom this report is addressed — educationalists, parents, and those concerned with the provision of resources centrally and locally — will consider how far the standards of performance revealed in this report are acceptable.

The APU is undertaking a series of annual surveys which should build up a clear picture of what children can achieve in science at the ages of 11, 13 and 15. It would be unwise to draw firm conclusions on the strength of the results of a single survey.

This report is intended for the non-specialist reader as well as for those with a professional interest in the subject. We hope that readers will find the report interesting in itself, and will also be encouraged to relate it to APU reports of surveys in other areas of the curriculum. A report on the performance of 11 year olds in science was published in December 1981 and a report on 15 year olds' performance will follow later this year.

Jean Dawson   John Graham
Joint heads of the Assessment of Performance Unit

Acknowledgements

The work described in this report is the product of planning and development in which many members of the monitoring teams and of the Steering Group for Science have taken part. The teams were based at two centres: at Chelsea College, University of London and at the University of Leeds. Responsibility for monitoring at ages 11 and 13 is held at Chelsea and for monitoring at age 15 and for data processing and analysis at Leeds.

We should like to acknowledge the help of visitors from academic institutions overseas and, in particular, that of Dr John Theobald of Monash University, Australia, who worked at Chelsea over an extended period on the development of the bank of questions used at age 13.

We are indebted to Mrs Barbara Bloomfield and to other members of the Monitoring Services Unit at the National Foundation for Educational Research for drawing the sample, corresponding with the survey schools, organising itineraries for administrators of practical tests and arranging for the distribution, administration and return of the written tests.

Officers of strategically situated local education authorities helped to arrange the release of science teachers from school duties so that they were able to conduct the practical tests involved in the survey. Their cooperation and support, and that of Headteachers and staff of schools involved, were an essential element of the monitoring exercise. The teachers who undertook to administer the practical tests played an important and strenuous part in the survey. Thanks are also due to those who marked the written tests.

Help in the form of criticism and advice has been received from many areas of science education, including liaison groups of teachers who have worked regularly with members of the teams to improve the quality of the monitoring. Many of our colleagues at the Centre for Science and Mathematics Education at Chelsea have contributed expertise in fields as widely different as question shredding and the video-taping of pupils' investigations. Others have given us patient support over technical matters — preparation of apparatus, typing questions, and the like. The large-scale provision of apparatus for practical testing was undertaken by Philip Harris Ltd. and the flexibility shown by the members of staff responsible in the face of the steadily increasing scale of the exercise has been very much appreciated.

None of the work would have been fruitful without the cooperation of the pupils who took part in the survey and the teachers in the sample schools who administered the tests.

Introduction

The survey

This report describes the design and results of the survey which was carried out in England on behalf of the Department of Education and Science in June 1980 to assess the performance in science of boys and girls aged 13. The corresponding surveys of pupils aged 11 and 15 were carried out in Wales and Northern Ireland as well as in England. In future, surveys at age 13 will also cover all three areas.

The design of the assessment was the responsibility of the monitoring teams which are based at Chelsea College, London University, and at Leeds University. The teams worked within guidelines established by the Science Steering Group set up by the Assessment of Performance Unit. The preparation of the tests used in this particular survey was the responsibility of members of the Chelsea team, while the analysis of the results was carried out at Leeds.

Earlier APU surveys, in mathematics and language, have not been conducted with pupils aged 13 but only with those of 11 and 15. The decision to include assessment at age 13 was taken because many pupils of this age will have had a similar course in science for two years, whereas at ages 11 and 15 there is great variation in science provision.

The object of the assessment was not to report the performance of individual pupils, but rather to give an overall picture of performance of 13 year old pupils. For this purpose, a sample of about 11 000 pupils was randomly selected. It included boys and girls from all kinds of schools scattered over the whole of England.

Many different packages of questions, both written and practical, were used in the survey, reflecting a number of different aspects of performance in science. Different packages were given to different sub-samples of pupils, so that although few pupils were tested for more than an hour, the composite effect was similar to that of a 'test' lasting for about 19 hours.

Individual pupils who took part in the survey remain anonymous. Their names are known only to a few teachers in their own school. Similarly, neither individual schools nor individual local education authorities can be identified with the results. Indeed, the results of individuals are meaningless since no single pupil, and no single school, saw more than a small fraction of the complete range of questions used in the survey. It is not until the results are assembled that a comprehensive picture emerges.

The purpose of the assessment

Public examinations give information about the performance of some pupils with respect to certain clearly defined content areas at age 16. Even here, however, there is no one test in science to which every pupil can be referred; and the same level of attainment, in terms of GCE or CSE grades, may be achieved by the application of quite different skills and abilities. At age 13 (and, of course, age 11) there are in any case no nationally applied tests. One of the purposes of the survey was to make available information about the general spread and level of response of pupils of all abilities and school backgrounds to a set of common questions. To make this information more useful questions were divided into groups each designed to assess a different specified aspect of scientific activity. As a consequence, the result is a profile report: a profile not of one pupil, but of the population as a whole.

The assessment categories

In order to fulfil the purpose described, it is necessary that the wide variety of activities which contribute to scientific performance be separated and sorted into a number of categories, each of which can be separately assessed. The profile is then built up from the results, category by category.

Initially six main categories were identified. (See the summary which follows) However, it soon became clear that they were too broad for the purpose, and so most of them were further sub-divided. This report describes performances for the 17 sub-categories which resulted, and it is these which constitute the facets of the profile.

In certain sub-categories all the questions appear to contribute to a coherent whole. Most of these are represented in the survey by many questions and in such cases overall sub-category performance levels are reported in addition to those for a few illustrative questions. In some, however, it was not possible to include a sufficient number of questions in a single year to justify the reporting of an overall performance level for the sub-category. In such cases the questions are reported individually. In other sub-categories it does not seem sensible to generalise — for example when a question appears to test something unique to itself; in such cases the sub-category is represented by one or two questions only, and the questions are reported separately and in detail.

Some of the skills and abilities involved can be assessed only by asking pupils to perform a practical task, and so in three of the main categories, this mode of testing is used.

However, the first monitoring of one of these (ie category 6) was deferred for age 13 until the 1981 survey. A full account of the categories used and their relationship to content is given in Chapter 6.

Sampling procedures

[1] Pupils' ages ranged from 12 years ten months to 13 years nine months.

For the purpose, it is not necessary to test every pupil in the age group. A sufficiently random balanced sample can adequately represent the whole population of 13 year olds.[1] In the 1980 survey, such a sample of about 11 000 pupils was divided into sub-samples, chosen so that each reflected the composition of the whole with respect to several relevant facts. It was arranged, for example, that each contained the same proportion of pupils from given geographical areas as did the whole. The complete science test can also be split, and each section given to a different sub-sample. It is now possible to relate performance on each section of the test to each of the chosen factors, or stratifying variables.

Table 0.1 *Framework of categories and sub-categories*

Main categories	Sub-categories
1. Using symbolic representations *(written tests)*	α Reading information from graphs, tables and charts β Expressing information as graphs, tables and charts γ Using scientific symbols and conventions
2. Using apparatus and measuring instruments *(practical tests)*	α Using measuring instruments β Estimating quantities γ Following instructions for practical work
3. Using observation *(practical tests)*	α Using a branching key β Observing similarities and differences γ Interpreting observations
4. Interpretation and application *(written tests)*	(4α, β and γ are *not* dependent on taught science) α Describing and using patterns in information β Judging the applicability of a given generalisation γ Distinguishing degrees of inference (4δ and ε are dependent on taught science)* δ Making sense of information using science concepts ε Generating alternative hypotheses
5. Design of investigations *(written tests)*	α Identifying or proposing testable statements β Assessing experimental procedures γ Devising and describing investigations
6. Performance of investigations *(practical tests)*	

* A list of science concepts relevant to these sub-categories can be found in Chapter 6.

In the 1980 science survey, a two-stage process was used in the selection of the sample of pupils. In the first stage a random selection of schools was made, and in the second a random selection of 27 pupils from each of those schools. Details of the sampling procedure is to be found in Appendix 3. Some schools declined the invitation to take part in the survey. It was not possible, on this occasion, to take account of this, but investigations designed to assess the effects of such refusals on the sampling procedure are in progress. At least three different kinds of test package were sent to each of the schools that agreed to take part. A typical sub-sample of pupils, all receiving the same batch of questions, was made up of 720 pupils spread between 80 schools. Smaller sub-samples of about 500 pupils were used for practical tests, for financial reasons.

The drawing of the samples, correspondence with the schools and the printing, delivery and collection of the tests were organised by the Monitoring Services Unit of the National Foundation for Educational Research; the planning of the itineraries of the practical testers and the arrangement for their reception by the relevant schools in the sample were also undertaken by this Unit.

The school questionnaire

The purpose of the APU survey is not only to describe the pattern of performance which exists, although that in itself may be valuable, but also to relate that performance to certain of the circumstances in which pupils learn. In order to measure some of the factors which may influence performance, schools were asked to complete a questionnaire. This is reproduced in Appendix 4. It was designed to elicit information about those variables which apply to the year group as a whole, rather than to an individual pupil. It requested information about numbers and qualifications of members of staff teaching science, about laboratory provision, technician support and money spent on apparatus and other materials.

In addition, the school was asked to name the type of science course currently being followed by each pupil in the survey; to say, for example, whether it was a general science course or one composed of separate subjects.

Organisation of the report

It seems likely that different readers of this report will wish to focus their attention on different features, at least in the first instance. Some will look first at results and others at illustrations of questions.

However, in order to make sense of either it will be necessary to view them in relation to the purpose of the survey, to the sampling procedures and to the assessment framework. Brief references to each of these have already been made, but readers may well find it useful to turn to the full discussions which appear later in the report before studying either questions or results in any detail.

In Chapters 1 to 5 of this report the pupils' performances on the tests within categories one to five respectively are discussed.

Several questions are used to illustrate each sub-category. Such questions, and their corresponding mark schemes, are reproduced on a reduced scale (the original question occupies an A4 page), and a histogram showing the percentage of pupils obtaining any given score, or a chart indicating the percentage of responses falling into any particular category, is included.

Values are also given for the number of pupils to whom the question was set, the mean of their raw scores for the question and the proportion of pupils not responding to the question (This proportion includes a negligibly small number of pupils who failed to reach the question in the time allowed; steps taken to reduce the incidence of such failure are discussed in Appendix 2.) The relative size of the group of pupils who did not respond to the question is indicated on the histograms by the shaded area of the zero column. In some questions pupils were required to select one response from several; the proportion who instead gave a multiple response, and so scored zero, is indicated in such cases.

Readers will find that questions vary in the maximum number of marks that a pupil can achieve on the basis of the associated mark scheme; this is often true even for closely similar questions. For technical reasons, it is preferable for questions to be identically weighted when contributing to overall sub-category scores. In order to achieve this equal weighting the raw scores achieved by pupils on individual questions were transformed, where necessary, onto a common mark scale of 0−3 (or, in some cases, onto a scale of 0−1). An account of the transformation process can be found in Appendix 1. Whenever the term *mean score* appears without qualification in Chapters 1−5, it can be taken to refer to the arithmetic average of the pupils' transformed scores. Where, for questions which are discussed in detail, the transformed mean score differs from the raw mean score, both values will be indicated.

Table 0.2 summarises the notation used to refer to the factors described above.

Table 0.2   *Key to notation used to describe question results*

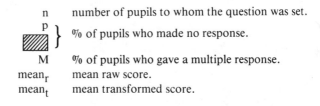

n	number of pupils to whom the question was set.
p	% of pupils who made no response.
M	% of pupils who gave a multiple response.
mean$_r$	mean raw score.
mean$_t$	mean transformed score.

Chapter 6 traces the development of the assessment framework. The categories and sub-categories are described in detail, and the types of question involved are indicated by the lists of question descriptors, which are yet further sub-divisions of the sub-categories. The chapter ends with a list of science concepts which constitutes an orthogonal though essential dimension of the framework.

In Chapter 7 there is a full description of the characteristics by which the schools and pupils in the survey can be distinguished from one another. These include not only those characteristics which were considered in drawing the samples, but also those which emerge from the data collected by questionnaire from schools which actually took part. The many factors reviewed range from geographic region through laboratory provision to the science curriculum followed by the pupil.

Chapter 8 is devoted to the discussion of the relative performance of different groups of pupils with respect to certain areas of the assessment framework. In those sub-categories where the type and the number of representative questions seem to justify the procedure, a mean test score for each of the pupils tested has been calculated. An estimate of the performance to be expected for the whole population of 13 year olds has then been made based on these mean scores, weighted to take account of the two-stage method of sampling and of sample in-balance due to differential school participation rates. Performance estimates are also given for boys and girls separately, and for a number of other sub-groups of pupils distinguished by some of the characteristics described in Chapter 7.

In the final chapter of the report, an attempt is made to interpret the results of the survey. The meaning of differences of performance from one sub-category to another is discussed, and questions are raised in connection with the significance of reported differences — or lack of differences — between sub-groups with different backgrounds. Finally, the strengths of the assessment framework for the purpose in hand, the limitations it imposes on reporting, and the implications of the results for those concerned with school science are considered.

Category 1: using symbolic representations

1.1 Introduction

Nature of the category   In questions from this category pupils were required to use conventional representations. (A discussion of the reasons for including questions of this kind in a science survey is to be found in Chapter 6). Some of them required the use of graphs and charts commonly used in everyday communication, as well as in science and other lessons; others were probably identified by pupils as 'science questions' even though they were in fact restricted, as far as possible, to testing pupils' ability to translate to or from specialised varieties of symbolic representation.

The questions were designed to highlight the difficulties of this translation process: they did not, therefore, exploit opportunities to probe into pupils' ability to interpret data. This was tested by questions from category 4: using interpretation and application.

Each pupil answered questions drawn from three sub-categories which are discussed in turn below. None of the questions demanded the use of science concepts mentioned in the introductory chapter and discussed more fully in Chapter 6. However, knowledge of certain conventions used in scientific drawings was required in the third of these sub-categories.

Administration   The test, lasting about an hour, was administered by a teacher in the pupil's own school, who was asked to offer help in reading either whole questions or individual words within them. Other pupils in the group being tested may have been answering a different set of questions. (Details of the administration and the marking of tests can be found in Appendix 2.1)

Fifty seven questions were used altogether. Each pupil was given a booklet containing 19 of these questions, with spaces in which to write the responses. The mode of response varied; some questions required a simple tick or cross in the appropriate box, some a short phrase or sentence and others a drawing of some kind.

Experienced science teachers were appointed to mark the scripts, since few questions could be marked objectively. They attended a training meeting and took part in a limited reliability check, using sample scripts, before undertaking the bulk of the marking. All questions had a numerical mark scheme. In addition, in selected questions, responses were allocated to categories defined by reference to error or misconception.

1.2 Sub-category 1α: reading information from graphs, tables and charts

The range of questions used   Eighteen questions from this sub-category were used in the survey. In order to answer them pupils had to obtain information from graphs, tables and charts. Different kinds of demand were made by different types of question, usually, in this sub-category, because of differences

[1] The types of question used in this and other sub-categories are summarised in a list of question descriptors. This list can be found in section 6.4.

in presentation of data. [1] A few representative questions have been chosen to illustrate the nature of the sub-category; the results obtained for these questions are also given. Any general patterns of response are also indicated.

Tabulated information   'Fish calendar' is one of a group of questions in which pupils are required to read information presented in tabular form. In this particular question representational symbols were used.

Fish calendar

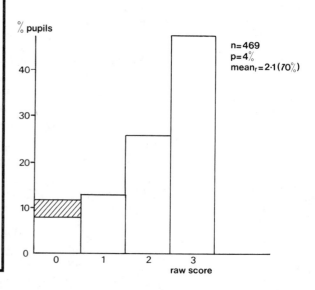

This is part of a chart that appeared in "Which?" magazine in August 1979. It is to help people when they are shopping for fish.

	JAN FEB MAR APR MAY JUN JUL AUG SEP OCT NOV DEC
PILCHARD(1)	
PLAICE	
POLLACK	
REDFISH	
ROCKFISH (catfish)	
SAITHE (coley)	
SALMON	
SARDINE(1)	
SEA BREAM	
SKATE	
DOVER SOLE	
LEMON SOLE	
SPRATS	
SQUID	
BROWN TROUT	
RAINBOW TROUT	
SALMON TROUT	
TURBOT	
WHITEBAIT	
WHITING	
WITCH(1)	

Key: ● good quality   fair quality   blank: unlikely to find

Use the chart to answer these questions:

a) In some months you can't find sprats for sale at all.
    Which months are these? . . . .

b) Name one fish that is of good quality only in March, April
    and May. . . . .

c) One fish is for sale all year round but is never likely to
    be of good quality. Which one is this? . . . .

Mark scheme

a) April–August   1

b) Sardine or saithe (coley)   1
   (Give one mark only for either or both)

c) Squid   1
   (Deduct the mark if any extra name is given)

                                                       ③

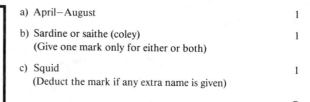

% pupils

n=469
p=4%
$mean_r=2.1(70\%)$

Other questions in which information was tabulated using either symbols (as in 'Fish calendar'), figures or words were set in different contexts; one was concerned with world consumption of oil, one with the cost of central heating and one with the consequences of agricultural improvement, for example. Mean scores varied from 33 to 77 per cent of the maximum, the lower scores relating to the tables containing the most detailed numerical information.

Bar charts   In a second type of question, information is presented in the form of a bar chart. 'Braking' is an example of this type.

Braking

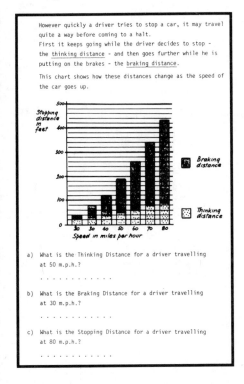

However quickly a driver tries to stop a car, it may travel quite a way before coming to a halt.

First it keeps going while the driver decides to stop – the thinking distance – and then goes further while he is putting on the brakes – the braking distance.

This chart shows how these distances change as the speed of the car goes up.

a)   What is the Thinking Distance for a driver travelling at 50 m.p.h.?

   . . . .

b)   What is the Braking Distance for a driver travelling at 30 m.p.h.?

   . . . .

c)   What is the Stopping Distance for a driver travelling at 80 m.p.h.?

   . . . .

Mark scheme

a) 50 feet   2
    (Reasonable range — 45–55 feet

b) 50 feet   2
    (Reasonable range — 45–55 feet

c) 430 feet (or up to 440)   2
    (Reasonable range 420–450 feet)

                            ⑥

N.B. In each case 1 mark is for the unit — but not unless the numerical value is in the reasonable range.

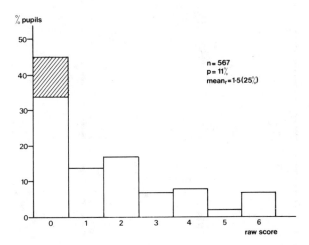

$n = 567$
$p = 11\%$
$\text{mean}_r = 1\cdot5 (25\%)$

The low mean score for this question (30 per cent) reflects the fact that 11 per cent of the pupils failed to respond and that another 27 per cent failed to include any units.

Other questions of the same type (in which pupils read information from a bar chart), had higher mean scores of about 57 per cent of the maximum. There were two possible sources of difficulty in 'Braking' which were not present in the others. The first was the need to look for the *difference* between two values in order to find the braking distance in part b) of the question; and the second was the fact that the vertical scale, though marked with horizontal lines every 20 feet, was labelled only at intervals of 100 feet.

Schematic representation   A third type of question is represented by 'Okapi'. In this type, a process, relationship or series of linked events is represented by a diagram or flow chart.

Okapi

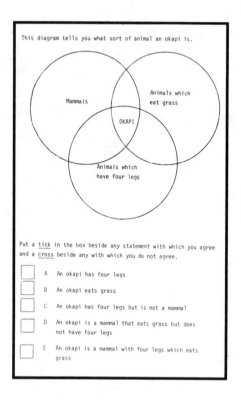

Mark scheme

A ✓   1
B ✓   1
C X   1
D X   1
E ✓   1

                      ⑤

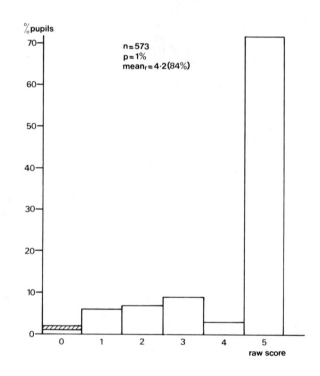

[1]See page 5 for a note on transformed scores, and Appendix 1 for further detail.

The mean scores for all questions of this type were above 60 per cent of the maximum but was highest (77 per cent)[1] for the one illustrated. The non-response rate was low; this was usually the case for coded answer questions of which this was an example.

Line graphs   In a fourth type of question, of which 'Storage radiator' is an example, pupils were required to read information from data presented in the form of a line graph.

Storage radiator

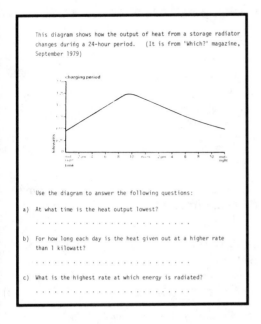

Mark scheme

a) Midnight   1

*b) About *7 hours*   2

*c) *1.25 kilowatts*   2

⑤

*in b) and c) marks should only be given for units if the values are reasonable – b) between 6 and 7 hours,

– c) between 1 and 1.5 kilowatts

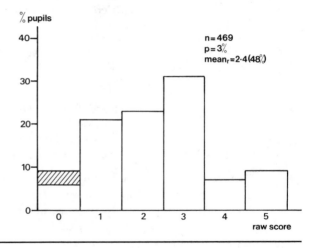

A common error was to misread the horizontal scale — to count two hours as one; many pupils gave answers which were numerically correct but without units. Other questions of the same type had higher mean scores.

Other types of question   Two other types of question were used in the test. In one type information was presented in the form of a pie chart; the mean scores for these were about 85 per cent, the lowest mean score being associated with the case where proportions were described numerically as well as visually. In the other type pupils were asked to provide suitable labels for the axes of line graphs said to illustrate a given event. The mean scores in these questions were about 45 per cent; many pupils provided a label with a suitable quantity without including reference to any units.

Summary of results for sub-category α   Sub-category 1α was represented in the survey by a total of 21 questions, seven in each of three different test packages containing similar mixtures of 1α, 1β and 1γ. (Three questions appeared in more than one package). Over 1 500 children attempted one or other of these test packages. All but six gained at least one mark for 1α performance. The mark distributions for the three packages were similar; they were bell shaped, with a mean mark about three-fifths of the maximum and spread across the complete scale. There was no consistent difference between results for boys and girls, and no clear relationship between mean scores and types of question.

Lowest mean scores tended to be associated with questions with numerical data, whatever the method of presentation.

1.3 Sub-category 1β: expressing information as graphs, tables and charts

The range of questions used   In the 18 questions from this sub-category which were selected for use in the survey, pupils were required to put information presented in words or numbers into various graphical, tabular or symbolic forms; sometimes they had to construct such forms entirely for themselves, and sometimes they had to add to partially completed ones.

Four different types of question are illustrated.

Adding results to tables   In the first type, of which 'Slope' is an example, pupils were asked to add four numerical results from a simple investigation to a partially completed table.

In this question pupils tended to score high or low rather than in the middle of the range. The resulting horse-shoe shaped distribution means that in general if they could do the question at all they could do it well. Nine per cent of the pupils failed to respond, contributing to the 31 per cent with a zero score.

This question was also set for 11 year old pupils. For that age group, the non-response rate was 19 per cent and the mean raw score 1.7 (42 per cent) of the maximum. The distribution of scores, compared with that for 13 year old pupils is shown in Figure 1.1

Figure 1.1 *Distribution of scores at ages 11 and 13 for 'Slope'*

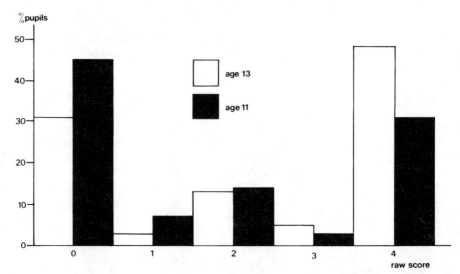

Slope

John and Pauline measured how far their truck travelled
after it left the end of the board (Distance D cm).
They changed the height of the end of the board (H cm).
They put different weights in the truck.
These are some of their results:

Height of raised end in cm. (H)	Distance travelled in cm (D)				
	Nothing in truck	100 g in truck	200 g in truck	300 g in truck	400 g in truck
5	70	80	85		
10	85	95	103		
15	140	145	150		
20					
25					

a) They also got these results for the truck loaded with 300 g:

When H = 5 cm,   D = 105 cm

H = 15 cm,   D = 160 cm

Add these results to the table above.

b) They put the height of the raised end up to 25 cm and found
these results:

For 100 g in truck, D = 195 cm

For 200 g in truck, D = 200 cm.

Add these results to the table above.

Mark scheme

a)

Height	Distance					
	Nothing	100 g	200 g	300 g	400 g	
5				105 g		1
10						
15				160 g		1
20						
25						

b)

Height	Distance					
	Nothing	100 g	200 g	300 g	400 g	
5						
10						
15						
20						
25	195	200			1,1	④

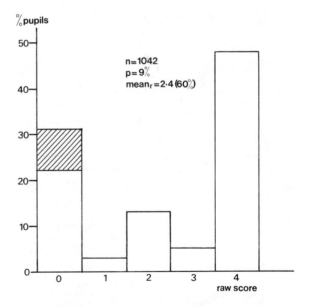

n=1042
p=9%
mean$_r$=2·4 (60%)

Pie charts   'Travel choice' was one of several questions in which pupils were asked to complete a pie chart in order to represent tabulated information.

Travel choice

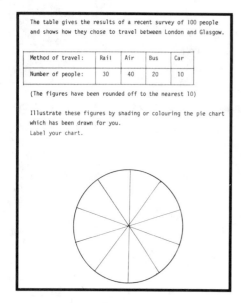

The table gives the results of a recent survey of 100 people and shows how they chose to travel between London and Glasgow.

Method of travel:	Rail	Air	Bus	Car
Number of people:	30	40	20	10

(The figures have been rounded off to the nearest 10)

Illustrate these figures by shading or colouring the pie chart which has been drawn for you.
Label your chart.

Mark scheme

The maximum score of 3 was given when the four sectors were clearly defined by shading or colouring and identified by label or key. Less complete responses received a proportion of the marks

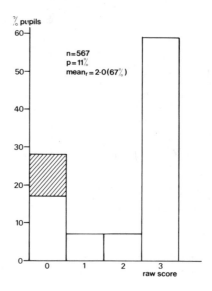

n=567
p=11%
$mean_r = 2.0 (67\%)$

There was a high non-response rate (11 per cent of the pupils), a high proportion of pupils with a zero score (28 per cent) and a horse-shoe shaped distribution of scores. In other questions of the same type the pattern of response was similar, with non-response rates of between 9 and 17 per cent of pupils and with between 28 and 57 per cent of pupils scoring zero. A low score was generally caused by failure to identify the different sectors of the completed chart.

Line graphs: axes not labelled   Several questions were included in which pupils were to represent tabular data in the form of a line graph, with no help given in relation to drawing, labelling or scaling the axes. 'Bean height' is an example of this type, in which the marking was focussed not so much on accuracy as on the organisational aspects of the task.

Bean height

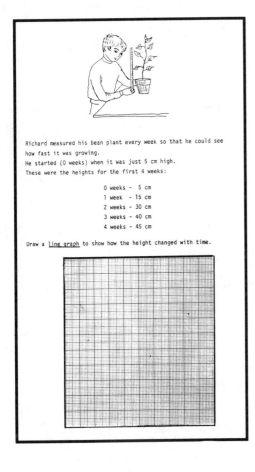

Richard measured his bean plant every week so that he could see how fast it was growing.
He started (0 weeks) when it was just 5 cm high.
These were the heights for the first 4 weeks:

    0 weeks - 5 cm
    1 week - 15 cm
    2 weeks - 30 cm
    3 weeks - 40 cm
    4 weeks - 45 cm

Draw a <u>line graph</u> to show how the height changed with time.

Numerical mark scheme

Preparation

Direction of axes conventional, whether labelled or implied   1

Axes labelled *height* in *cm*   2
              time in *weeks*   2

Suitable linear scale on x axis   1
                        y axis   1

Although there is no need to include the point (0.0), do not penalise for a small scale if this results from such inclusion.

Plotting (scale to maximum shown) One mark for each point correctly plotted with respect to a linear scale   2

Completing

Points joined by smooth curve   2
Points joined by ruled lines (1)   Total   ⑪

Other possibilities

(1) If, with conventional direction of the axes a *vertical bar chart* is drawn with lines (or very thin bars) of the right height and correctly placed on the x scale, give marks corresponding to plotting points.   Maximum mark...   ⑨
(2) If, with conventional direction axes a *horizontal bar chart* is drawn, give no marks for plotting points.   Maximum mark...   ⑧
(3) Pupils who mark out one axis with a non-linear scale get no marks for plotting or completing.   Maximum mark...   ⑥

n = 469
p = 6%
mean$_r$ = 5.3 (48%)
mean$_t$ = 43%

The mean score for the question was 43 per cent, with 22 per cent of the pupils scoring zero, including 6 per cent who did not respond. 'Bean height' was one of the questions referred to earlier for which markers allocated answers to categories as well as awarding a numerical score. The question was set at age 11 as well as at age 13; since the same category mark scheme was used, it is possible to compare the incidence of different types of response at the two ages. The categories were related to the six criteria listed over.

Criteria for category marking of 'Bean height'

1. The direction of the axes is conventional (ie independent variable along the horizontal axis); this can be indicated by labels or implied.
2. A linear scale is used on both axes; this can be labelled or implied.
3. An uncramped scale is used on both axes (ie down to 1cm representing 1 year and to 1cm representing 10cm).
4. The axes are sufficiently well labelled (apart from figures alone) to be identified by quantity or unit or both.
5. At least 3 points are correctly plotted with respect to the scale used — even if non-linear.
6. The points are connected by a line, implying that one quantity varies continuously with the other.

Table 1.1 *Categories of response: 'Bean height'*

Nature of response	% of pupils	
	Age 13	Age 11
Met all six criteria	24	15
Met all criteria except No. 4 (axes not labelled)	16	1
Met all criteria except No. 6 (no line joining points)	18	12
Met all criteria except No. 2 (used at least one non linear scale)	7	3
Met criteria 5 but joined points to both axes with vertical & horizontal lines	5	4

The figures on the table of responses (Table 1.1) show that more 13 year olds than 11 year olds were able to complete the task in a satisfactory manner (24 per cent compared with 15 per cent). In addition, more of them met all criteria except that they used at least one non-linear scale (7 per cent compared with 3 per cent). Many pupils at both ages, having plotted the points successfully, failed to join them with a continuous line (18 per cent and 12 per cent respectively). Most of these pupils drew bar graphs. Other questions of the same kind had similar mean scores of about 40 per cent.

Other types of question   Questions of the type in which pupils were required to complete a bar chart or a line graph, with axes already labelled and in some cases scaled, were also included. In contrast to the case just described, the emphasis in marking was on accuracy of plotting. The mean score for such questions was about 45 per cent of the maximum where a line graph was required, and about 70 per cent for bar charts.

Summary of results for sub-category 1β Twenty-one of the questions contained in the three category 1 test packages belonged to sub-category 1β — seven questions in each package. (Again three questions appear in more than one package). The mean mark for each test package was about half-way along the mark scale and 4 per cent of the 1 600 pupils who took one or other of these packages failed to score a mark for 1β performance.

The distribution was flat rather than bell-shaped, and covered the complete scale. There were no clear patterns relating performance to question type apart from the relatively low mean scores associated with the drawing of line graphs; and there were no general differences in performance between boys and girls.

1.4 Sub-category 1γ: using scientific symbols and conventions

Range of questions used Thirteen questions were randomly selected from this sub-category, all of which required some degree of familiarity with conventions used in conveying information in science. The two kinds of symbolic representation involved were the drawing of section diagrams of general laboratory equipment, notably glassware, and simple circuit diagrams. At age 15, questions using other conventions, such as chemical symbols, were included, but this was not appropriate at age 13.

Five different types of question were used, some testing identification of apparatus drawn in the question, and others requiring pupils to draw conventional diagrams of apparatus, or of an arrangement of apparatus from some other kind of illustration.

Matching names to diagrams In this type of question, pupils were required to label a set of section diagrams of common laboratory glassware using names from a list provided. The list had more names than was required. The mean scores for such questions were above 55 per cent of the maximum and the non-response rate was less than one per cent.

Proposing names for general apparatus   In questions of this type, pupils were presented with section diagrams of an experimental set-up, and were required to label the components parts indicated. 'Thistle' is an example of such a question.

Thistle

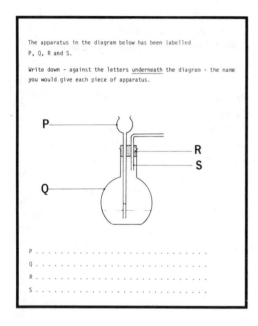

Mark scheme

(Give credit in spite of spelling mistakes if the intention is clear)

P Thistle funnel   1

Q Flask   1
   (allow round flask, but not conical flask)

R Cork or bung   1
   (but not stopper)

S (Delivery) tube   1

④

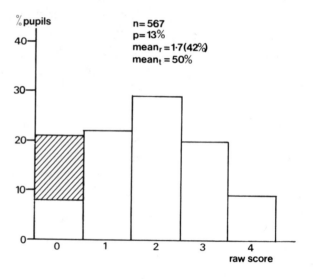

Mean scores for questions of this type averaged 60 per cent (for this question the transformed score was 50 per cent) and non-response rates six per cent.

Proposing names for components of a simple circuit   This type of question is very similar to the last, but the context is different. 'Ammeter' exemplifies the type.

Ammeter

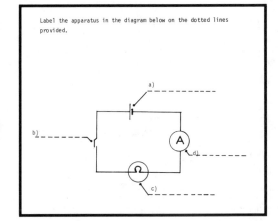

Mark scheme

(Give credit in spite of spelling mistakes if the intention is clear)

a) Cell (allow battery)   1

b) Switch   1

c) Lamp, or bulb   1

d) Ammeter   1

④

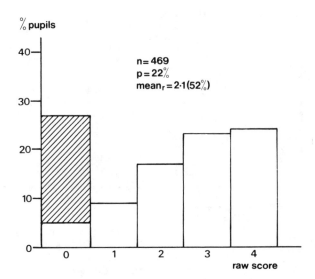

In a similar question in which a voltmeter featured, the non-response rate was higher (27 per cent of pupils) and the mean score much lower (27 per cent of the maximum).

Representing general apparatus Pupils were asked to represent in a conventional way an arrangement of equipment presented to them as a three-dimensional line drawing. The mark scheme is detailed but was found to be more reliable than other ways of arriving at a numerical score such as impression marking.

CO_2 test

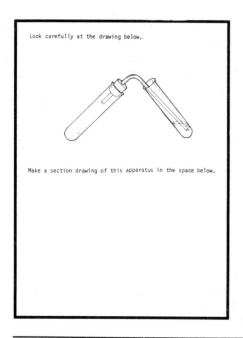

Look carefully at the drawing below.

Make a section drawing of this apparatus in the space below.

Mark scheme

(Mark only if the right hand tube is open at the top. No marks if apparatus is not assembled)

Thin tube open at left-hand side	1
closed by bubble at right	1
Liquid level in right-hand side horizontal	1
not inside tube	1
Tube ending below liquid on right	1
cork on left	1
Tube not blocked by cork on left	1
Cork with top and bottom straight lines	1
Reasonable proportion — height to width of t.ts.	1
Test tubes similar in size	1
Proportion of tube to test tubes	1
Use of ruler where appropriate	1
Neat enough to be clear	1

Total ⑬

Table 1.2 indicates the nature of some of the responses.

Table 1.2 *Categories of response: 'CO_2'*

Nature of response	% of pupils	
No response	17	
An attempt with zero score	51	$n = 46$
An attempt to copy the drawing in the question	19	$p = 17\%$
A drawing showing separated components	18	$mean_r = 22\%$

The mean score for this question and for others of the same type was 23 per cent of the maximum, and the pattern of response was similar in terms of the categories in Table 1.2.

These results suggest either that the task is not one normally expected of 13 year old pupils, or else that the instructions are usually phrased differently.

Representing simple circuits   In questions of this type, pupils were given a three dimensional drawing of the circuit and asked to draw a circuit diagram instead. The example shown, 'Double meter', involves a circuit board of the kind in common use in schools for pupils aged 13.

Double meter

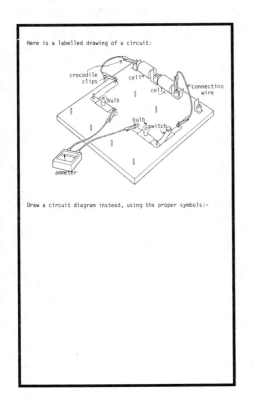

Mark scheme

(The layout need not be rectangular)

Do not score unless at least one acceptable symbol is used.

Accept.  for bulb
for ammeter.

Any complete series circuit	1
All 6 components represented	1
Components in correct order (allow mirror image)	1
Acceptable symbols for cell	1
bulb	1
ammeter	1
switch	1

⑦

Code D if the drawing in the question is copied without symbols, whether with or without the circuit board.

The mean score for this question was 27 per cent. Types of response are indicated in Table 1.3.

Table 1.3 *Categories of response: 'Double meter'*

Nature of response	% of pupils	
No response	30	$n = 573$
An attempt with zero score	21	$p = 30\%$
An attempt to copy the drawing in the question	12	$mean_r = 2.2(31\%)$
		$mean_t = 27\%$

Other questions of the same type showed this pattern of response

Summary of results for sub-category 1γ   Sub-category 1γ performance was assessed using 15 questions — five per category 1 test package (two were used in more than one package). The raw mark distributions were similarly symmetrical, with mean marks below half of the maximum. About one per cent of 1 609 pupils who attempted one or other of these packages failed to gain a single mark for their 1γ performance. The distribution was bell shaped and covered the complete scale.

The rate of non-response was high for most types of question in this sub-category. The exceptions were those in which pupils matched names to apparatus, or proposed names for general apparatus.

Very low mean scores were obtained for the two types of question in which pupils had to translate *to* conventional symbolic representations rather than *from* them, and these also had a very high non-response rate.

Boys consistently obtained higher mean scores than girls for both these types of question, and also for all other questions involving circuits.

1.5 Patterns in performance in category 1

The non-response rate was generally low for questions in 1α (less — usually much less — than 10 per cent of the pupils) and only slightly higher for those in 1β. It was much higher (between 10 and 30 per cent) for 1γ questions with the exception of those involving simple matching of name to diagram.

There were no consistent sex differences apparent with respect to any types of question from 1α or 1β, but on two types of question from 1γ, both involving translating *into* symbolic representation, boys performed better, on average, than girls.

It seems that when a question involves specifically scientific conventions (as in 1γ) the demand to translate into symbolic representations differentiates between the sexes, although there is no such differentiation when the direction of translation is reversed. When the conventions are mathematical or general, as in 1α and 1β, no differentiation appears to occur.

2   Category 2: using apparatus and measuring instruments

2.1   Introduction

Nature of the category For the assessment of performance in this category, pupils were given a variety of practical tasks to perform. Some demanded the use of measuring instruments or laboratory apparatus, while others were concerned with everyday materials and equipment. In some pupils had to use practical techniques they had learned in the school laboratory, in others they had simply to follow instructions; and in yet another group they were asked to estimate quantities of material without the use of measuring instruments.

There was no great emphasis on the use of science concepts, although clearly in order to measure a physical quantity it is necessary to have some idea of its nature. All questions inevitably involved the pupils in a degree of observation, but they were not left in any doubt about what it was they needed to observe: the ability to make use of self-directed observation was asssessed in category 3.

Administration The test was organised as a circus of nine stations, with equipment for one or more tasks set out at each station. During the course of the test, which lasted for about 1¼ hours, each pupil in the group of nine participating, moved round from station to station at intervals of eight minutes until all pupils had visited all stations. In order to facilitate the organisation of

The circulation pattern

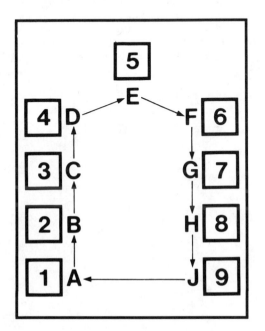

Pupils' written instructions

About this 'circus'

This is a practical test. Sometimes you will use science apparatus, and sometimes other simple equipment.

The things you will need have been set out for your at nine *stations* in a *circus*. It is called a circus because, wherever you start, you will move round so that you visit all the stations in turn.
The supervisor will tell you when you are to move.
By the end of the test, you will have visited every station.

In some questions, you will be told to use a letter of the alphabet — the supervisor will tell you which letter you should use.

Write your letter
in this space→

If you need help to read a question, put up your hand.

Read every question carefully and be sure to follow the instructions given.

the circus, pupils were given lapel badges marked with a letter of the alphabet and the stations were marked with a large numbered card. Before the test began the administrator spent some time making sure that pupils understood how and when pupils were to move; the movement was described by a diagram like the one on page 23. They also read through the first page of the pupils' test booklets (which is also shown), helped them to fill in the necessary particulars on the cover, and offered to help them with any reading difficulties.

The test booklets, in which the tasks were described, were similar to those used in written tests, but the mode of response varied from task to task. Thus a pupil's performance was variously assessed by inspection of a written answer, of an arrangement of apparatus, or of a 'product' resulting from the performance. In one case, assessment was by direct observation of a pupil's actions during the performance of the task.

Each test was administered in the pupils' own school by one of twelve practising science teachers, each based in a different area of the country. They had earlier spent a day at Chelsea College, training in preparation for their task. The trained administrator was assisted by a science teacher from the school itself, who was given the responsibility of assessing performance in the one task where direct observation of the pupil's action was required.

Four hundred and fifty nine pupils, from 51 different schools, were all given the same group of tasks, each of which is described and reported separately. They were drawn from three sub-categories which are discussed in turn below.

'Scale readings'

Seven different measuring instruments have been set up all ready for you to look at.   Do not change them in any way.
Answer as many of the questions below as you can.
Don't forget to say what units you are using.
The first question has been answered to show what we mean.

How wide is this booklet? | 21 cm

a) How much water is there in the measuring cylinder?

b) How big is the force with which the rubber band pulls on the hook?

c) What is the pressure of the gas at this gas-point?

d) What is the temperature of the water in the flask?

e) How long had the stop-clock been running before it was stopped?

f) Press the push-button to switch on the current. Read the current through the circuit on the ammeter.

g) Press the push-button again.   Read the voltmeter.

Mark scheme

For *each* question at this station, there are 2 marks for the value and 1 for the unit, giving a possible total of ③.

Note, however, that the correct unit scores a mark only if the value given lies within the wider of the two ranges specified. (Do not penalise for using capital letters or the plural form (e.g. Newtons).

Marks:	Value	Close range 2	Wide range (1)	Units 1	Total 3
a) measuring cylinder	42	± 1	± 2	cm^3 or cubic centimeter (not cc)	
b) forcemeter	27	± 1	± 2	N or newton (allow Newtons)	
c) manometer	?	± 1	± 2	cm of water (not just cm)	
d) thermometer	35	± 1	± 2	°C or °Centigrade or °Celsius. (or degrees in full)	
e) stop-clock	2m 23s	± 1	± 2	m and s or minutes and seconds (allow min. and sec.)	
f) ammeter	0.38	± 0.02	± 0.04	A or amp or ampere	
g) voltmeter	3.8	± 0.1	± 0.2	V or volt	

2.2 Sub-category 2α: using measuring instruments

The range of questions and their purpose   Three types of question were used to assess the ability to use measuring instruments and other laboratory apparatus in clearly defined situations. In the first, it was only necessary for pupils to record the scale reading of an instrument and supply appropriate units; in the second, they had to supply written evidence of ability to use magnifying instruments; while in the third they were required to measure out specified quantities of material.

Recording scale readings   The seven instruments involved were set up as though in actual use. The values of the quantities being measured had been preset by the administrators (or in some cases by the suppliers), so that all the pupils had to do, apart from pressing a push-button in two cases, was to read the scale and record the reading and the units.

The results obtained are shown on the bar charts (over). The instruments are listed in order of decreasing mean scores.

Pupils who gained the maximum score recorded a value within the range designated close (generally within one scale division either side of the actual value) and also stated the units in a satisfactory manner. Those with zero score recorded a value more than two scale divisions from the actual value and failed to give satisfactory units. Pupils who failed to give a written response also came within this group; but the non-response rate was less than three per cent of the pupils even in the case of the manometer. There were several factors which may have affected performance, for example:

1) the relationship between a single scale division and the corresponding unit
2) the shape of the scale — whether it was linear or circular
3) the familiarity of the pupil with the instrument
4) the need to note the difference between two readings rather than a single reading

Familiarity appears to be related to the use of units rather than to overall mean score, for the thermometer, measuring cylinder and stopclock are probably in more common use than the other instruments at age 13 and the link between this group and a low incidence of lack of units is apparent on the relevant chart. On the other hand there was a higher mean score for the voltmeter than for the ammeter, although it is certainly the less familiar instrument.

There was no clear pattern linking performance to the shape of the scale. The voltmeter, stopclock and ammeter had circular scales, while all the others were linear. However the fact that the ammeter had its smallest scale division related to 0.02 units rather than to 0.1 units like the voltmeter, or to a single unit as in all other cases, may account for the low mean score of 17 per cent.

Using a manometer involves reading the difference between two scale readings and this, together with lack of familiarity, seems to be reflected in the low mean score of ten per cent.

Mean scores as a percentage of the maximum

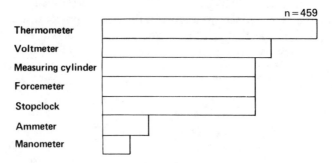

Percentage of responses gaining the maximum score

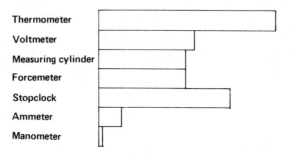

Percentage of responses gaining zero score

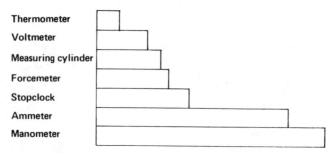

Percentage of responses with no satisfactory units

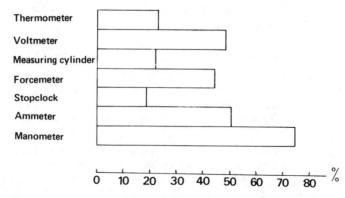

Use of hand lens and microscope   In this group of questions, pupils used a lens in order to read some very small capital letters on a card, and then a microscope to read two more sets of letters on microscope slides. The letters had been reduced in size so that it was impossible to read them with the naked eye.

'Lenses'

Mark scheme

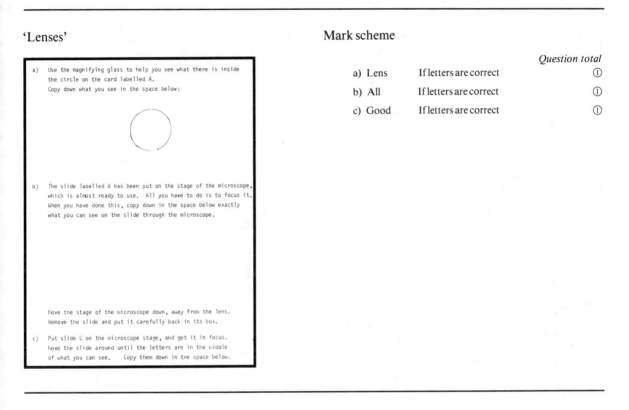

Question total

a) Lens   If letters are correct   ①

b) All   If letters are correct   ①

c) Good   If letters are correct   ①

Table 2.1 shows the percentage of pupils performing in the manner indicated.

Table 2.1   *Categories of response: 'Lenses'*   *n = 459*

Type of performance	Lens	Microscope: focussing	Microscope: positioning slide and focussing
Satisfactory use of instrument	74%	73%	73%
Incorrect letters recorded	23%	16%	9%
No written response	3%	11%	18%

The mean score (about 73 per cent) was much the same for all three tasks. As the task became more complex and possibly less familiar, the rise in the non-response rate was balanced by the fall in the incidence of incorrect letter.

Measuring out samples of material   This group of tasks demanded the use of a rule graduated in millimetres, a measuring cylinder, and a lever-arm balance.

'Deliver'

> *This question is to find out how well you can use the kind of apparatus you measure things with.*

a) Cut off a length of paper tape 47.3 cm long.
    Put it in the envelope which has your letter on it,
    and leave it on one side.

b) Measure out 55 cm³ of water as accurately as you can and
    pour it into the small beaker which has your letter on it.
    Put this to one side.

c) Put the piece of filter paper with your letter on it on the
    balance to protect the pan.   Put on to it 68 g of plasticine.
    Be as accurate as you.   Leave it on the filter paper, to
    one side.

d) Put the metal can with your letter on it on the balance, and
    put into it 82 g of sand.
    Leave the sand in the can and put it to one side.

Mark scheme

Each question has a total of ③ marks, as shown; the score depends on how near the pupil's sample is to the required value.

	Quantity required	Close range (3)	Wide range (1)	Total ③
a) Tape	47.3 cm	± 0.1	± 0.3	
b) Water	55.0 cm³	± 1.0	± 3.0	
c) Plasticine	68.01g	± 1.0	± 3.0	
d) Sand	*(x = 82) g	± 2.0	± 6.0	

* Mass of the can (x g) varies by more than 1 g: so to check pupil's performance, use a container the mass of which you have already determined — or use a plastic cup with negligible mass.

Performance on these tasks was assessed by administrators after the session.

'Non-response' in this case means failure to leave behind a measured-out quantity of material. The incidence of this was highest with the most complicated task (measuring out sand) in which the mass of the can had to be taken into account as well as the mass of the sand itself.

It is worth noting that almost half of the pupils tried and failed to use the balance to measure out a specified mass of plasticine within the limits allowed (in this case a range of six grams). The balance used had a smallest scale division of one gram and the top of the pointer was just below, rather than in front of, the scale.

The highest mean score (77 per cent) was obtained for the use of a measuring cylinder. This is higher than that of 57 per cent for the task involving a measuring cylinder described on page 25 in which all that pupils were required to do was to read the level of the water already inside the measuring cylinder. The higher score may have been due to the greater permissible range of values allowed in the more complex 'measuring out' task; but it could also have been related to the fact that the pupils were not required to state the units used.

Mean scores for the four tasks in 'Deliver'

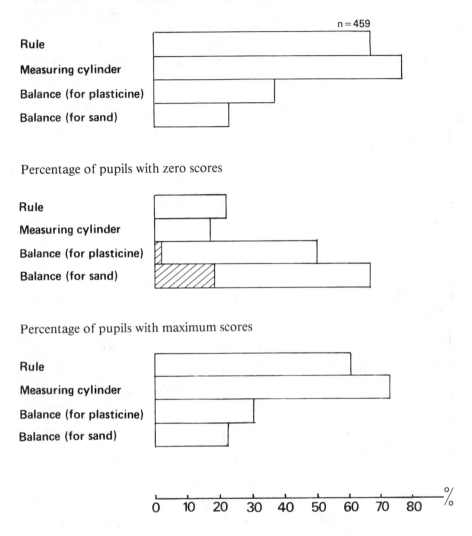

Percentage of pupils with zero scores

Percentage of pupils with maximum scores

Summary of results for sub-category 2α   One category 2 practical circus was administered in this survey to 459 pupils and this test package contained a mixture of 2α, 2β and 2γ questions. Sub-category 2α was represented by 14 questions. Every pupil scored at least one mark, and the mean score is about half-way along the mark scale.

2.3 Sub-category 2β: estimating quantities

The range of questions used   All the questions in this sub-category were of the same type. Materials already prepared to predetermined specifications were set out for the pupils to look at and to handle. No measuring instruments were provided, and pupils were prevented from using any of their own. Instead they had to make an estimate of the values of quantities such as length, mass, time and temperature associated with the materials provided.

'Guesstimate'

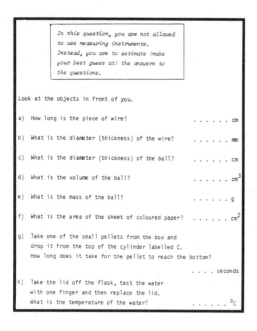

Mark scheme

Each question has a maximum of ③ marks; the score depends on how close the pupil's estimate is to the actual value (units are given in the question).

	Actual value	Close range (3)	Wide range (1)	Total ③
a) length of wire	15 cm	13.5–16.5	7.5–22.5	
b) diameter of wire	1.5 mm	1.3–1.7	0.8–2.2	
c) diameter of ball	3 cm	2.7–3.3	1.5–4.5	
d) volume of ball	14.1 cm³	12.7–15.5	7.1–21.2	
e) mass of ball	2.1 g	1.9–2.3	1.1–3.1	
f) area of paper	2401 cm²	2160–2640	1400–3400	
g) time of fall	1.75*	1.5–2.0	1.0–2.5	
h) temperature of water	40°C	35–45	20–60	

* This varies according to how well the ball is centred to start with, but is within the 'close range' given.

A 'wild' guess was defined for the purposes of this exercise as an estimate which was out by a factor of ten or more, except in the case of temperature where any estimate below ten degrees centigrade or above 80 degrees centigrade was deemed to be 'wild'.

The only two cases where the mean scores were approaching 50 per cent involved the measurement of length. The relatively high rates of non-response (ten per cent) for volume of ball and mass of ball suggest that the concepts of mass and volume were not well understood. The rate of non-response was lower (four per cent) for the 'area' task, which suggests that pupils are more familiar with this concept, but the mean score was lower than for any other task, and nearly 60 per cent of the pupils made estimates that were more than ten times too big or ten times too small.

Mean score as a percentage of the maximum for the eight estimating tasks

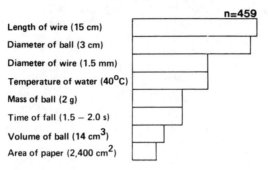

Percentage of pupils making various responses to the eight tasks:
Values within 'close' range (maximum score)

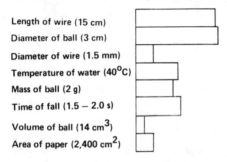

Values outside 'wide' range (zero score)

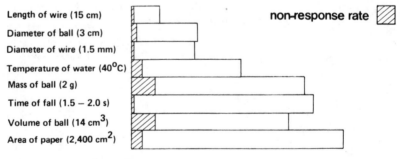

'Wild' guesses as defined on page 30

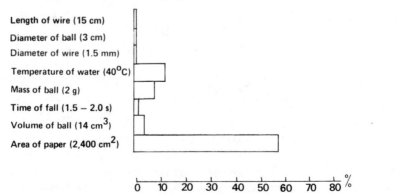

General comments about tasks in 2β   The single category 2 practical circus administered in this survey contained eight questions belonging to 2β (the rest were 2α or 2γ questions), and 459 pupils attempted this test package.

Correlation of results for tasks in the 'Guesstimate' group with those for other kinds of task set in category 2 was low; pupils who were good at using laboratory instruments or following instructions were not necessarily good at making estimates. In addition most of the 'wild' guesses were made not by those who scored low on category 2 tasks as a whole but by those in the middle of the range.

2.4 Sub-category 2γ: following instructions for practical work

Range of questions used   The six tasks drawn from this sub-category were all designed to investigate the ability to follow instructions. For some tasks the instructions were given with the help of conventional diagrams; for some they were written and for others a mixture of words and diagrams was used. Success in following the instructions was judged by looking at the pupil's written records, by inspecting the tangible products which resulted, or by direct observation of the pupil's actions.

Diagrammatic instructions   In the two tasks of this type included in the test, pupils were asked to set up some apparatus in accordance with a conventional representative diagram. In each case the results were marked by the administrator in the course of the circus, as soon as the individual pupil had indicated that the task was finished.

In the first example, the pupil was required to fix a boss and clamp on a retort stand, to put liquid into a test tube and to fix the test tube in the clamp ready for heating by a Bunsen burner.

The percentage of pupils satisfactorily performing various parts of the task are shown in Table 2.2.

Table 2.2   *Categories of response: 'Clamp'*   *n = 459*

'Clamp'	% of all pupils
Fixing boss and clamp	94
Fixing test tube in clamp	86
Tilting test tube at a suitable angle	74
Test tube at suitable height, relative to burner	69
Burner in position under tube (unlit)	59
Liquid in test tube, less than half full	60

Not all the pupils cleared the first hurdle, that of fixing the boss and clamp, and as the figures in the table show, there was then a progressive fall in success rate. However very few pupils failed to attempt this task (less than one per cent) and the mean raw score was 73 per cent of the maximum.

In the second example of this kind, a circuit diagram was used.

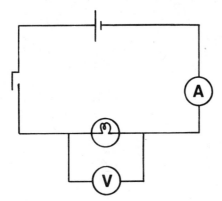

The five components were all fitted with 4mm sockets, and six leads ending in 4mm stacking plugs were supplied. It is of course possible that some pupils would have been more familiar with circuit boards, but experience in trials sugested that an equal number might have been quite unfamiliar with them. It was not possible, on this occasion, to test performance with both types of equipment.

Table 2.3   *Categories of response: 'Circuit'*   *n = 459*

'Circuit'	% of all pupils	% of all girls	% of all boys
Series circuit including lamp, switch and one or other of the meters	48	41	55
Voltmeter in parallel with the lamp	23	20	27
Polarity of ammeter and voltmeter correct with respect to the cell	22	20	25

The non-response rate for this task, in contrast to 'Clamp', was high (11 per cent) with 16 per cent of the girls and seven per cent of the boys making no attempt. Half the pupils failed to score. It seems likely, from feedback from administrators, that many pupils were not used to handling electrical equipment. On this task, girls performed less satisfactorily than did boys, and the mean raw score was 29 per cent of the maximum.

Written instructions   The next two examples are of tasks in which instructions were given mainly in words, with a little help from drawings. In each case, performance was judged from the written record.

In the first task, 'Pink fizz', the purpose suggested for following the instructions was the identification of four colourless liquids. These were presented in 'squeezy' wash bottles, while the two test liquids Q and V were in smaller flip-top dropping bottles. This was to reduce the risk that one pupil would contaminate the supplies of Q and V and so ruin the chances of those who followed. As indicated in the question, each pupil had access to an ample supply of clean test tubes.

'Pink fizz'

You have been given 4 colourless liquids labelled W, X, Y and Z.
One of them is plain water.
If you follow the instructions below you will be able to find out
which one is water, because water is the only one that does not
react with either of the two 'tester' liquids labelled Q and V.

Test 1

Label 4 clean test tubes, as shown, with the special pencil provided.
Put a little of liquid W into
tube W so that it is not more
than ¼ full.
Put the other liquids into the
tubes X, Y and Z.
Add a few drops of the liquid
called Tester Q to each tube
in turn.
Write down what happens in
this table:

	W	X	Y	Z
Tester Q				

Put all your used test tubes into the
container marked 'USED TEST TUBES'

Test 2

Repeat test 1, but use Tester V instead of Tester Q.

	W	X	Y	
Tester V				

Which liquid do you think is plain water? [   ]

Put all your used test tubes into the
container marked 'USED TEST TUBES'

Mark scheme

The point of this question is to find out if the pupil has followed
the instructions, not to see if he can describe the results: so give
credit if the answers indicate that instructions *were* followed.

	W (dil. Na_2CO_3)	X (water)	Y (dil. $NaHCO_3$)	Z (dil. citric acid)	
Q (dil. HCl)	fizz	—	fizz	—	4
V (phenolphthlein solution—slightly alkaline ∴ pink)	red	pink	pink	colourless	4
		Water = X			1

N.B. No marks for 'X' unless X column is correct.

⑨

Some alternative offerings:

Q	bubbles (gas)	neutral did not react	bubbles gas	neutral no reaction
V	dark pink	discolours a little	discolours a little	clear
	pink with one drop			nothing
	purple (look for *contrast* with next column)	watery purple	watery purple	neutral
				no reaction

The mean raw score for the question was about 46 per cent and the non-response
rate relatively high, over six per cent of the pupils failing to record any results.
Pupils in this group may, of course, have been taking some unrecorded action.
Among the pupils who *did* make a record of their results, were four per cent who
identified the liquid X as water although this was contrary to the evidence
described in their record.

The element of observation in this task and the next is not of the self-directed
kind that would place them into category 3. The mark schemes emphasise that, in
these two cases, inspection of the record is to be regarded simply as a substitute
for watching the action of the pupil; it is to determine whether the instructions
have been followed, rather than to assess observation or descriptive powers.

In the second example of this type of question, 'Blackout', an appeal is made to the pupil's curiosity to provide a purpose for following instructions.

'Blackout'

Some very strange things happen when you look through the bits of plastic in this kit.   We want you to follow the instructions to find out about them.
First check the kit.   You should have:

- *three greyish plastic strips labelled A, B and C*
- *one bit of clear food wrapping film labelled P*
- *one bit of aluminium foil labelled F*

Use them like this:

a) Hold the strip A upright in front of one eye (close the other eye)
Hold strip B several cm behind A and look through
them both at the window.

What do you see when B is held sideways?

. . . .

What do you see when B is held upright?

. . . .

Now hold B still and move A round instead.   If you hold B
upright and A sideways, what happens?

. . . .

b) Now hold A and B so that they touch one another and make a cross:

Slide the plastic film P in between the strips to make a sandwich
and hold it up to the light.   Crinkle the film up slightly to
make some pleats.

What do you see?

. . . .

. . . .

c) Put the plastic strip A down on top of the aluminium foil F.
Twist it round, keeping it flat on the foil.   Then turn it
over, and twist it round again.

What difference did turning it over make?

. . . .

Now do the same with strip C.   What difference does turning
C over make?

. . . .

Lift C up 10 cm above the foil and look at the foil through C.
Does it make any difference if you now turn C over?

. . . .

Comment

The strips A and B were plane polarised and C was circularly polarised. Pupils of 13 are not likely to be familiar with the properties of these materials, and even if by chance they were, it would be unlikely to affect their responses.

Mark scheme

N.B. This question is to find out if instructions have been followed, not to judge ability to record results; so give credit if answers indicate that these instructions *were* followed.

Marks

		Marks
a)	(i) Nothing through centre 'or dark'	1
	(ii) See through to window	1
	(iii) as (i)	1
b)	Colours or light and dark streaks	1
c)	(i) No difference	1
	(ii) 'Purple' one way up, not the other way	1
	(iii) No	1
		⑦

The mean raw score was about 59 per cent of the maximum, and less than one per cent of the pupils failed to respond.

Making a product   In this type of task, instructions were given for making an object which was marked by the administrator after the session was over. Considerable use of diagrams was made in giving the instructions, which were complete in themselves.

The example used in the test, 'Kaleidoscope' did not in fact require pupils to be familiar with the laws of reflection, or even with mirrors, in order to follow the instructions to make the model.

One of the difficulties of including this kind of activity in a circus is that pupils are apt to use their predecessor's attempt as a model instead of following instructions independently. In order to prevent this a 'post box' was provided to screen the complete product from view.

'Kaleidoscope'

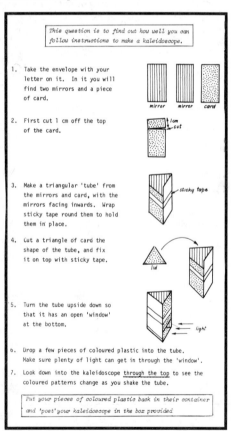

Mark scheme

(Marking is by inspection of the finished product)

	Marks *	
Top '1 cm' of card cut off	2	
(but not 1 cm)		(1)
Tube fixed together	3	
(but badly		(2)
but edges not in line)		(1)
Δ cut from card	2	
(but wrong shape)		(1)
Δ fixed to tube	4	
(but not firmly		(3)
but wrong end — i.e.		(2)
'even' end		
but both above faults)		(1)
	⑪	

*N.B. Numbers in brackets are the reduced marks allowed for the operation, if the faults suggested occur.

The mean score for the question was about 73 per cent of the maximum. About three per cent of the pupils failed 'to post' an identifiable product. (In this task, as in others where marking was carried out after the testing session was over, the letter on the lapel badge handed to the pupil at the start was used to link product to pupil. This letter was not only on the envelope referred to in the question: it was also printed on the middle of the card inside. Even so some pupils cut the card into such small pieces that the identification letter was missing from their model).

Two per cent of the sample ended up with mirrors facing outwards, instead of inwards, and six per cent fixed the triangle at the wrong end of the tube. Making the kaleidoscope calls for considerable manual dexterity. Nevertheless 70 per cent of the pupils had very nearly completed the task from printed instructions alone in the eight minutes available.

The observed task   This task is one of a type in which the pupil is required to follow instructions which are not complete in themselves, since they refer to techniques taught in school science.

In this task, 'Blue', performance was assessed by a teacher from the pupil's own school, who filled in a check list while observing the actions of the pupil. The check list provided was necessarily straightforward since the teacher had no opportunity to study it for more than a few minutes prior to the beginning of the circus.

'Blue'

This question is to see how well you can follow instructions.

1. Take a clean test tube and put a spatula-full of the black powder labelled P into it.

2. Put the test tube in the rack and quarter fill the tube with dilute acid from the bottle labelled Q.

3. Light the Bunsen burner and adjust the flame so that it is suitable for heating the test tube and its contents.

4. Heat the mixture in your test tube gently until it is boiling. Put it back in the rack to cool down for a minute.

5. Adjust the bunsen burner until you have a yellow flame.

6. Filter the liquid from your test tube into the flask provided.

Put your dirty apparatus into the container provided.

Comment

The task involved adding dilute sulphuric acid to copper II oxide in a boiling tube, and then heating and filtering.

The teacher at the station had the following written directions, and used a fresh check list for each pupil.

Using the check lists

Please tick if the pupil acts as indicated. If you have to prompt, either for safety's sake or to get some action, write P instead of a tick and make a note on the right-hand side of the paper. Any action not anticipated in the check list should be noted in the space at the side.

If pupils are entirely unfamiliar with a particular technique, do not over-prompt. (Say something like "Don't worry, if you can't remember it or have never done it, just stop".)

Preparing the station

Before *each* pupil begins, please check the following:

(1) The Bunsen burner should be connected, but not lit; the collar should be turned so that the hole is wide open.

(2) The spatula should be clean and resting on a spare filter paper by the side of container P, which has its lid on.

(3) A clean boiling tube should be put in the rack, with the test tube holder at the side.

(4) A clean funnel and flask should be placed separately on the bench behind the rack.

(5) Used boiling tubes can be put in the container provided. Funnel and flask should be rinsed ready for the next customer. One spare of each is provided to allow time for this.

```
B 1245  'Blue' Check List
                                      Pupil letter
                                      Pupil number

                                   P or ✓        Notes

Uses safety goggles . . . . . . . . . . .  [    ]

Handling Chemicals
  1.  Adds powder P to test tube, with spatula  [    ]
  2.  Puts spatula down in suitable place. .     [    ]
  3.  Puts test tube in rack . . . . . . . .     [    ]
  4.  Puts lid on container . . . . . . . .      [    ]
  5.  Adds acid Q to test tube . . . . . . .     [    ]
  6.    - ¼ full . . . . . . . . . . . . . .     [    ]

Heating
  7.  Lights Bunsen burner . . . . . . . . .     [    ]
  8.  Adjusts flame by rotating collar . . .     [    ]
  9.          - by turning tap . . . . .         [    ]
 10.  Holds test tube in holder. . . . . . .     [    ]
 11.    - angled . . . . . . . . . . . . .       [    ]
 12.    - in safe direction . . . . . . . .      [    ]
 13.    - using top half of flame . . . . .      [    ]
 14.    - keeps it moving. . . . . . . . .       [    ]
 15.    - till boiling . . . . . . . . . . .     [    ]
 16.    - stops when boiling . . . . . . .       [    ]
 17.    - puts in rack . . . . . . . . . .       [    ]

Filtering
 18.  Puts filter funnel in flask . . . . .      [    ]
 19.  Folds filter paper suitably . . . . .      [    ]
 20.  Inserts it in funnel . . . . . . . . .     [    ]
 21.  Pours in mixture . . . . . . . . . . .     [    ]
 22.    - without over-filling . . . . . . .     [    ]
 23.    - without by-passing filter paper        [    ]
```

An overall score for the task was arrived at by counting ticks, whether earlier prompting had been needed or not. On this basis the mean raw score for the task was about 75 per cent.

Pupils were allocated to categories if they had difficulties with particular aspects of the task. The results are shown in Table 2.4.

Table 2.4   *Categories of response: 'Blue'*   n = 459

Type of performance	% of all pupils	% of all girls	% of all boys
Inability to light bunsen burner without prompting	20	24	17
Inability to use filter paper without prompting	43	49	37
Inability to light burner *and* to use filter paper	10	10	10

**2.5 General
impressions of
category 2 tests**

Administrators and teachers expressed surprise at the high speed at which most pupils worked. The fact that they were being tested goes some way to explain this. They were also working on their own rather than with a partner or in a group, which is a more common arrangement at age 13. They were generally reported to have enjoyed taking part in the practical tests, and in many cases stayed behind to ask the administrators for more information about the tasks they had been asked to perform.

3 Category 3: using observation

3.1 Introduction

Nature of the category In this category performance is measured on tasks which essentially demand one of the following abilities or a combination of them: the ability to observe using a range of senses; the ability to select the relevant observations; and the ability to use observations to classify objects, to sequence or explain events and to make predictions. The tasks set to the pupils fall into three sub-categories:

3α - Using a key
3β - Observing similarities and differences
3γ - Interpreting observations

Form of the tests Within each sub-category the tasks varied according to the outcome expected from the pupil, the resource used and the setting or context of the question. The range of resource used included apparatus and other objects, photographs and live materials where appropriate. In addition pupils were given instructions to use equipment so that they could observe events. A balance was established between the three different types of resource ie 30−40 per cent photographs, 30−40 per cent objects and 30−40 per cent events, and this is reflected in the questions used. The setting of the tasks and the choice of resource were varied to ensure a spread across physical, chemical and biological contexts as well as those that could be seen as associated with everyday situations or other school subjects.

Three packages of questions were used, each package combining a random selection of questions from all three sub-categories. Constraints were imposed on the selection to ensure that each sub-category was appropriately represented and that there was a balance across different resources and context.

Each package was organised as a practical circus, an arrangement which allows the most efficient use of pupil testing time and resource. Each circus was composed of nine stations, with eight minutes' testing time allowed per station. This meant that nine pupils could be tested in 72 minutes. As they circulated round the nine stations of the circus, each pupil saw 14 different tasks.

Test administration The tests were administered and marked by science teachers released from the schools for 12 days. This period included one training day and one debriefing day. In the training session the teachers were able to go through each circus that they were to administer, question by question, and to make notes of relevant administrative details. Part of the training involved the organisation of the administrative work load; this needed careful planning in order to ensure that each pupil would have suitable and similar resources for the task in hand. Mark schemes were discussed and marker reliability trials were carried out on sample scripts. Each teacher had two different circuses to administer and was responsible for all the apparatus and any replacement needed, for both of them. The apparatus for each task was boxed in a separate kit; the kits were delivered to the administrators' homes.

The schools included in the sample had been asked to provide a laboratory with the usual services and to free a science teacher from normal duties in order to assist in the administration.

Details of administration   The administrator, by reading through the first page of the test booklet, introduced the pupils to the test, its purpose and intent. This page is reproduced below.

The way in which pupils were to move around in a circus was explained; each one was given a lettered badge which linked him or her to a particular station number at a given point in time. The pupils were told of the time allowed at each station and the number of tasks to be completed at each one. They were told when they had had half their allotted time at each station, and were warned when they had only one minute left. It was made clear to the pupils that any necessary help with reading would be given. In contrast to category 2 both the administrator and science teacher were instructed to assist pupils who had manipulative difficulties with any of the apparatus. The help was to be given when the difficulty was apparent: the pupils themselves did not have to request help.

A number of tasks from the tests have been chosen to illustrate the nature of the sub-categories and the range of resources and contexts employed.

3.2 Sub-category 3α: using a branching key

At age 13 the use of a simple identification key was included in the assessment, since keys feature in many major science courses used at this age. It was difficult

'Flower key'

You have been given four different flower pictures P, Q, R and S.
Try to name each flower by working through the sets of 'clues' below,
always starting at number 1.
Write the name of the flower next to its label at the bottom of the page.

1. Each flower has four petals — if YES go on to 2
   Each flower has five petals — if YES go on to 3
   Each flower has more than five petals — if YES go on to 4

2. Leaves are slightly jagged — GERMANDER SPEEDWELL
   Leaves are very jagged — TORMENTIL

3. Flowers are found singly or in groups of two — if YES go on to 5
   Flowers are found in groups of three or more — if YES go on to 6

4. Leaves grow from the bottom of the stem — HAWKWEED
   Leaves grow singly on alternate sides
   of the stem — if YES go on to 7

5. Leaves grow singly on alternate sides
   of the stem — BELLFLOWER
   Leaves grow in pairs along the stem,
   opposite one another — if YES go on to 8

6. Leaves grow in clusters on the stem — HERB ROBERT
   Leaf or leaves grow from the bottom of the stem. — FALSE OXLIP

7. Leaves are heart-shaped — LEOPARD'S BANE
   Leaves have jagged edges — MARSH RAGWORT

8. Leaves are oval — GREATER PERIWINKLE
   Leaves are long and thin — LESSER SPEARWORT

P is called . . . .
Q is called . . . .
R is called . . . .
S is called . . . .

Comment

In the example shown four flowers were to be identified — False Oxlip, Tormentil, Greater Periwinkle and Leopard's Bane. The pupils were presented with coloured photographs of real specimens of flowers and their leaves, labelled respectively P, Q, R and S.

Mark scheme

Flower key	Mark scheme
P — False Oxlip	1
Q — Tormentil	1
R — Greater Periwinkle	1
S — Leopard's Bane	1
Total	④

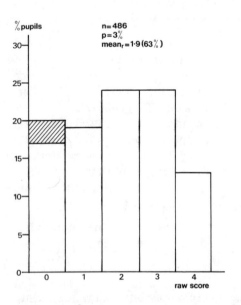

%pupils

n= 486
p= 3%
mean$_r$ = 1·9 (63%)

raw score

to decide in which category such tasks should be included, there being a burden on observation skills which suggested that they should be placed in category 3, accompanied by the necessity to follow written instructions, which makes for overlap with category 2. This dilemma was resolved partly by ensuring, during question trials, that — for the majority of pupils — the main burden in the tasks chosen was dependent on the pupils' ability to observe the similarities and differences referred to in the key.

Each test included one such task. The non-response rate varied between one per cent and five per cent.

The score distribution on the question 'Flower key' appears to be related to the number of observations required to identify a given specimen. Of the 24 per cent of pupils who scored three marks, the largest proportion failed to identify R (Greater Periwinkle). As can be seen from the question, identification of R demanded that four separate distinctions be made, which was more than was required for the other three specimens. Only two per cent of this group of pupils who scored three marks failed to identify Q (Tormentil) which required only two of the specified observations. The relationship between successful identification of the specimen and the number of observations required was also obvious amongst the 24 per cent of pupils who scored 2 marks. Seventeen per cent identified Q (Tormentil) and P (False Oxlip) or S (Leopard's Bane) and only seven per cent scored two by identifying R (Greater Periwinkle) and one other. Similarly the highest proportion scoring one did so by identifying Q (Tormentil).

On the task 'Shell key' about 70 per cent of the pupils scored in the lower ranges, ie 0–2 marks. Consideration of the question shows that to identify two of the specimens, P and Q, between three and four distinctions had to be made whereas at least five observations had to be made in order to identify samples S and R. Thus it was very much easier to score the first two marks than to score the second two. This task had the highest proportion of pupils scoring zero (25 per cent) of the three key tasks.

Summary of results for sub-category 3α

Table 3.1   *Summary of results for sub-category 3α*

Task	Mean score (Max. = 4)	Proportion of pupils giving no response
Flower key	1.9	3%
Crystal key	2.2	1%
Shell key	1.7	5%

The differences on the three key tasks in terms of mean score, non-response rate and score distribution appear to be due to a combination of two factors: the number of specific observations required to identify the specimen and the nature and difficulty of the individual observations involved.

'Crystal key'

You are given a hand lens and a collection of substances all labelled on watch glasses.
Try to name each substance by working through the pairs of 'clues' below, always starting at number 1.
Write the name of the substance next to its label at the bottom of the page.

1. The substance is in crystal form   if YES go on to 2
   The substance is in powder form   if YES go on to 3

2. The crystal is colourless   if YES go on to 4
   The crystal is coloured   if YES go on to 5

3. The substance is a white powder   LIMESTONE
   The substance is a green powder   COPPER CARBONATE

4. The crystal face is shaped like a squashed
   oblong (parallelogram)   CALCITE
   The crystal face is shaped like a
   rectangle   ROCK SALT

5. The crystal is blue   if YES GO ON TO 6
   The crystal is not blue   if YES go on to 7

6. The crystal face is shaped like a diamond.   COPPER SULPHATE
   The crystals are rod-shaped with
   hexagonal ends   CALCIUM COPPER ACETATE

7. The crystal is flat and shaped like
   a diamond   RHOMBIC SULPHUR
   The crystal is shaped like
   needles   MONOCLINIC SULPHUR

   P is called . . . .
   Q is called . . . .
   R is called . . . .
   S is called . . . .

Comment

In the second example of a key task, the objects to be identified were four specimens of seed crystals. The crystals were displayed on watch glasses and a hand lens was provided.

Mark scheme

Crystal key	Mark scheme
P = copper sulphate	1
Q = calcite	1
R = rhombic sulphur	1
S = calcium copper acetate	1
Total	④

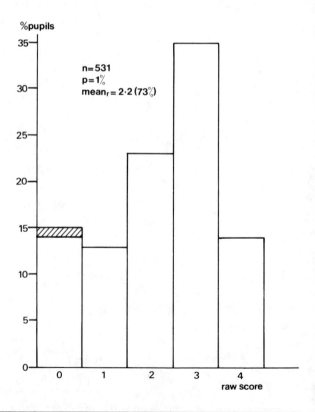

%pupils

n=531
p=1%
$mean_r = 2.2$ (73%)

raw score

'Shell key'

You are given four different shells P, Q, R and S.
Try to name each shell by working through the sets of 'clues'
below, always starting at number 1.
Write the name of the shell next to its label at the bottom of
the page.

1. Shell has ridges that can be clearly seen   if YES go on to 2
    Shell has no clearly seen ridges   if YES go on to 3

2. Shell has slit up the side   EMARGINULA RETICULATA
    Shell has no slit up the side   if YES go on to 3

3. Shell is oval shaped   PATELLA VULGATA
    Shell is not oval shaped   if YES go on to 4

4. Shell has bright blue spots   PATINA PELLUCIDA
    Shell is speckled and banded with colour   CREPIDULA FORNICATA
    Shell is not speckled but has shades or
      bands of colour   if YES go on to 5

5. Shell is less than 5 cm at widest point   if YES go on to 6
    Shell is more than 5 cm at widest point   if YES go on to 7

6. Shell is spiral-shaped and like an ice-cream
      cone   TURRITELLA COMMUNIS
    Shell is spiral-shaped but with a widely-spread
      base   APORRHAIS PELECANI

7. Shell has no regular shape   CRASSOSTREA ANGULATA
    Shell has a fan-like shape   PECTEN MAXIMUM

P is called . . . .

Q is called . . . .

R is called . . . .

S is called . . . .

Comment

In the third example the objects to be identified were four actual shell samples. The shells were presented on a white background and labelled P, Q, R and S respectively.

Mark scheme

Shell key	*Mark scheme*
P = Crepidula Fornicata	1
Q = Patella Vulgata	1
R = Pecten Maximum	1
S = Turitella Communis	1
Total	④

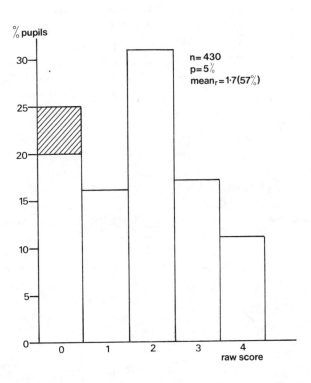

% pupils

n= 430
p=5%
mean$_r$=1·7(57%)

raw score

'Crystal key' had the highest mean score and the lowest non-response rate. The score distribution shows that 58 per cent of the pupils achieved between two and three marks. The number of observations necessary to identify a crystal varied between three and four. The nature of the observations required included distinguishing between a crystal and a powder, between colours and between simple shapes.

On the 'Flower key' task the non-response rate was higher (three per cent) and more pupils scored zero than on the 'Crystal key'. The number of observations necessary for identification of the flowers ranged from two to four but only 48 per cent of the pupils scored two or three marks compared to 58 per cent on 'Crystal key'. The observations the pupils had to make were less obvious and more detailed than those needed in 'Crystal key'. Distinctions that had to be made included those between the number of petals, leaf shape, degree of raggedness of the leaves and the method of leaf formation on the stem.

'Shell key' had the highest non-response rate (five per cent) and 20 per cent of the pupils scored zero on this task. Like 'Flower key', the observations required covered a wider range and were more detailed than those involved in 'Crystal key'. The mean score on this task was the lowest (1.7). Far fewer pupils (28 per cent) scored three or four marks, compared to (37 per cent) on 'Flower key' and (49 per cent) on 'Crystal key'. In order to gain these marks on 'Shell key' six different observations had to be made to identify each of the shells R (Pecten Maximum) and S (Tormentil Communis).

The nature of the resource did not appear to affect the performance, as both 'Crystal key' and 'Shell key' depended on the identification of real objects.

There were no consistent differences between the performances of the boys and girls on these tasks. The girls did better on 'Flower key' and 'Shell key' which might suggest a context effect as both these tasks are in biological settings. On the 'Crystal key' task the boys achieved a raw mean score of 2.4 compared to 2.0 for the girls.

3.3 Sub-category 3β: observing similarities and differences

The range of questions used   A range of different types of task was considered necessary in order to assess pupils' ability to observe similarities and differences. The tasks varied in the demand made on the pupil and included grouping and classifying, recording changes, matching drawings and verbal descriptions and sequencing events. There were also tasks in which differences and/or similarities between objects or between photographs had to be stated. The mode of response varied from coded answer to an extended response and in some cases scientific drawings were required. A number of questions have been selected to illustrate pupils' performance on different tasks and across different types of question.

Classification   One question type had two distinct parts. The first part involved pupils in identifying the rules which had been used to classify objects. The objects were presented already arranged in three groups to exemplify the rules.

Performance on this part of the task depended on the nature and complexity of the observations demanded.

For example in one task, 'Solid sorting', the pupils were presented with 18 phials filled with different substances (powders, eg zinc dust, irregular solids, eg silica gel, and man-made regular shapes, eg marbles) placed in three groups of six by mass. In order to identify the rule used in the classification the pupils had to employ the sense of feel.

The score distribution for this task is shown beside the question.

'Solid sorting'

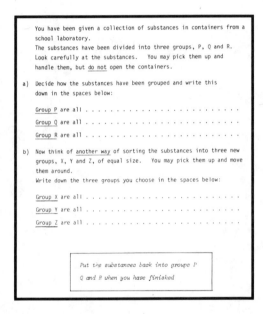

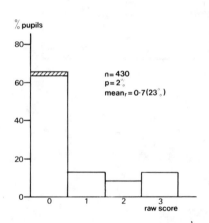

A similar task in which buttons had been classified by number of holes had the score distribution shown for part (a) (over).

A similar score distribution as that for part (a) of 'Buttons' was obtained for a task where a number of groceries had been classified according to their packaging. The raw mean score for this task was 2.5 which was 83 per cent of the maximum.

The second part of this example involved the pupils in establishing their own rules for classifying the objects. The objects were so chosen and the question so phrased that there was only one alternative method of classification. For each of the tasks this part proved to be more difficult and a higher proportion of pupils scored zero.

The second histogram illustrates the point in the case of the 'Buttons' task.

'Buttons'

Mark scheme

You have been given a collection of buttons.
The buttons have been divided into three groups, P, Q and R.
Look carefully at the buttons.   You may pick them up and
handle them.

a)   Decide how the buttons have been grouped and write this down
in the spaces below:

Group P are all . . . .
Group Q are all . . . .
Group R are all . . . .

b)   Now think of another way of sorting the buttons into three new
groups, X, Y and Z, of equal size.   You may pick them up and
move them about.
Write down the three groups you choose in the spaces below:

Group X are all . . . .
Group Y are all . . . .
Group Z are all . . . .

Put the buttons back into groups
P, Q and R when you have finished.

Buttons

		Mark scheme
a) P — 2 holes		1
Q — 1 hole		1
R — 4 holes		1
	Total	③
b) X—metal		1
Y—plastic		1
Z—wood		1
	Total	③
	Question total	⑥

a) and b) parts of question scored separately.

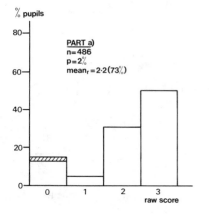

PART a)
n=486
p=2%
mean$_r$=2·2(73%)

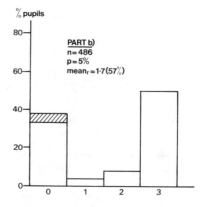

PART b)
n=486
p=5%
mean$_r$=1·7(57%)

The raw mean score on the second part of 'Buttons' was about 55 per cent of the maximum compared to 70 per cent on the first part. Similarly in the task 'Groceries' in which groceries were classified there was a 20 per cent drop in performance level on the second part of the task. There was also an increase in the number of pupils who did not attempt to answer this part of the question. In the case of the 'Buttons' task it increased from two to five per cent and in the 'Solid sorting' from two to 18 per cent of the pupils.

Observing similarities and differences The two question types which involved statements of similarities and differences were attempted by virtually all the pupils. In the case where as many differences as possible had to be stated the performance level was about 50 per cent for all tasks. The only consistent difference between results for these tasks and those for types in which a specified number of differences and similarities was required was that a larger proportion of pupils scored at the extremes in the latter case. The latter kind also appeared to be easier, with a performance level around 60 per cent of the maximum.

Observing changes A number of tasks which involved the pupils in observing events and recording changes showed similar score distributions with the majority of pupils scoring in the middle range or just below. The distribution appeared to be affected by the demands on the different senses and the degree of direction given in the question with regard to what observations should be made. The following example employs the sense of sight and very little direction is given to indicate what to observe.

'Swindle'

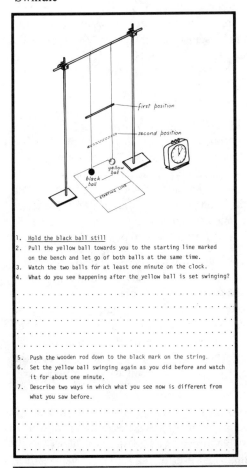

1. Hold the black ball still
2. Pull the yellow ball towards you to the starting line marked on the bench and let go of both balls at the same time.
3. Watch the two balls for at least one minute on the clock.
4. What do you see happening after the yellow ball is set swinging?

. . . .
. . . .
. . . .
. . . .

5. Push the wooden rod down to the black mark on the string.
6. Set the yellow ball swinging again as you did before and watch it for about one minute.
7. Describe two ways in which what you see now is different from what you saw before.

. . . .
. . . .
. . . .
. . . .

Mark scheme

Swindle	*Mark scheme*
a) Black sphere starts moving	1
Black sphere swings further each time	1
Yellow sphere slows	1
Yellow sphere (nearly) stops	1
Wood starts to move	1
Cycle repeats itself	1
Black swings about as far as yellow	1
(any of above points) Max.	5
b) The same changes in movement, but quicker	1
Sideways movement less	1
Cycle repeats itself (rapidly)	1
Max.	2
Total	⑦

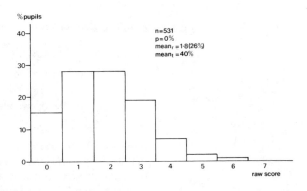

% pupils

n=531
p=0%
mean$_r$ =1·8(26%)
mean$_t$ =40%

raw score

The pupils were presented with the apparatus as shown in the diagram and help was given to operate the stop clock if needed. The mark scheme outlines the observations possible. Of the total number of observations made 44 per cent of the pupils observed the black sphere beginning to move but only 16 per cent observed the yellow sphere slowing. The detailed observations relating to the movement of the spheres were noted by only five per cent of the pupils. A similar proportion observed the repetition of the cycle and only one per cent recorded the movement of the wooden rod. When the wooden rod was lowered to the second position 30 per cent of the observations related to the decrease in sideways movement, 13 per cent to the changes in movement being the same but quicker and again four per cent observed the repetition of the cycle.

The mean score on this task was about 40 per cent of the maximum. Other tasks of the same question type had a mean score around 50 per cent but in these cases more direction was given about what to observe and the changes involved were more obvious.

Matching   Another question type required pupils to match drawings to real objects or photographs of them. Here again the mean score varied according to the number and the difficulty of the observations to be made. For example the matching of an insect's leg (enclosed in resin) to one of nine drawings had a mean score of 40 per cent of the maximum, whilst matching a photograph of a telephone to six possible drawings had a mean score of 60 per cent. Matching an actual plant to a drawing of five possible ones had a mean score of 80 per cent of the maximum.

Summary of results for sub-category 3β   Three category three practical circuses were administered in this survey, each containing a similar mixture of 3β and 3γ questions (with a sole 3α question). Sub-category 3β was in fact represented by a total of 27 questions — nine per circus. The raw mark distribution resulting from the administration of these three 3β sub-tests was normal with a mean score about half-way along the mark scale. Almost 1 500 pupils attempted one or other of these practical circuses, and no child failed to achieve at least one mark for 3β performance. The maximum score obtained was about 90 per cent.

Pupil performance on individual tasks appeared to be affected by several factors; however, the number of tasks used means that any discussion about the relationship between pupil performance and these factors is rather tentative. Tasks depending upon the sense of touch tended to have mean scores below 50 per cent of the maximum. Similarly where the sense of smell was involved the performance level on the tasks dropped. Pupils appeared to perform better when the tasks depended on sight alone. However, as in the 'Swindle' example, the mean score achieved was lower when little direction about what to observe was given.

Another factor apparently affecting pupil performance was the number and detail of observations required. In the question type which required pupils to match an object to one of several possible drawings of it, the mean score varied from 40 to 80 per cent of the maximum. The lowest mean score was achieved on

'Insect legs'

You have been given a specimen of an insect's leg and drawings
of nine different insects' legs.
Use a hand lens to look carefully at the specimen.

Which <u>one</u> of the drawings, P, Q, R, S, T, U, V, W or X, is most
like the leg of your specimen?

The drawing most like the specimen is drawing . . . . . .

Comment

Detailed observation of the actual specimen is required in this
task and the pupils were provided with a hand lens. The drawings
used were twice the size of those shown on the right.

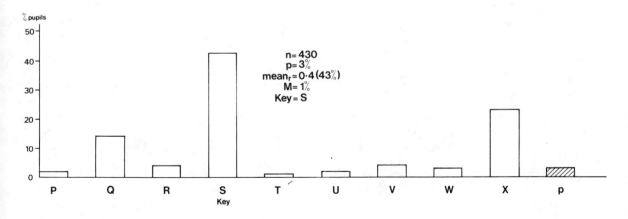

n= 430
p= 3%
mean_r= 0·4 (43%)
M= 1%
Key= S

'Telephone match'

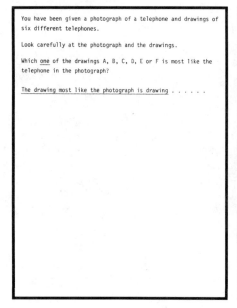

You have been given a photograph of a telephone and drawings of six different telephones.

Look carefully at the photograph and the drawings.

Which <u>one</u> of the drawings A, B, C, D, E or F is most like the telephone in the photograph?

<u>The drawing most like the photograph is drawing</u> . . . . . .

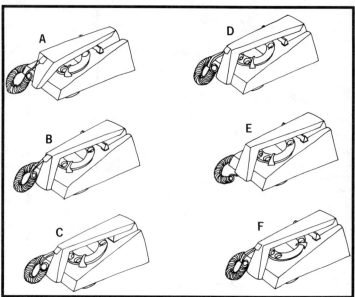

Drawings are reduced to a quarter of the actual size.

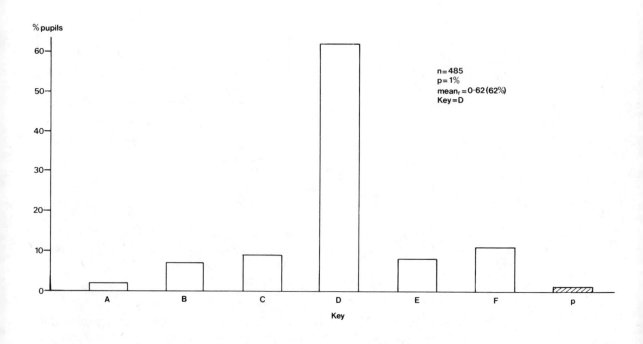

n=485
p=1%
mean$_r$=0·62 (62%)
Key=D

the task which had the most drawings (nine) to be considered. The highest mean score was for the task with the fewest drawings. In the question type which asked for as many differences as possible to be stated between two objects or photographs, the lowest mean score was 47 per cent of the maximum. This task required many more observations to be made compared to the others in order to select those relevant for the solution of the problem.

In one question type an enlarged part of a photograph had to be identified and marked on a copy of the whole. Pupils appeared to find this type of task difficult and the mean scores varied from 20 to 45 per cent of the maximum. The mean score decreased as the amount of detail to be considered in the individual photographs increased.

Performance varied with the type of task set to the pupil. The mean scores achieved when pupils had to identify the rules used to classify objects were considerably higher (by about 20 per cent) than when they had to establish their own rules. Tasks which required pupils to state as many differences between objects as possible had a performance level around 53 per cent. When the number of differences to be stated was fixed, the mean scores increased to around 62 per cent. The type of question with the lowest performance level was the one already mentioned where a magnified part of a photograph had to be matched to the whole. The average mean score for this type was 30 per cent of the maximum, compared with 60 per cent for most other types. The group of tasks with the next lowest performance level (≈ 45 per cent) required pupils to observe events and record changes. In this type of question very little direction was given to the pupils as to what they should observe and the events chosen offered a wide variety of changes.

In this sub-category the girls' mean scores were higher than the boys' on tasks that involved stating as many differences as possible. On tasks where an object or photograph had to be matched to a drawing or a written description there was little difference between boys and girls, even with respect to the proportions opting for different distractors. The slight difference between the performance level estimates for boys and girls in 3β — in favour of the girls — is not statistically significant.

3.4 Sub-category 3 γ: interpreting observations

Range of questions used   In the previous sub-category 3β pupils had to make observations and then select the relevant ones. In 3γ a further step is demanded in that once the selection has been made the pupil must then generalise to do one of the following: create a hypothesis; identify a pattern; give an explanation or make a prediction. The tasks in this sub-category involved the pupils mainly in practical activities. Care was taken that the manipulation skills necessary were minimal and did not act as a hurdle to the observations required.

Making predictions   In one question type pupils were asked to record changes and then make predictions based on the relationships observed. Again the performance level varied according to the nature and complexity of the

'Liquid ball'

You have been given three long tubes filled with different liquids, four different balls, a stop-clock and three bottles containing a sample of the liquids P, Q and R.

You may pick up the bottles but do not take their tops off.

Your job is to find out how long it takes for the different balls to fall down through the liquids.

a) Take a marble, drop it into tube P and time its fall:

Time taken in tube P . . . .

Repeat using a new marble in each of the other two tubes:

Time taken in tube Q . . . .

Time taken in tube R . . . .

What do you notice about the thickness of the liquid and the time it takes a ball to drop?

. . . .

. . . .

b) Take metal ball 1 and drop it into tube P.   Time its fall

Time taken by metal ball 1 . . . .

Take metal ball 2 and drop it into tube P.   Time its fall:

Time taken by metal ball 2 . . . .

What do you notice about the balls and the time they take to drop?

. . . .

. . . .

c) Pick up the metal ball X.

DO NOT DROP IT in a tube.

About how long do you think this ball would take to drop —

in tube P ? . . . .

in tube Q ? . . . .

in tube R ? . . . .

Mark scheme

Apparatus

4 × 1 metre plastic tubes (1 spare) containing:

Glycerol	—P
Dimethylsilicone	—Q
Water	—R

3 phials containing the above liquids and labelled.
1 stop-clock
3 funnels
30 marbles
10 metal balls 1
10 metal balls 2
2 metal balls X
1 paper towel
4 clampstands

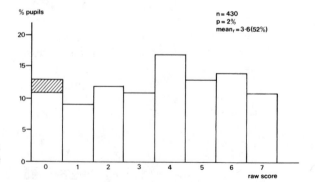

Comment

In this task pupils were presented with the listed apparatus. Each of the three tubes was filled with a different liquid — P being the most viscous and R the least

observations required. For example two tasks involved the sense of sight; in one the prediction was based on the relationship between two observable variables and the mean score was around 80 per cent of the maximum; in the other task the relationship depended on three observable variables and had a mean score around 70 per cent of the maximum. A similar task in terms of question type involved relating observations of sound and sight and had a mean score around 50 per cent of the maximum. An example of this question type is 'Liquid ball'.

In part (a) of the task the pupils were asked to observe and state the relationship between the time of fall and the thickness of the liquids. Thirty four per cent of the pupils failed to score anything on this part. Eighteen per cent recorded specific observations but did not relate them and 47 per cent correctly stated the relationship. There was a six per cent non-response rate and the overall raw mean score was around 50 per cent of the maximum.

In part (b) of the task the pupils were asked to observe and state the relationship between the time of fall and the size of the balls. Forty per cent of the pupils failed to score and 20 per cent recorded specific observations. For example, metal ball 2 falls slowly. Forty per cent of the pupils correctly stated the relationship. There was a 17 per cent non-response rate and the raw mean score was around 50 per cent of the maximum.

In part (c) of the task the pupils were asked to link the two observed relationships and make predictions based on them. Thirty-four per cent of the pupils scored zero, 12 per cent made one correct prediction, 26 per cent made two correct predictions and 20 per cent made three correct predictions. The non-response rate on this part had increased to 26 per cent of the pupils and the raw mean score was around 50 per cent of the maximum.

Selecting explanations   In the question type in which pupils were to record changes during an event and select an appropriate explanation, the performance level varied according to the nature of the observations required. One task, which depended on the senses of touch and smell, had a mean score around 50 per cent of the maximum whereas one which depended on direct observation by sight had a higher mean score of 60 per cent.

In the last example, 'Curdled milk', the pupils had to add different solutions (each labelled with its name and pH value) to milk in a test tube. After observing and recording any changes they were then asked to select an appropriate explanation with the aid of a pH chart.

On the first part of the task, which involved recording changes, three of the possible changes had something in common, as did the other three. This explains the peaks in the score distribution at three and six, for more pupils who spotted one change tended also to notice the other two associated with it.

The score distribution for the whole task, which included three marks for selecting the appropriate explanation, demonstrates how that ability appears to differ from the one involved in recording changes. Two per cent of the pupils who scored no marks for recording changes selected the correct explanation. The

'Curdled milk'

You have been given six liquids each labelled with its name and pH
number, a test tube rack with six clean test tubes, a bottle
of milk and an indicator chart.

a) Place about 1 cm of milk in each test tube.   To one test tube
add a few squirts of vinegar.   Shake the tube and notice what
happens.   Using a fresh test tube of milk each time, repeat this
for each of the other liquids.
Make notes below about what happens.

Liquid	What happens to milk when liquid is added
Vinegar	. . . .
Baking soda	. . . .
Lemon juice	. . . .
Water	. . . .
Wine	. . . .
Caustic soda	. . . .

b) Which one of the following best explains what you noticed about the
liquids and the milk?   Tick in the box next to the one you choose.

Milk is curdled (made to go lumpy) by:

☐   A   acids only

☐   B   alkalis only

☐   C   alkalis above pH 10 only

☐   D   acids below pH 4 only

☐   E   acids below pH 4 and alkalis above pH 10

☐   F   both acids and alkalis

*Empty the test tubes and put them
in the container provided.*

Mark scheme

Curdled milk   *Mark scheme*

a) Vinegar — lumpy or bitty or curdled   1
   Baking soda — no change   1
   Lemon juice — lumpy or bitty or curdled   1
   Water — no change or gets thinner   1
   Wine — lumpy or bitty or curdled   1
   Caustic soda — no change   1

                          Total   ⑥

b) Key A   3

                   Question total   ⑨

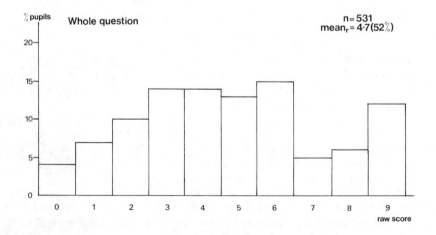

% pupils   **Whole question**   n = 531
                                         mean$_r$ = 4·7 (52%)

'Curdled milk'

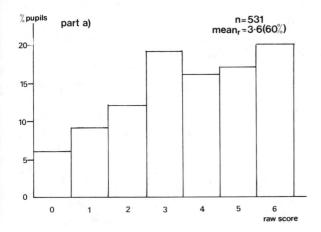

score distribution in Figure 3.1 shows the proportions of pupils who selected the correct explanation in part (b) and the score they obtained on recording changes in part (a).

Figure 3.1 *Relationship between scores on parts (a) and (b) of 'Curdled milk'.*

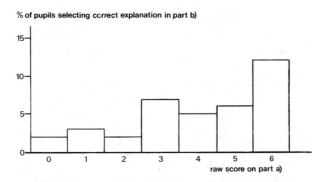

Boys and girls varied in their choice of key and distractor on other tasks of this type. This is best illustrated by considering a task, 'Polyglass', in which a plastic bottle and a glass bottle of the same volume were placed together in hot and then in cold water for fixed times. The bottles contained the same volume of dye solution, the level of which could be read off from calibrated capillary tubes in the necks of the bottles. When the bottles are placed in hot water the level in the plastic bottle decreases markedly and in the glass bottle there is a small initial fall and then the dye rises. The levels change again when the bottles are transferred from the hot water to the cold water. The dye rises in the plastic bottle back to the original level and falls in the glass bottle. The correct explanation for the changes in levels in terms of differential expansion was selected by 24 per cent of the boys and only 14 per cent of the girls. However 27 per cent of the girls, compared with only ten per cent of the boys, selected the explanation that the atmospheric pressure had a differential effect on the bottles.

Summary of results for sub-category 3γ   Five questions in each of the three category three practical circuses provided a total of 15 questions for assessment of overall 3γ performance. The mean raw scores for each sub-test were about half of the maximum possible mark for 3γ performance. The maximum score obtained was around 85 per cent.

In the whole of this sub-category, 3γ, of which these tasks are examples, the performance level and score distribution varied with the individual task rather than the type of task set. Unlike 3β the performance across a question type was not consistent: the greatest range in mean scores was from 20 to 83 per cent. A variation of between 20 to 30 per cent was common for most question types. No one question type appeared more difficult than another. In this sub-category the type of observation that the task depended on eg sight, sound, etc., did not appear to be significant. The performance on the tasks seemed to be most affected by the number of observations required and the content and setting of the task.

Two tasks which involved recording changes and identifying a pattern varied both in mean score (from 30 to 60 per cent of the maximum) and distribution. In the first task the pattern involved three variables whereas in the second only two variables had to be observed and related. The majority of pupils scored in the lower-middle ranges on the first task with only two per cent of pupils failing to score. On the second task around 68 per cent of the pupils scored on the upper range of the scale but 24 per cent failed to observe and identify the pattern.

On the question type which involved noting differences and making predictions the performance again varied across tasks. One task of this type required the pupils to relate the diameter of bore of different capillary tubes firstly to the level to which one liquid would rise and secondly to the level to which liquids of different viscosity would rise. The pupils were able to note individual differences but failed on the whole to observe the relationship between them. As a result very few were able to make the prediction based on this relationship. The mean score for this task was around 20 per cent of the maximum — with 50 per cent of the pupils failing to score and 37 per cent scoring only one or two out of a possible five marks.

A different task but from the same question type as above required the pupils to observe the differences between the notes made when stretched strings of different thicknesses were plucked. The second part of the task then required the pupils to relate the length of the strings to the sound produced. The final part of the task was to make a prediction by relating both the thickness and length of the string to the sound produced. The score distribution for this task showed that many pupils were able to do all three parts with 59 per cent scoring nearly full marks. The proportion failing to score was only three per cent and the mean score was about 80 per cent of the maximum.

Two tasks which looked at the same ability as the ones mentioned above but differed in that the prediction had to be selected not generated, had a performance level around 50 per cent of the maximum. However, in one in which the pupil had to decide the likely environment of a bird from drawings of birds' feet, the score distribution was normal, more pupils scoring in the middle range than at the extremes. In the other, in which the method of seed dispersal had to be decided by observing photographs of the plant and seeds, the score distribution was linear, with almost equal numbers of pupils getting each possible score from 0 to the maximum.

In this sub-category, 3y, there were no consistent differences between the performances of boys and girls. The slight performance difference in favour of girls did not reach statistical significance. There was variation in the relative performance of girls and boys with the content of the question but it was small and insignificant.

4 Category 4: interpretation and application

4.1 Introduction

The nature of the category   This category is concerned with the overall ability of interpretation and application. It is divided into two very different parts. In one part the questions have all the information necessary for an answer in the question itself. The questions involve interpretation of data and require pupils to identify patterns or trends, whereas the other part has questions which require the recall and application of science concepts in given situations.

Within these two divisions there are further sub-categories which occur, as in previous categories, because of the nature of the questions and the demands made on the pupil.

The five sub-categories relate to the two main divisions as follows:

Interpretation not requiring science concepts	4α:	describing and/or using patterns in presented information.
	4β:	making judgements about the application of a given generalisation to a presented situation.
	4γ:	distinguishing between the degree of inference in different statements about the same event.
Interpretation and application of science concepts	4δ:	making sense of new information using science concepts.
	4ε:	generating alternative hypotheses about presented situations.

Test administration   The questions in this category were presented in hour-long paper and pencil tests. The number of questions per package varied and was based on the criterion that the majority of pupils would be able to finish within an hour. As in all other categories pupils were told that help would be given with reading. The first page of a test booklet is reproduced below.

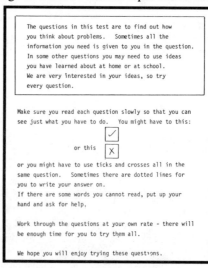

The questions in this test are to find out how you think about problems. Sometimes all the information you need is given to you in the question. In some other questions you may need to use ideas you have learned about at home or at school. We are very interested in your ideas, so try every question.

Make sure you read each question slowly so that you can see just what you have to do. You might have to this:

or this

or you might have to use ticks and crosses all in the same question. Sometimes there are dotted lines for you to write your answer on.
If there are some words you cannot read, put up your hand and ask for help.

Work through the questions at your own rate - there will be enough time for you to try them all.

We hope you will enjoy trying these questions.

It was clear during the trials of these questions that the language could and did in some cases act as a hurdle to the abilities being tested. Efforts were made to reduce the dependence on reading skills but by the very nature of the subject under test this was not always possible. The tests were administered by teachers within the school who had instructions about the degree and type of help which could be given to the pupils.

> We should like every pupil to have sufficient time to do all of which he or she is capable, so there is no time limit for the tests. However, we expect most pupils to finish within one hour. Please provide for those finishing early by arranging some quiet work for them.
>
> Each pupil will need a pencil or pen and a ruler.
>
> Before the pupils begin the test, help them fill in the boxes on the cover. Write the date on the board and give any assistance necessary to write their age.
>
> When the cover has been completed, tell the pupils to turn to the next page and to read the instructions carefully. Please note that different tests have different instructions.
>
> We are anxious that pupils' responses should not be unduly affected by poor reading ability. Therefore, if any pupil asks for help, please read the instructions or any of the questions to him or her privately, once slowly whilst pointing out words, and a second time at normal speed. For pupils who ask for individual words, these can be read without giving the whole question.
>
> Emphasise that the pupils should try all the questions and thus if they are stuck on certain questions they should leave these, go on and possibly return to the difficult ones later.

Within this category there was inevitable overlap with other categories. For example, in some questions the ability to read a graph was needed in order to make the appropriate interpretations. An overlap with category 1. The questions were written so that the burden was on the ability to interpret and use the presented information. Where observation of a drawing was necessary to collect information the drawing emphasised the features that the pupils had to observe.

4.2 Sub-category 4α: describing and/or using patterns in information

The range of questions used   A number of different question types were used in this sub-category. The questions differed from each other in several ways, for example in the nature and method of presentation of the data which could be in pictorial, graphical or tabular forms. The question in addition could have a selection of patterns and/or predictions from which the pupils had to choose the correct interpretation. In other types of question the pupils had to give explanations or make predictions based on the pattern discerned in the data. A variety of ways of getting pupils to describe patterns was also included in the questions.

There were 27 questions used in the survey from this sub-category which were divided so that there were nine in each of three packages. A number of questions are illustrated, followed by general discussion of results of similar questions.

In the example 'Elastic band', the pattern was presented in a table of results. Pupils had to discern the pattern by identifying the 'odd man out'. The methods that could be used to discern the pattern were also presented and the pupils had to select an appropriate one. Several methods were equally applicable and so no marks were awarded in part (a).

Seven per cent of the pupils successfully identified the error after drawing a complete or partially complete line graph. All of these pupils used two equal interval scales and scored between 2 and 3 marks. Three per cent of pupils who got full marks did so by either plotting a correct and complete bar chart, or by identifying the intervals between the numbers and stating them. The 15 per cent of pupils who scored two marks were made up of eight per cent who plotted a line graph and seven per cent who plotted a bar chart. Most of these pupils failed to identify the error. Pupils scored one mark by either attempting to work out the intervals between the figures and thus identifying the error (seven per cent) or by making a reasonable attempt at part (b) in terms of plotting a graph or calculating the intervals but failing part (c) of the question.

Fifty−six per cent of pupils failed to score. Among these were 12 per cent who made no attempt at any part of the question and 12 per cent who only attempted (a) for which no marks were given.

Overall the pupils who attempted part (b) and/or part (c) of the question did so as shown in Table 4.1.

Table 4.1   *Categories of response: 'Elastic band'*

Nature of response	% of pupils who attempted part b) and/or part c)
Line graph	29
Bar chart	20
Pattern in numbers	46
Writing an equation	4
Pie chart	1

The largest proportion of pupils elected to look at a pattern in numbers (46 per cent). This included nine per cent who identified the error, nine per cent who attempted to work out the intervals but incorrectly identified the error and 28 per cent who made no attempt at part (b) and made an incorrect guess for part (c).

Sixteen per cent of the boys failed to attempt the question compared to ten per cent of the girls. The raw mean scores were very similar. Girls appeared to be more successful at drawing line graphs than bar charts and the reverse was true for the boys.

Discerning patterns

'Elastic band'

A group of pupils was investigating the way a thick rubber band stretches. They hung the rubber band with a light pan on the end of it from a hook. They added marbles one at a time to make the band stretch. The marbles each had the same mass. Every time a marble was added the length of the rubber band was measured. The results are shown in the table below.

Number of marbles N	1	2	3	4	5	6
Length in cm (l)	5	11	10	12	13	13.5

A mistake has been made in one of their measurements. You are to find out which one it is.

a) Tick which one of the following methods you would use to find this out.

- [ ] A   Drawing a bar graph
- [ ] B   Looking at the pattern in the numbers
- [ ] C   Drawing a pie chart
- [ ] D   Drawing a line graph
- [ ] E   Writing an equation between N and l.

b) Use the method you have chosen to find out which result is the mistake.

c) Which result is the mistake?

. . . .

Mark scheme

Elastic band   *Mark scheme*

a) No marks

b) Appropriate sketch, graph (bar or line or number   2
   pattern)
   (Reasonable attempt score 1)

c) Incorrect result—2 marbles   1
   11cm length

                                           Maximum Total ③

Mark distribution

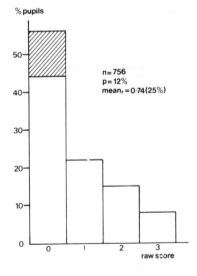

% pupils

n = 756
p = 12%
mean$_r$ = 0·74 (25%)

raw score

'Food needs'

This table is about the mass of food some animals need.

	Mass of animal	Food needed each day	Mass of food divided by mass of animal
Guinea-pig	667 g	95 g	$\frac{1}{7}$
Rabbit	2,000 g	67 g	$\frac{1}{30}$
Man	70,000 g	1,400 g	$\frac{1}{50}$
Whale	120,000 Kg	120,000 g	$\frac{1}{1,000}$

A mouse has a mass of 250 g.

About how much of its mass would it need in food each day?

Tick in the box next to the one you choose:

A   About $\frac{1}{2}$

B   About $\frac{1}{7}$

C   About $\frac{1}{8}$

D   About $\frac{1}{10}$

E   About $\frac{1}{20}$

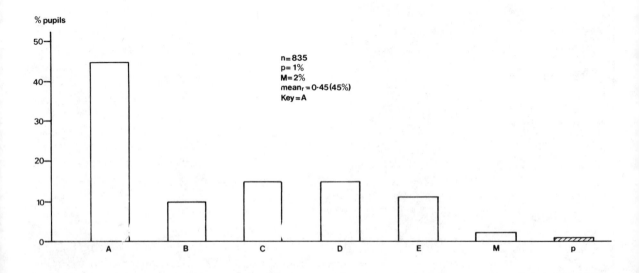

% pupils

n = 835
p = 1%
M = 2%
mean$_r$ = 0·45 (45%)
Key = A

Selecting a prediction   In this type of question the pupils had to select a prediction based on their interpretation of the presented data.

In the example, 'Food needs', three different columns of figures had to be related. Once the pattern between them had been discerned only one of the answers given was possible and no further interpretations were necessary.

In another question of the same type, 'Celery', the pupils had to link a trend in the time taken for ink to rise up a stem to the degree of leaf formation. The mean score for this question (33 per cent) was lower than 'Food needs' although the latter was mathematically more complex. The difference in performance can possibly be explained because discerning the pattern in 'Celery' was only the first step in the interpretation of the data. Once this was accomplished a finer judgement was required between three of the options, all of which were possible, in order to select the correct prediction. In the previous example, 'Food needs', there was only one possible answer.

In other questions of this type but in which data was not presented in a numerical form the performance level was around 80 per cent of the maximum.

In the example 'Bacteria' over, the information was presented in prose and a simple pictorial table. As in the 'Food needs' example, once the initial deduction had been made there was only one possible answer and the mean score was 84 per cent of the maximum. The results indicate that pupils' ability to select a prediction based on a pattern depends on the complexity and content of the information and the range of possible answers to be considered.

Making a prediction   Questions asking for a prediction to be made rather than to be selected had a lower performance level overall.

All of these questions required one word answers, sketches or numerical responses. Some of the questions involved the relating of observed size to numerical values. An example of this sort involved pulley systems made from 'cotton reels' of different sizes and connected together by bands. In order to make the necessary prediction about the direction, speed and distance moved by different reels the pupils had to relate the size of the two reels and the way in which they were connected. The mean score for this question was 57 per cent of the maximum which was higher than the mean score for another question of the same type about birds' eggs (50 per cent). In this question pupils had to consider two sets of figures and the size of different birds' eggs. They had to deduce from these three variables the fact that they could not predict from the size of an egg the likely number to be laid, but that they could predict the average number of days it would take to hatch.

In two other questions of this type the information to be interpreted was presented in a simple sketch graph form. In one question once the interpretation relating the graphical data to the written data had been made the predictions

'Bacteria'

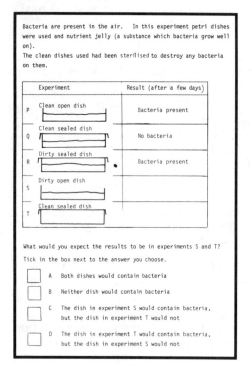

Bacteria are present in the air.   In this experiment petri dishes were used and nutrient jelly (a substance which bacteria grow well on).
The clean dishes used had been sterilised to destroy any bacteria on them.

Experiment		Result (after a few days)
P	Clean open dish	Bacteria present
Q	Clean sealed dish	No bacteria
R	Dirty sealed dish	Bacteria present
S	Dirty open dish	
T	Clean sealed dish	

What would you expect the results to be in experiments S and T?

Tick in the box next to the answer you choose.

A   Both dishes would contain bacteria

B   Neither dish would contain bacteria

C   The dish in experiment S would contain bacteria, but the dish in experiment T would not

D   The dish in experiment T would contain bacteria, but the dish in experiment S would not

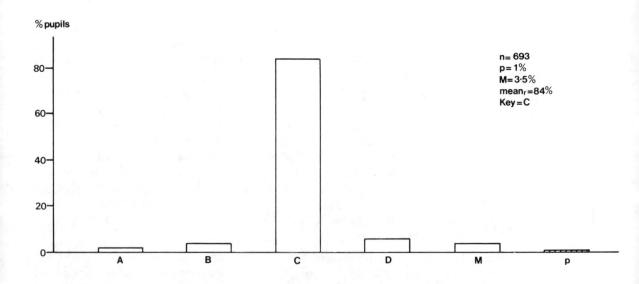

% pupils

n= 693
p= 1%
M= 3·5%
mean$_r$ = 84%
Key = C

could be read from the graph. In the other question one prediction could be read from the graph but the next two involved using the interpretation to predict the outcome in two new situations. In the first example the mean score was 78 per cent compared to 47 per cent in the second example.

The lowest mean score (42 per cent) occurred in a question which required the pupils to relate the length and thickness of guitar strings to the note they produced. The pupils then had to predict, in the light of this relationship, the length that strings of different thickness had to be in order to produce an equivalent note. A question in category 3, 'Using observation', requiring the same relationship to be discerned and a very similar prediction to be made, but set in a practical situtation with a sonometer, had a mean score of 78 per cent of the maximum. The non-response rate for this question in its paper and pencil form was high (seven per cent) compared to around three per cent for other questions of this type. Pupils' success in this type of question appeared to be related to a combination of different factors: the form of the content ie whether the data was numerical, pictorial, etc.: the number of variables to be related or rejected in order to establish the pattern, and whether the prediction was projected to a new, hypothetical situation.

Making a prediction, giving reasons   The question type which required pupils to make predictions and in addition to describe the pattern upon which they based them had a much lower performance level. The highest mean score achieved was 60 per cent and the lowest 17 per cent. In general on questions of this type over half the pupils failed to score. The majority of pupils who scored marks did so by making the correct prediction. Only a very small proportion were able to state the complete pattern and pupils tended to refer only to certain aspects of it, which was consistent with the findings at age 11. The score distribution appeared to be affected by the content and presentation of the question. In general the performance level was lower on questions where the pattern had to be described first and the prediction made afterwards, than on those for which the order was reversed. Although the performance level was lower when the pattern had to be described before the prediction was made, more pupils scored marks for stating the pattern in these cases than in questions where the format was reversed.

The question 'Candles' over, had the lowest mean score for questions of this type. From the mark scheme it can be seen that only a full description of the generalisation scored marks. The prediction was set in abstract terms and not a real situation. The nature of the response on the first part of the question is indicated in Table 4.2 and on the second part in Table 4.3 (see page 69).

The pupils who made the correct prediction in part (b) of the question (five per cent) had not all been able to state correctly the generalisation in part (a). Only 40 per cent of this group scored marks on the first part of the question.

'Candles'

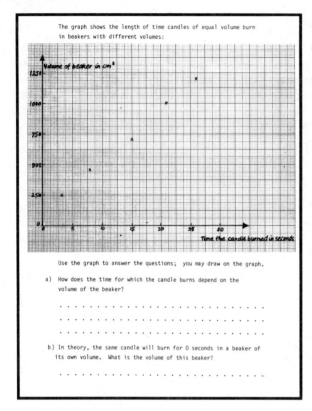

The graph shows the length of time candles of equal volume burn in beakers with different volumes:

Use the graph to answer the questions; you may draw on the graph.

a) How does the time for which the candle burns depend on the volume of the beaker?

· ·
· ·
· ·

b) In theory, the same candle will burn for 0 seconds in a beaker of its own volume. What is the volume of this beaker?

· ·

Mark scheme

Candles	Mark scheme
a) The larger the volume the longer the candle burns for or vice versa	2
b) Approximately 125 cm^3	1
	Total ③

Comment

In this example the pupils had to describe a pattern in the presented information and then use the pattern to make a prediction.

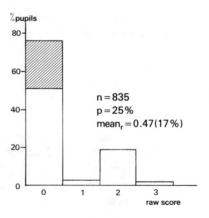

%pupils

n = 835
p = 25%
mean$_r$ = 0.47 (17%)

raw score

Table 4.2   *Categories of response: 'Candles', part (a)*

Nature of response on part a) of the question	% of pupils
Response in which the relationship between the time of burning and the volume of the beaker was correctly stated	20
Relationship expressed in reverse	1
Response in which specific observations were made e.g. a small beaker has less air, no mention being made of the time variable	13
Response in which an attempt was made to explain the generalistion rather than to describe it	7
Response in which values were read off the graph e.g. the candle burns for 28 seconds	4
Irrelevant response	30
Non-response	25

Table 4.3   *Categories of response: 'Candles', part (b)*

Nature of response on part b) of the question	% of pupils
Correct prediction—volume about $125 cm^3$	5
Volume of the beaker $= O cm^3$	29
Volume of the beaker $= 50 cm^3$	2
Volume of the beaker given as below $250 cm^3$ but not near to the actual value	13
Volume of the beaker $= 250 cm^3$	5
Volume of the beaker given as above $250 cm^3$	5
Response in which information in the question was repeated e.g. the same volume as the candle	12
Non-response	29

Selecting predictions, giving reasons

'Planets'

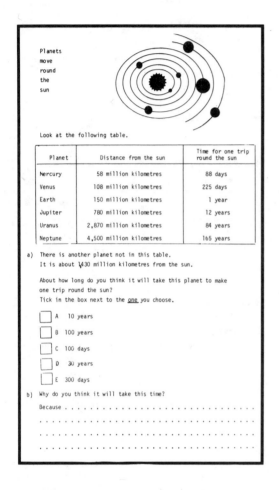

Mark scheme

Planets   *Mark scheme*

a) Key D   1

b) The planet is in between Jupiter and Uranus   1

The further from the sun the longer the trip ∴   1
more than 12 years but less than 84 years.

Total ③

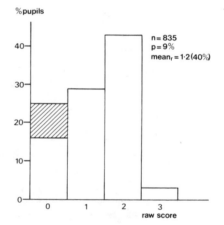

In the example 'Planets', the data had to be interpreted in order to discern the relationship between the distance of a planet from the sun and the time taken for it to orbit the sun. Once the pattern is established the pupils have to select a prediction consistent with it. The final part of the question required the pupils to describe the pattern they used. The same question was set to the 11 year olds and comparisons between the responses at the two ages are shown in Table 4.4.

The non-response rate on this group of questions where predictions had to be selected and reasons given varied from one to 12 per cent and seemed to depend on the method of presentation of the data ie numerical data — higher non-response rate.

Table 4.4   *Categories of response: 'Planets'*

Nature of response	% of 11 year olds	% of 13 year olds
Response including the complete generalisation that the further from the sun the longer the time of orbit, and that as the distance of the planet was in between Jupiter and Uranus it would also be between them in orbit time	1	3
Response not including a description of the generalisation but a statement that as the planet was between Jupiter and Uranus in distance it was therefore between them in time	27	27
Response including reference only to distance or time with respect to Jupiter and Uranus	0	7
Statement that the planet was 'in between Jupiter and Uranus'	0	9
Response including reference only to one of the planets and a statement that the distance was about half the distance of Uranus from the sun and so the orbit time would be half of the time for Uranus	14	16
Response including an incorrect reference to the other planets e.g. 'it must be further away than all of them' or 'it must be further away from the sun than all the others'	14	8
Response in which no reference was made to the planets	21	8
Response in which pupils said they 'guessed' or 'did not know'	3	1
Irrelevant response	6	12

Summary of results for sub-category 4α   Sub-category 4α was represented in the survey by 27 questions in total — nine of each of three category 4 test packages (the other questions in these packages belonging to one or other of the 4δ sub-categories described later in this chapter.) The resulting sub-test mark distributions were similarly symmetrical, with mean marks about two-fifths of the way along the mark scale. About 800 pupils attempted each test package, and only 25 pupils (one per cent) failed to achieve at least one mark for 4α performance. The maximum mean score obtained was around 80 per cent.

Pupil performance on questions in this sub-category varied with the type of question being asked. In general questions which required pupils to select answers rather than generate them had higher performance levels. Whether this performance difference is due to the higher proportion of pupils responding to these questions or is a consequence of 'guessing' is unknown.

Other factors which operated independently of the question type and varied from question to question also appeared to affect pupil performance. For example, in questions where pupils had to select a prediction based on the pattern, the mean scores varied from 30 per cent to over 80 per cent of the maximum. The lowest scores were achieved on questions where, once the pattern had been established, pupils were required to assess a range of answers several of which were possible. Pupils' performance was higher on questions where, once the pattern had been discerned, only one of the given answers was possible.

On questions where predictions had to be made pupil performance differed according to the number of variables which had to be assessed in order to establish the pattern. Pupil performance was also adversely affected when one of the variables presented had to be rejected as not contributing to the pattern.

Another factor which appeared to affect pupil performance was the kind of situation to which the prediction related. If it was projected to a new, hypothetical situation, rather than the one originally presented, the performance was lower.

Questions which required pupils to make or select predictions and describe the pattern upon which they were based had lower mean scores than questions in which the pattern did not have to be described. In general on questions of this type pupils scored marks by making the correct prediction. Only a very small proportion of the pupils stated the complete pattern and pupils tended to refer only to certain aspects of it.

The performances of boys and girls in this sub-category were very similar and any differences in mean scores were insignificant. Girls did better than boys at describing patterns but boys did better in four out of six questions where they had to make predictions and describe a pattern. There were no consistent differences in the performance levels of girls and boys on other question types.

4.3 Sub-category 4β: judging the applicability of a given generalisation

In this sub-category there is only one question type. The questions included all involve the pupils in considering presented data about a situation or event in conjunction with a hypothesis based on the data. The pupil had to select the relevant information in order to assess the hypothesis. These questions were not included in the α sub-category as the interpretation required did not entail establishing a pattern in the data or using a pattern.

In the example 'Mushrooms', the information was presented diagrammatically. The diagram indicated the distribution of mushrooms and five-day old cow droppings in a meadow and included contour lines and compass directions. A key was given to ensure that all pupils understood the symbols without having to have had previous experience of them.

'Mushrooms'

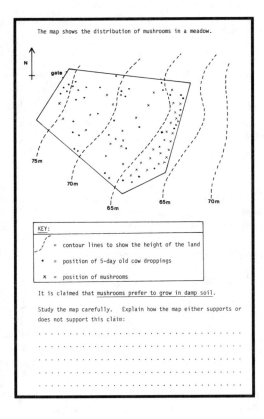

The map shows the distribution of mushrooms in a meadow.

KEY:

⌇ = contour lines to show the height of the land

• = position of 5-day old cow droppings

✗ = position of mushrooms

It is claimed that mushrooms prefer to grow in damp soil.

Study the map carefully. Explain how the map either supports or does not support this claim:

. . . .

. . . .

. . . .

. . . .

. . . .

Mark scheme

Mushroom	*Mark scheme*
Supports	
East end lower	1
Water will drain to it	1
More mushrooms appear to grow nearer this wall/or on land	1

or

If not supported

Not enough information to decide The soil may be well drained and no damper at any point in the field than any other	1
There are mushrooms growing all over the meadow	1

Total ③

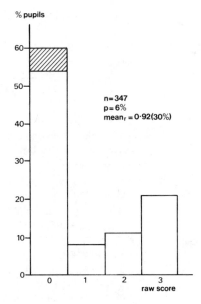

% pupils

n = 347
p = 6%
mean$_r$ = 0·92 (30%)

raw score

Forty per cent of the pupils who attempted the question succeeded in scoring. The responses given by these pupils varied in the ways shown in Table 4.5.

Table 4.5   *Categories of response: 'Mushrooms' (scoring)*

Nature of response	% of pupils
Response in which the distribution of mushrooms was linked to the contour lines and drainage in the meadow. The evidence selected supported the hypothesis	25
Response in which the evidence selected similarly supported the hypothesis but in which no reference was made to drainage, only to contour lines and number of mushrooms.	10
Response in which pupils argued that on the basis of the contour lines the hypothesis was correct but did not state the relationship between the contour lines, mushroom distribution and dampness	2
Response in which pupils scored by selecting information which failed to support the hypothesis	3

Fifty-four per cent of the pupils failed to score and the proportions giving different responses are shown in Table 4.6.

Table 4.6   *Categories of response: 'Mushrooms' (non-scoring)*

Nature of response	% of pupils
Response which included no generalisation but which listed specific observations eg the mushrooms grow near the wall. No attempt was made by this group to assess the validity of the hypothesis.	15
Response in which contradictory evidence was selected in support of the hypothesis arguing that more mushrooms grew near the cow droppings which were the source of damp	5
Response in which it was claimed that mushrooms did prefer damp soil but equated higher ground with damp ground	3
Response in which pupils used the same argument as the previous group to say that the hypothesis was not supported by the evidence as more mushrooms grew on low land	5
Response in which pupils failed to assess the hypothesis and which was irrelevant or incomprehensible	20

Boys performed better on this question, achieving a mean score of 33 per cent compared with 27 per cent for girls. The pattern of scoring for boys and girls was similar in many respects but the proportion of boys linking the distribution of the mushrooms to the contour lines and drainage of the land and thus scoring full marks was 30 per cent, whereas for girls it was 19 per cent.

Two other questions in the same sub-category had performance levels around 30–35 per cent of the maximum and high proportions (48–50 per cent) of pupils scoring zero.

4.4 Sub-category 4γ: distinguishing degrees of inference

Range of questions used   There is only one question type in this sub-category, which was excluded from 4α as the skills being tested did not rely on the discernment and use of patterns. The method of presentation of the information and the demands made on the pupils were seen to be sufficiently different to warrant reporting the questions individually.

The events to be assessed were often presented pictorially. To avoid overlap with category 3 the information to be observed was emphasised using simple line drawings (often of a cartoon type).

The pupils who failed to score on the question, 'Vase of Flowers', tended to select distractors A (26 per cent) or B (15 per cent). The same question was set to 11 year olds and the differences in their responses compared to 13 year olds are illustrated in the score distribution. The additional information on the chart refers to 13 year old pupils.

The performances of 11 and 13 year olds were very similar. Distractors A and B were the most frequently chosen at both ages. More 13 year olds selected the key than 11 year olds (43 per cent and 30 per cent respectively). A larger proportion of 13 year olds (11 per cent) than 11 year olds (seven per cent) chose distractor E. This distractor represented an explanation of the whole situation including extraneous factors rather than referring to the illustrated details of the event.

In the question, 'Candle', the event presented was simple and one that most pupils would have experienced. The distribution across the distractors shows that only E was chosen by a significant proportion of the pupils in preference to A. It is clear that this distractor involved only a slight and very plausible assumption in comparison to the others. The performance of boys and girls did not differ on this question.

The question, 'Sheep', was used in the survey at age 11 as well as in the survey at age 13.

The mean score for this question was 48 per cent of the maximum at age 13, compared to 28 per cent at age 11. The other main difference between the performance at the two ages was in the very large proportion of pupils (44 per cent) making a multiple response at age 11. More 13 year old pupils selected distractors A and B, in total 34 per cent; at age 11 only 20 per cent chose one of these two.

At age 13 a greater proportion of girls chose distractor A compared to boys, 22 per cent and 13 per cent respectively. The difference in the number of boys and

'Vase of flowers'

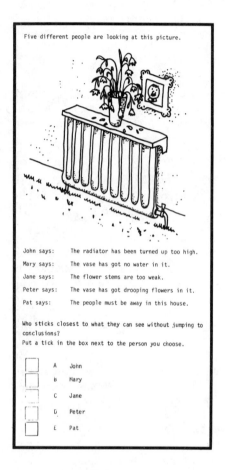

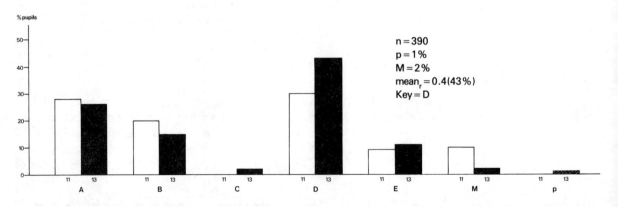

n=390
p=1%
M=2%
$\text{mean}_r=0.4(43\%)$
Key=D

'Candle'

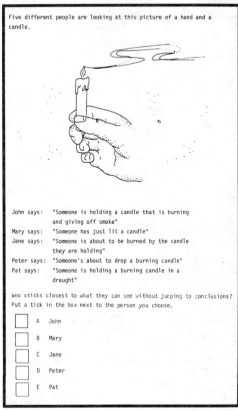

Five different people are looking at this picture of a hand and a candle.

John says: "Someone is holding a candle that is burning and giving off smoke"
Mary says: "Someone has just lit a candle"
Jane says: "Someone is about to be burned by the candle they are holding"
Peter says: "Someone's about to drop a burning candle"
Pat says: "Someone is holding a burning candle in a draught"

Who sticks closest to what they can see without jumping to conclusions?
Put a tick in the box next to the person you choose.

☐   A   John

☐   B   Mary

☐   C   Jane

☐   D   Peter

☐   E   Pat

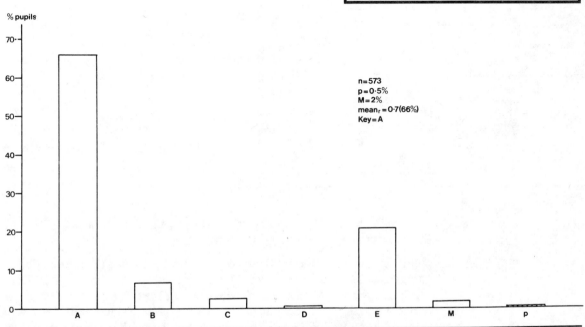

% pupils

n=573
p=0.5%
M=2%
mean$_r$=0.7(66%)
Key=A

'Sheep'

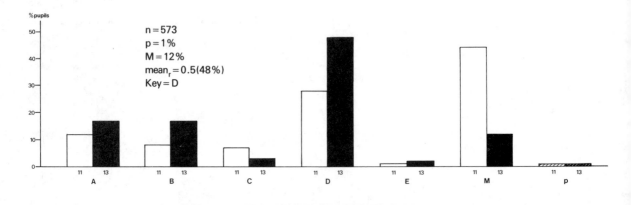

girls selecting the correct response at age 11 (girls 32 per cent, boys 24 per cent) did not occur at age 13 (boys 49 per cent, girls 46 per cent).

Another example of this question type, 'Election', presented the information in writing and the mean score was 52 per cent of the maximum. The score distribution was very similar to those obtained for the other question examples. No one distractor attracted a higher proportion of pupils but all of them were chosen by around ten per cent of the pupils tested. The multiple response rate was low as was the case in the example 'Vase of flowers'. The method of presenting the situation was clearly very different but appeared not to affect the pupils' performance significantly.

'Election'

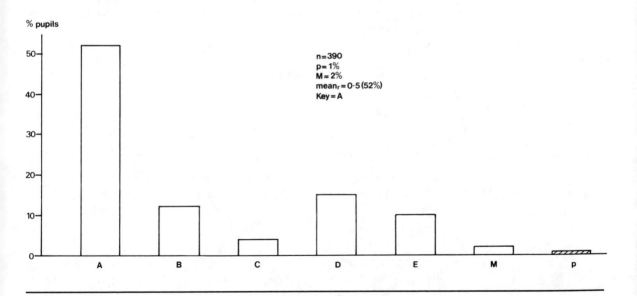

Five different people read this election manifesto:

> If this party is elected at the next election we will see to it that every effort is made to build more houses than ever before so that none of our citizens will need to be housed in poor conditions.

John says: "This political party claims that more houses may be built if they are elected"

Mary says: "More houses will be built when the next election is won"

Jane says: "The Labour Party says they will build more houses"

Peter says: "Everyone agrees that more houses need to be built"

Pat says: "The Labour Party claims more houses may be built after the election"

Who sticks closest to what they can see without jumping to conclusions? Put a tick in the box next to the person you choose.

A   John
B   Mary
C   Jane
D   Peter
E   Pat

% pupils

n = 390
p = 1%
M = 2%
mean$_r$ = 0·5 (52%)
Key = A

Summary of results for sub-category 4γ   Two factors seem to effect performance on these questions. The first is whether the situation is a 'known' everyday event, as for example in the 'Vase of flowers', 'Sheep' and the one which involved a motorway collision. In these circumstances pupils tended to explain the event rather than describe it. The result of this is two-fold and leads to a greater spread across distractors and thus a decrease in performance level and sometimes to an increase in multiple responses. This effect was noted in the 'Sheep' and 'Motorway' questions. The other factor which affects performance is the plausibility and degree of assumption within the individual distractors. If all the distractors include small equivalent assumptions, the performance level is lower than if only one distractor is like this, as demonstrated in the 'Candle' question.

4.5 Sub-category 4δ: making sense of information using science concepts

Introduction　This sub-category and the following one, in addition to demanding interpretation of information as in 4α, also require the pupil to recall and apply science concepts. The questions in these sub-categories do not emphasise simple recall but performance on them depends on the pupils' understanding of basic science concepts.

The concept base　A list of concepts to be used in writing and classifying the questions was prepared in consultation with teachers from different parts of the country. The list (given in Chapter 6) was developed in such a way as to contain concepts to which most 13 year old pupils will have been exposed in their science lessons, and so it reflects current practice rather than prescribes it. A corresponding list was prepared for use at age 11 and age 15. The concepts listed for age 13 are a sub-set of the concepts given for age 15. The lists represent a consensus view of the teachers and other educationalists consulted. To help in arranging for an adequate, balanced coverage of all the concepts the list was divided into six concept areas:

A　Interaction of living things with their environment

B　Living things and their life processes

C　Force and field

D　Transfer of energy

E　The classification and structure of matter

F　Chemical interaction

The ultimate aim was that the bank of questions which represent this sub-category, 4δ, would be balanced across these six areas. For reporting purposes the areas were then paired into regions which were designated biological (A and B), physical (C and D) and chemical (E and F).

Variety of the questions and the nature of the tests　There were 81 questions used in this sub-category, 27 from each of the three concept regions. Pupil performance will be reported within each of these regions and no overall 4δ figure will be given.

The questions used varied across question type, as in 4α; that is they varied with respect to the demands made on the pupil to make or select predictions either with or without an explanation, to state or select explanations or to assess the validity of generalisations in the light of presented information.

The other large variation between the questions used in 4δ was related to the concept base. Within the one concept region from which questions were selected, there were two distinct and quite different concept areas, as indicated above. Associated with each concept area were several different but related sections, each defined by a set of concept statements. It was to these individual concept statements that questions were written.

Apart from the wide variety inherent in such a concept base, questions written for the same single concept statement varied in the level at which the concept was involved. For example, in order to make a prediction a pupil may need simply to be aware of the underlying concept in order to answer the question correctly. Another question written to the same concept statement might require the pupil to explain a phenomenon in terms of the concept. Marks would be given, in the latter case, for each point which demonstrated the pupil's understanding of the concept.

The 27 questions used in each concept region were selected at random from the item bank and no controls were placed on the diversity of the question. The questions were presented in groups of nine to three different samples of pupils. A consequence of this design was that detailed data about performance on individual concepts within any one region occurred by chance rather than by prescription.

4.6 Sub-category $4\delta_{AB}$: making sense of information using biological concepts

Biological concept region   The two main areas in the biological concept region were concerned with the 'interaction of living things and their environment' (area A) and 'living things and their life processes' (area B).

The questions randomly selected in this region reflected the early composition of the item bank when questions on certain concept statements were not yet present. In addition such selection also meant that some sets of concept statements were either not represented at all or that only a few questions relating to them occurred by chance. The 27 questions selected were spread over five different sets of biological concepts with a maximum of seven questions in any one section. Some questions have been chosen to illustrate pupil performance on different sets of statements within the biological concept region. In addition general discussion of pupil performance on other concepts and on different types of question within the biological concept region is given where the numbers of questions (≈ 5) allow some generalisations to be made.

Interdependence of living things   In this section one question, 'Food chain', is described in detail followed by other examples eg 'Food web' in which performance is discussed in less detail and is used to facilitate the general discussion which follows.

'Food chain'

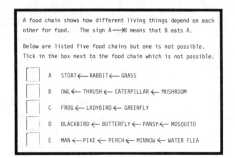

A food chain shows how different living things depend on each other for food. The sign A⟶B means that B eats A.

Below are listed five food chains but one is not possible. Tick in the box next to the food chain which is not possible.

A   STOAT⟵ RABBIT⟵ GRASS

B   OWL⟵ THRUSH⟵ CATERPILLAR ⟵ MUSHROOM

C   FROG ⟵ LADYBIRD ⟵ GREENFLY

D   BLACKBIRD ⟵ BUTTERFLY ⟵ PANSY⟵ MOSQUITO

E   MAN ⟵PIKE ⟵ PERCH⟵ MINNOW ⟵ WATER FLEA

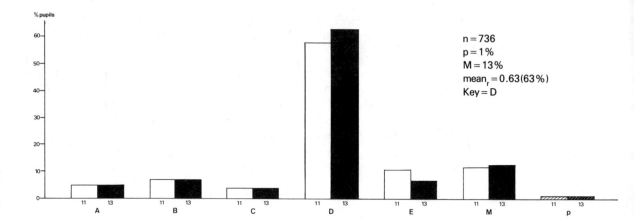

n = 736
p = 1%
M = 13%
mean$_r$ = 0.63(63%)
Key = D

In the above example the interpretation of a food chain involves understanding aspects of the interdependence of living things and the ultimate dependence of animals on green plants for their food. The concept demand in the question was small and the question was included in the survey at age 11 as well as that at age 13.

The performances at the two ages on this question were very similar. Five per cent more of the 13 year olds chose the correct answer than did the 11 year olds. The raw mean scores were 0.63 and 0.58 respectively; seven per cent of 13 year olds compared to 11 per cent of 11 year olds opted for distractor E, which was the only food chain in which 'MAN' featured.

At both ages the performance of boys and girls showed little difference, with the exception that at age 13, six per cent more boys than girls gave a multiple response.

Another question which involved aspects of the concept of interdependence presented information in the form of a food web. In this case predictions had to be made, not selected, about the effect of the increase or decrease of one of the populations in the food web on the other groups of animals in the web. The mean score on this question was 50 per cent of the maximum compared to 60 per cent on the previous one — 'Food chain'. There was no difference in the performances of boys and girls.

'Food web'   Mark scheme

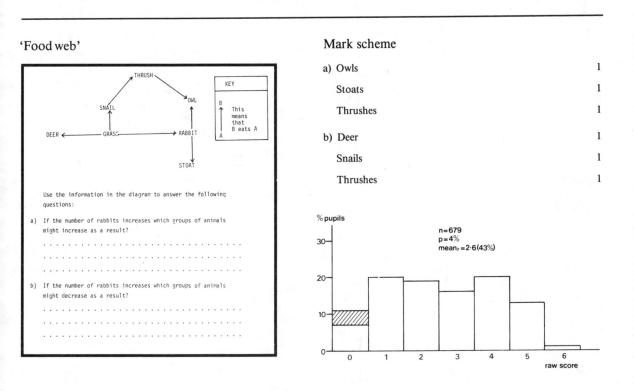

The lowest mean score (33 per cent) was achieved on a question which asked pupils to select all the likely occurrences when a pest which attacked vegetables was introduced into a country where it had never existed before. The question itself was more complex as it required the pupils to assess five different hypotheses and it also relied on the pupils appreciating that adaptation of organisms is a slow process. Only a small proportion of the pupils appeared to appreciate this factor.

Performance on questions based on the concept of interdependence of living things was consistently higher than on questions for any other biological concept area.

Respiration and Photosynthesis In this section two questions, 'Gas balance' and 'Field of grass' are described in detail including the different types of response given by the pupils. Other questions eg 'Breathing rate', are included with less detail and there is general discussion on the performance within the section.

'Gas balance'

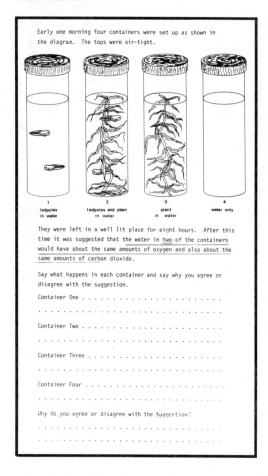

Early one morning four containers were set up as shown in the diagram. The tops were air-tight.

1 tadpoles in water
2 tadpoles and plant in water
3 plant in water
4 water only

They were left in a well lit place for eight hours. After this time it was suggested that the water in two of the containers would have about the same amounts of oxygen and also about the same amounts of carbon dioxide.

Say what happens in each container and say why you agree or disagree with the suggestion.

Container One . . . .
. . . .
Container Two . . . .
. . . .
Container Three . . . .
. . . .
Container Four . . . .
. . . .
Why do you agree or disagree with the suggestion?
. . . .
. . . .

Mark scheme

Container One	Oxygen removed, replaced with carbon dioxide (respiration in tadpole)	1
Container Two	Oxygen removed by tadpole and plant replaced by carbon dioxide (respiration)	
	Carbon dioxide removed by plant and replaced by oxygen (photosynthesis)	1
Container Three	Carbon dioxide removed, replaced with oxygen (Net result of photosynthesis and respiration in plant)	1
Container Four	Balance remains the same	1
agree	Container Two and Four contain same amount if balance assumed	1
OR		
disagree	No two containers have the same amounts if balance not assumed	1

Total ⑥

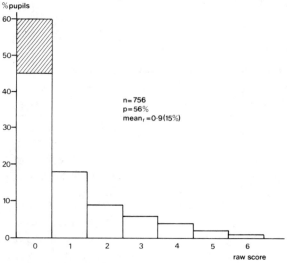

%pupils

n=756
p=56%
mean$_r$=0·9(15%)

raw score

In the example, 'Gas balance', the pupils' responses were categorised to see at what point their understanding of the concepts involved broke down. The percentages of pupils giving different responses are shown in Table 4.7.

From these responses it can be seen that over half of the pupils tested failed to score either because they appeared not to understand the question or else demonstrated no understanding of the processes of respiration and

Table 4.7 *Categories of response: 'Gas balance'*

Nature of response	% of pupils
Complete response including both photosynthesis and respiration and the balance between the two	1
Response including both photosynthesis and respiration but failure to link the two together	5
Correct response about photosynthesis and respiration but not that water contains dissolved gases	2
Response about the actual gases that plants produce and use in water but no reference to the animals	1
Correct response about respiration but not photosynthesis	5
Response about respiration alone but only in terms of carbon dioxide and air, not oxygen	2
Statement of only some of the gases used or expelled by plants and animals, eg tadpoles give out carbon dioxide, or plants take in carbon dioxide	25
Response indicating no understanding of photosynthesis or respiration	28
Response indicating no understanding of the question	16
Non-response	15

photosynthesis. A further 25 per cent of pupils were able to score marks by knowing some of the gases involved but they showed no understanding of the individual processes and could not say how they were linked.

The question 'Fields of grass' further illustrates pupils' performance on concepts related to the life processes. The pupils were not expected to know or to be able to explain the processes involved in the photosynthesis and respiration of plants. In order to select the correct graphs pupils had to understand which gases are taken in or expelled by plants; as a combined effect of the two processes, respiration and photosynthesis, during the day and night. The histogram for part (a) shows that 26 per cent of the pupils selected the day and expected plants to take in carbon dioxide during the day and thus lower the concentration of that gas in the air. A higher proportion (34 per cent) of the pupils thought the reverse and selected the graph, distractor B, which suggests that plants give out carbon dioxide in the day. Of the pupils selecting the right answer, key A, for part (a), only two-thirds chose the correct graph, key D, for part (b) of the question.

Another question in this section, 'Breathing rate', showed by means of a sketch graph the effect of exercise on the breathing rate of a person. The question asked

'Field of grass'

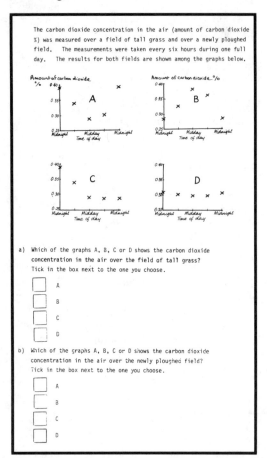

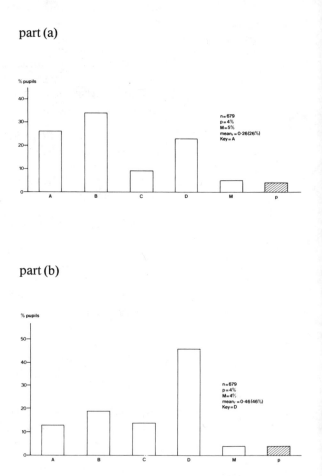

part (a)

part (b)

pupils to predict the graph showing the same person's heart rate. The axes were presented on the question paper with equal interval scales and were labelled.

Seventy-seven per cent of the pupils failed to score on this question of which eight per cent were those who made no attempt. The mean score for the question was 20 per cent of the maximum.

Performance on this group of questions concerned with respiration and photo-synthesis varied between 20 and 50 per cent of the maximum. It was generally the case that when understanding of the individual processes or the relationship between them was required in a question the performance level was low.

Nutrition   Pupil performance on questions which call on the understanding of animal and plant nutrition and the structural adaptation of animals to suit their food requirements was around 34 per cent of the maximum. Questions with the lowest mean scores required the pupils to demonstrate their knowledge of plant nutrition which was consistent with the results for the 'Field of grass' question. Pupils were able to state some of the factors involved in plant nutrition (eg sunshine and carbon dioxide) but could not explain the function of the component parts.

Physical and chemical principles   A similar performance level was achieved on questions which required pupils to consider the response of plants and animals to their physical and chemical environment.

In 'Goosegrass' overleaf 64 per cent of the pupils said that P is found in the hedge and Q on waste-land; 32 per cent thought the reverse.

Tables 4.8 and 4.9 show how the pupils responded (see page 89).

Twenty-five per cent of the pupils attempted to explain the shape in terms of support or obstructions. Twenty-six per cent explained the plant shape with respect to competition for light and/or nutrients.

The mean score for the boys was higher than for the girls on this question. The largest difference in the performance of boys and girls was that seven per cent more boys than girls said that P's shape was due to the support it receives from the hedge. Six per cent more girls than boys gave no explanation, just a description of observations.

Physical and chemical environment   The group of questions which depended on concepts about the physical and chemical environment, eg seasonal cycles, soil fertility, had mean scores which varied from 20 to 70 per cent of the maximum.

In the example 'Street lamp', the concept demand is small but the situation novel. The raw mean score on the first part of the question was 0.3. Of the pupils (31 per cent) who selected the correct answer for part (a), only 60 per cent were able to predict correctly the appearance of the tree. More pupils (37 per cent) were able to predict the appearance of the tree but were unable to select the correct answer for part (a).

Any difference in performance between boys and girls on this group of questions favoured the girls. In other cases in this group the same concept was required in questions of a different type. The concept involved was that plants take nutrients from both the air and soil. The question which required pupils to consider stated hypotheses about the difference in growth of two trees and to select all the correct ones had a mean score of 43 per cent of the maximum. The other question which demanded understanding of the same concept at a similar level stated one hypothesis about the growth of two trees. The pupils had to give an open response which assessed the validity of the hypothesis. This question had a mean score of 17 per cent of the maximum.

Summary of results for sub-category 4δ_{AB}   There were three different category 4 test packages and each contained nine questions relating to 4δ_{AB}, along with

'Goosegrass'

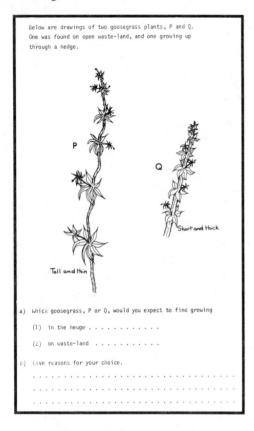

Below are drawings of two goosegrass plants, P and Q. One was found on open waste-land, and one growing up through a hedge.

P

Q

Short and thick

Tall and thin

a) Which goosegrass, P or Q, would you expect to find growing

(1) in the hedge . . . .

(2) on waste-land . . . .

b) Give reasons for your choice.

. . . .

. . . .

. . . .

Mark scheme

No marks for part a)

Part b)

If P found in hedge then P's poor appearance due to competition with the hedge for light and nutrients in the soil   3

or   P's poor or tall or thin appearance due to limited amount of light received (Q's strong appearance due to abundant light)   3

or   P's shape due to lack of space and obstruction (Q free to grow straight)   2

or   P's thin stem due to the support it received from the hedge (Q's thick stem due to no support)   1

If Q found in hedge then Q is stunted due to competition with the hedge   2

or   Q is trapped and stunted (P is free and grows tall)   2

or   P is taller therefore gets more sunlight — thus cannot be growing in the hedge   1

Total ③

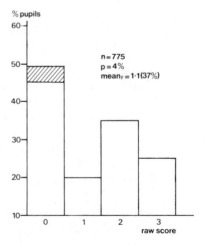

% pupils

n=775
p=4%
mean$_r$=1·1(37%)

raw score

Table 4.8 *Categories of response: 'Goosegrass' (type 1)*

Responses which say P is found in the hedge and Q on waste-land	% of pupils
P's thin stem is due to the support it receives from the hedge: Q's thick stem due to no support	9
P's poor (tall and thin) appearance due to the limited amount of light received (grows up to the light): Q's strong appearance due to abundant light	13
P's shape due to lack of space: Q is free to grow straight	16
P's poor appearance due to competition with the hedge for nutrients in the soil	2
Response which assumes the shape to be natural to cope with the environment, not as a result of the environment	9
Explanation based on irrelevant evidence, eg P has more leaves, Q is hardier, etc.	1
No explanation, just a description of observations eg P looks weak	5
Irrelevant response	9

Table 4.9 *Categories of response: 'Goosegrass' (type 2)*

Responses which say Q is found in the hedge and P on waste-land	% of pupils
Response in terms of association of *poor* appearance with *waste-land*	6
Q is stunted due to competition with the hedge: P is free and grows tall	10
P is taller so therefore gets more sunlight, nutrients, etc, therefore it grows on waste-land	1
No explanation, just a description of observations	3
Irrelevant response	12

questions relating to 4α or one of the other 4δ sub-categories described later. $4\delta_{AB}$ performance was assessed using a total of 27 questions. The three sub-test mark distributions were similarly shaped with the mean mark in each case being about two-fifths of the maximum possible mark. Between 650 and 750 pupils actually attempted each test package, and only 15 of the total 2 000 + pupils failed to achieve at least one mark for their performance on this particular sub-category. The maximum score achieved on each sub-test was about 75 per cent.

'Street lamp'

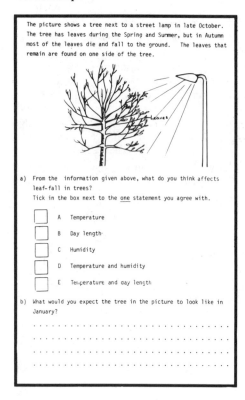

The picture shows a tree next to a street lamp in late October. The tree has leaves during the Spring and Summer, but in Autumn most of the leaves die and fall to the ground. The leaves that remain are found on one side of the tree.

a) From the information given above, what do you think affects leaf-fall in trees?

Tick in the box next to the **one** statement you agree with.

☐ A   Temperature

☐ B   Day length

☐ C   Humidity

☐ D   Temperature and humidity

☐ E   Temperature and day length

b) What would you expect the tree in the picture to look like in January?

. . . .
. . . .
. . . .
. . . .

Mark scheme

a) Key E   1

b) No leaves   1

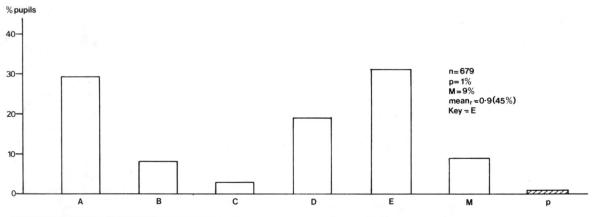

% pupils

n = 679
p = 1%
M = 9%
mean$_r$ = 0·9 (45%)
Key = E

From the results in this sub-category it was possible to make general comments about performance on certain groups of questions where there were sufficient data from which to generalise. The performance of pupils was highest on questions which required the application of concepts about the interdependence of living things. Any difference in performance on the questions between boys and girls favoured the boys but this was not significant.

The next highest level of performance was on questions involving pupils' understanding of the physical and chemical environment. In this concept section girls did better on some questions than boys. On no question did the boys perform at a higher level than the girls.

Three other groups of questions required the application of concepts related to plant and animal response to the environment and to plant and animal nutrition and respiration. It would seem that pupils found the application of these concepts more difficult than the previous ones even on similar questions. The performance level in each case was around 34 per cent of the maximum.

From individual question responses it appeared that 50–70 per cent of pupils had a reasonable grasp of the idea that organisms are dependent on the presence and activities of other organisms, and that all animals ultimately depend on green plants for food. They demonstrated their understanding by being able to use simple food chains and webs to make or select predictions or to generate explanations. Similarly they appreciated that plants take substances from the air and soil.

About half of the pupils tested appeared to have a reasonable understanding of animal nutrition and simple adaptation of animals to suit the kind of food they eat. Few pupils showed an understanding of the basics of plant nutrition, stating only that green plants use simple substances from their environment. They did not state all the substances involved and generally did not show an understanding of the process.

This was also the case with animal and plant respiration. About 50 per cent of the pupils knew some of the gases involved in both processes but only about ten per cent of the pupils appeared to understand clearly the individual processes. Virtually no pupils appeared to appreciate the link between the life processes of plants and animals.

The very marginal difference in the performance estimates for boys and girls did not reach statistical significance.

As noted previously, the type of question affected pupil performance. For example, pupils more often selected predictions correctly than made them correctly, the performance level on these questions being 50 per cent and 45 per cent respectively. Similarly the performance level on questions where explanations had to be generated was lower (30 per cent) than where the correct one had to be selected (40 per cent). The type of question which seemed the most difficult for the pupils required them to assess the validity of a given hypothesis in the light of the data and science concepts involved. An open response had to be given by the pupils and the performance level was around 20 per cent of the maximum. Questions which presented the pupils with a range of hypotheses to assess and required them to select the most likely had a performance level of 40 per cent of the maximum.

The results for the different question types set within the biological concept areas were consistent with the trends in performance observed over similar question types in sub-category 4α.

4.7 Sub-category 4δ_CD: making sense of information using physics concepts

Physical concept region The two main areas in the physical concept region were concerned with 'Force and field' (area C) and 'Transfer of energy' (area D). Twenty-seven questions were selected from the item bank and they spread across five of the seven sections of physical concepts.

Some of the questions used have been chosen to illustrate pupil performance on some sections within this concept region. In addition general discussion of pupil performance on particular concepts and on different types of questions is given where sufficient data exist.

'Freezing'

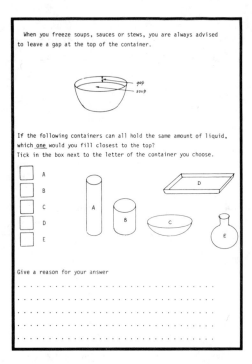

Comment

This question was concerned with concepts related to the 'properties of matter'. Pupils had to select a prediction by applying their understanding of the effect of the freezing of water and its accompanying volume increase.

Mark scheme

Freezing	Mark scheme
Key D	1
Largest surface area	1
Total volume increase will take up least depth	1

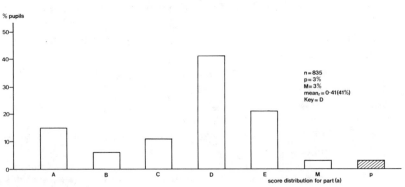

n = 835
p = 3%
M = 3%
mean_f = 0·41(41%)
Key = D

score distribution for part (a)

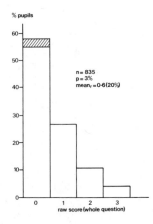

n = 835
p = 3%
mean_f = 0·6(20%)

raw score (whole question)

Properties of matter   In this section three questions — 'Freezing', 'Car tyre' and 'Watering can' are described in detail including the different types of response given by pupils.

On the question 'freezing' 41 per cent of the pupils tested selected the correct container. Only ten per cent of this group explained their choice both in terms of surface area and volume increase. Twenty seven per cent mentioned surface area alone and 63 per cent scored no marks on part (b).

It is interesting to note that the most frequently chosen distractor, E, (21 per cent) represents the least appropriate container. The second most popular distractor, A (15 per cent) also represents a container where the exposed surface has a small area. This may suggest that the pupils are attempting to apply their understanding of the effect of freezing of water but are failing in their application of the concept of volume.

Another question in this area, 'Car tyre', required pupils to apply the concept

'Car tyre'

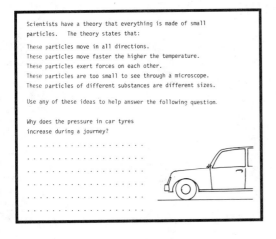

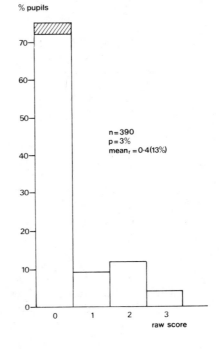

$n = 390$
$p = 3\%$
$\text{mean}_r = 0.4 (13\%)$

Mark scheme

Car tyre	Mark scheme
Tyres heat up	1
Air particles move faster as temperature rises	1
Greater force exerted on tyre wall (pressure increases)	1
Total ③	

that particles of matter are in constant motion. The pupils had to explain why the pressure in car tyres increased during a journey.

Some of the responses given to the question are shown in Table 4.10.

Table 4.10　*Categories of response: 'car tyre'*

Nature of response	% of pupils	score
Responses which say: Tyres get warmer and the particles of air move faster. As a result a greater force is exerted and the pressure increases	4	3
Tyres get warmer and the particles move faster—greater force/pressure in the tyre	10	2
Heat causes the air to expand so increasing the pressure in the tyres	2	2
The faster the car goes the warmer the tyres and the particles move around a lot/increase/expand so the tyres get harder/expand	8	0
The tyres get warm and the particles move faster	9	1
The pressure increases during a journey because of the load	5	0
No attempt to explain	33	0
Irrevelant argument e.g. The rubber tyres expand during the journey	17	0
Incomprehensible response	3	0
No response	3	0

Twenty–three per cent of the pupils scored marks by giving an explanation which referred to the particles of matter. Two per cent of the pupils incorrectly explained the situation in terms of the particles of matter and scored no marks. Nine per cent gained marks but made no reference to particles in their explanation. Five per cent of the pupils gave an incorrect description of the situation and the remaining 61 per cent made no attempt to explain or gave an irrelevant explanation.

There was a difference in the performance of boys and girls on this question. Twenty-one per cent of the boys compared to six per cent of the girls gave responses in the first two categories which corresponded to a complete or partially complete explanation. Sixteen per cent more girls than boys gave irrelevant explanations or did not attempt to explain at all.

'Watering can'

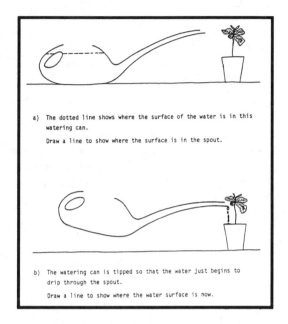

a) The dotted line shows where the surface of the water is in this watering can.

   Draw a line to show where the surface is in the spout.

b) The watering can is tipped so that the water just begins to drip through the spout.

   Draw a line to show where the water surface is now.

Mark scheme

Watering can   *Mark scheme*

a) Horizontal line at correct level   1

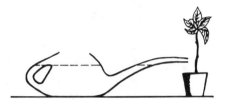

b) Horizontal line in body of can within range indicated   1

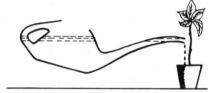

Horizontal line in spout within range indicated   1

Total ③

Comment

In this question pupils had to make a prediction by applying the concept that water tends to flow until the surface reaches a common level. The question was set to 11 and 13 year old pupils.

%**pupils**

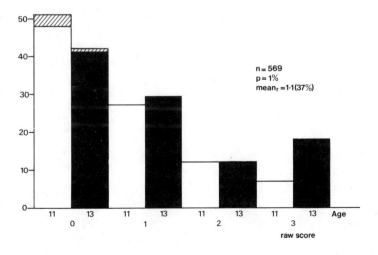

n = 569
p = 1%
mean$_f$ = 1·1(37%)

The mean score on this question was 37 per cent of the maximum at age 13 and 23 per cent at age 11. Thirty per cent of 13 year old pupils made no attempt at part (a) of the question compared to 47 per cent at age 11. Table 4.11 contrasts the types of response of 11 and 13 year olds who answered part (a).

The non-response rate in part (b) was much lower than on part (a) — one per cent at age 13 and three per cent at age 11. The success rate on part (b) was lower with only 33 per cent of the 13 year olds attempting the question achieving marks. The responses for the two age ranges are illustrated in Table 4.12.

On part (b) the main difference between the performance of 11 year olds and 13 year olds was in the proportion who only scored one mark because they failed to get the line in the spout correct (16 per cent of 11 years olds compared to seven per cent at age 13). More 13 year olds who drew the correct level in the can also drew the correct level in the spout and scored full marks. Apart from this difference the performance at the two ages was very similar. The most common error for both age groups was to draw a tilted line in the can, a high proportion at both ages, 16 per cent and 18 per cent respectively, drawing it tilted backwards with the right-hand higher or 14 per cent and 19 per cent respectively drawing a line tilted forward and parallel with the base.

There was a difference between the performances of boys and girls on this question at both ages. At age 13 the difference was noticeable on part (b). Twenty-nine per cent of the boys scored full marks compared to 13 per cent of the girls. In answering part (b), far more girls (54 per cent) than boys (36 per cent) drew a tilted line in the can.

Table 4.11   *Categories of response: 'watering can' (part a)*

Nature of response—part (a)	% of pupils age 11	% of pupils age 13
Correct response	53	70
Line tilted either left or right	22	14
Vertical line	9	—
Horizontal line too high	6	9
Horizontal line too low	3	2
Line blocking the end	2	2
Curved line	2	0
Responses not included in categories or multiple lines drawn	—	3

Table 4.12   *Categories of response: 'watering can' (part b)*

Nature of response—part (b)	% of pupils age 11	% of pupils age 13
Correct response	11	21
Correct line in can and not in spout	16	7
Correct line in spout and not in can	6	5
Incorrect line in spout, no line in can	11	2
Line in can only: horizontal line too low	3	3
Line in can only: horizontal line too high	1	2
Tilted line responses:	16	18

a)

Table 4.12   *(/contd.)*

Nature of response—part (b)	% of pupils age 11	% of pupils age 13
Tilted responses (contd.)	13	8
Parallel to the base	14	19
	2	3
Responses not included in the categories or multiple lines drawn	2	11
No response	3	1

Work and energy   In one question from this section pupils had to decide which would cost more — to heat the water in a kettle or the water in a bath.

Sixty−seven per cent of the pupils said that the bath water would cost more to heat compared to 28 per cent who thought the kettle would cost more. A small proportion of the pupils (five per cent) thought that there would be no difference in cost.

In Table 4.13 are examples of the responses and the proportions of pupils giving them.

Ten per cent of the pupils referred to both variables, the mass and temperature of the water, in their explanations. Sixty-nine per cent explained their choice by reference to only one of them.

As can be seen from the responses, of the 67 per cent of pupils selecting the correct answer ie the bath water, only two per cent were able to give an explanation which included both the relative amounts of water and the rise in temperature related to each one. Most pupils who scored were only able to state

'Kettle and bath'

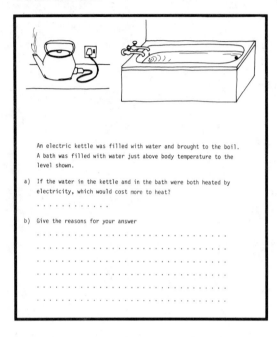

An electric kettle was filled with water and brought to the boil. A bath was filled with water just above body temperature to the level shown.

a) If the water in the kettle and in the bath were both heated by electricity, which would cost more to heat?

. . . .

b) Give the reasons for your answer

. . . .
. . . .
. . . .
. . . .
. . . .
. . . .

Comment

No marks were given in this question for the choice made only for the explanation as there was a 50 per cent chance of getting it right by guessing. Marks were gained in part (b) only if part (a) was correct.

Mark scheme

Kettle and bath   *Mark scheme*

a) Bath

b) —bath contains more water   1

   —kettle water raised to a greater temperature   1

   —ratio $\dfrac{\text{mass bath water}}{\text{mass kettle water}} > \dfrac{\text{Temp. rise in kettle}}{\text{Temp. rise in bath}}$ 1

   —therefore bath costs more   1

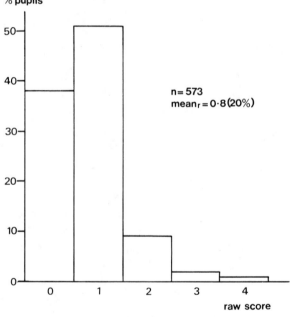

% pupils

n= 573
mean$_r$ = 0·8 (20%)

raw score

that there was more water to heat up in a bath and ignored the temperature rises involved.

The pupils who considered the temperature rise to be important ie the kettle water is brought to the boil and the bath water is not, opted for the kettle and scored no marks. In all these cases (17 per cent) the pupils did not take the mass of the water into account in their explanation.

There was little difference in the performance of boys and girls on the question.

Table 4.13   *Categories of response: 'Kettle and bath'*

Nature of response	% of pupils	possible score
Responses which said the bath water would cost more to heat than the kettle in part a)		
Response in which the relative amounts of water in the bath and kettle were related to the relative temperature rise	2	3—4
Explanation in terms of more water therefore more time and more electricity needed	27	1—2
Response which included a statement that there is more water in the bath and reference to the temperatures without taking them into account	5	1—3
Response which included a statement that there is more water in the bath but made no reference to the temperature of the water	27	1
Response which said there was more water in the bath and greater heat loss from it therefore more cooling	2	1
Irrelevant or meaningless response	4	0
Responses which said the kettle would cost more to heat than the bath in part b)		
Response in which it was stated that the water in the kettle is raised to a higher temperature	13	0
Explanation that the water in the kettle was at a higher temperature with reference to the bath having more water but failing to take it into account	3	0
The kettle takes longer to heat than the bath	1	0
There is cold water in the kettle whereas the water in the bath is already warm	2	0
Irrelevant or meaningless response	9	0
Explanation for both costing the same		
Both are heated by the same fuel i.e. electricity therefore the costs are the same	1	0
No understanding of the question e.g. kettle used to fill the bath	4	0

Movement and deformation   One question from this section asked pupils to decide what the force of a man's feet on the ground would be when he had raised a bucket of cement using a simply pulley.

'Man'

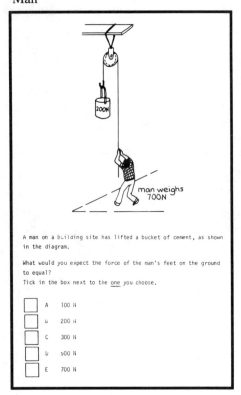

A man on a building site has lifted a bucket of cement, as shown in the diagram.

What would you expect the force of the man's feet on the ground to equal?
Tick in the box next to the one you choose.

- A 100 N
- B 200 N
- C 300 N
- D 500 N
- E 700 N

Comment

To answer this question correctly pupils had to understand that the tension in the rope ie 200 newtons, acts upwards on the man as well as pulling on the bucket to maintain its position. After trials the distractor 900 N was omitted as no pupils opted for it.

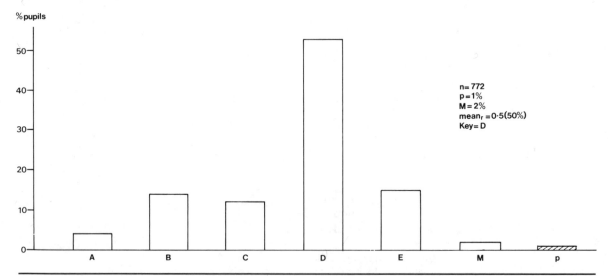

n= 772
p=1%
M=2%
$mean_r$ =0·5(50%)
Key= D

On this question 16 per cent of pupils opted for responses which could not be worked out directly from the data presented. Fifteen per cent of the pupils thought the force of the man's feet on the ground was unaffected by his raising the cement.

Similar proportions of pupils, 14 per cent and 15 per cent respectively, opted for the distractor B and distractor E, both of which could be read off the diagram.

Boys did better on this question than girls, six per cent more of them selecting Key D compared to girls. More girls (eight per cent) than boys thought the force would be unaffected and chose distractor E.

'See-saw'

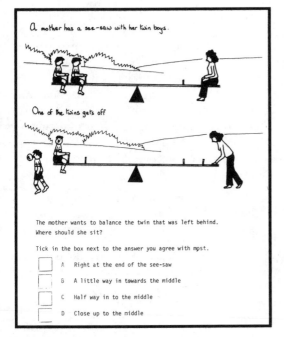

Comment

In this question pupils had to apply their understanding of the turning effect of a force about a point. The concept to be applied in this question features in most general science courses during practical work on simple beam balances.

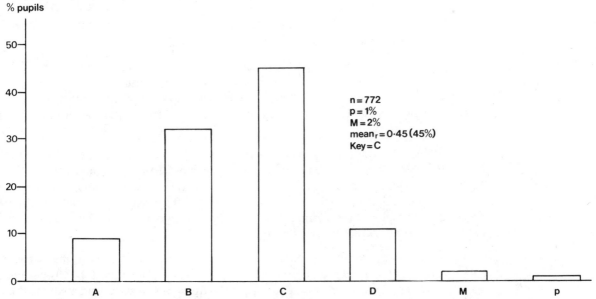

% pupils

n = 772
p = 1%
M = 2%
mean$_r$ = 0·45 (45%)
Key = C

From the histogram it can be seen that nine per cent of the pupils do not appear to know that the turning effect is larger when the line of action of the force is further from the turning point. Eleven per cent of the pupils opted for distractor D which suggests that the mother's weight is much greater than the data indicate. On the other hand 32 per cent of the pupils chose the distractor which said that the line of action should only be slightly decreased, indicating that the turning effect required was only a little smaller. Forty-five per cent of the pupils chose the answer which demonstrated an understanding of the concept and the data presented.

Summary of results for sub-category $4\delta_{CD}$ Sub-category $4\delta_{CD}$ was represented in the survey by a total of 27 questions — nine in each of three different packages (the other questions in the package either belonging to 4α or to $4\delta_{AB}$ or $4\delta_{EF}$). The three mark distributions were similarly-shaped, with more pupils achieving scores in the bottom half of the mark-range than in the top half. The mean marks were about one-third of the maximum possible total mark. Fewer than one per cent of the 2 000 + pupils who attempted a $4\delta_{CD}$ sub-test failed to achieve at least one mark for their performance on this sub-category. The maximum score achieved was about 75 per cent for each sub-test.

In this sub-category pupil performance was lowest on questions which required the application of concepts about the properties of matter. The mean scores for questions in this section varied from 13 per cent to 40 per cent of the maximum.

Only a small proportion of pupils (between 20 per cent and 30 per cent) demonstrated an understanding of the effect of temperature on the volume of materials — expansion and contraction. An even smaller proportion (15 per cent) explained the effect even when they correctly predicted it.

About half the pupils tested appreciated that water tends to flow until its surface reaches a common level. As one would expect, very few pupils (15 per cent) explained pressure in terms of particle motion and the subsequent effect of temperature on the pressure exerted.

The highest level of performance was in the section involving pupils' understanding of movement and deformation. The mean scores achieved on these questions were consistently higher than those obtained in other groups. The level for this group of questions was around 40 per cent of the maximum.

From individual question responses between 50 per cent and 70 per cent of the pupils demonstrated an understanding that speed was directly proportional to the distance travelled in a certain time. A much smaller proportion (about 15 per cent) showed a qualitative appreciation that acceleration was a change in speed in a given time. A similar proportion of pupils (50 per cent − 70 per cent) applied the concept that the turning effect of a force is larger when the line of action of the force is further from the point.

For questions which demanded the application of concepts about magnetism and the weight and mass of objects, the performance was around the 50 per cent level but there were only a few of these questions selected and used in the packages.

The group of questions which involved concepts related to work and energy had the second lowest performance level. The mean scores on the questions varied from 20 to 50 per cent of the maximum.

The difference in the performance levels of boys and girls — in favour of boys — this time reaches statistical significance, confirming, for general sub-category performance, differences that were noted earlier in this section for specific kinds of questions.

Within this concept region differences in performance due to question type were less obvious than in the biological concept region. This could be a result of the increased difficulty pupils appeared to have with the application of the concepts involved. As noted previously, the performance level on questions where explanations had to be generated was lower (16 per cent) than where the correct one had to be selected (65 per cent). It was noticeable when looking at different questions that the performance level for one type of question across different concept sections was much less varied than was performance on one section of concepts across different types of questions. The variation in mean scores for questions on a particular concept section was between 20 and 50 per cent of the maximum, and often greater. For questions of a particular type covering a range of concept sections the variation between mean scores was around ten to 20 per cent. This trend was consistent for questions set in the biological concept region.

4.8 Sub-category $4\delta_{EF}$: making sense of information using chemical concepts

Chemical concept region   The two main areas in the chemical concept region were concerned with 'the classification and structure of matter' (area E) and 'chemical interactions' (area F).

Twenty—seven questions from this concept region were selected from the item bank and they spread across eight of the ten sections of chemical concepts. There was a maximum of five questions in any one section. Some of the questions used are described below underneath the section heading.

States of matter   In this section one question, 'Melting ice', is described in detail including the different types of response given by pupils which are shown in Table 4.14.

From the pupil responses it appeared that 61 per cent of the pupils knew the changes of state from ice to water to steam and demonstrated some understanding that the temperature was constant whilst the change of state occurred. Of this group of pupils 79 per cent assumed that at the plateau the change of state had completely occurred rather than realising that the plateau represents the transition stage from one state to another. A further 4 per cent of the pupils attempting the question appeared to understand that the changes of state went from ice to water to steam; six per cent stated only that ice went to water. However, these pupils did not appreciate the temperatures at which the changes occurred or the significance of the plateaux in the graph. Twenty-four per cent of the pupils tested demonstrated an understanding of the sequence of the states of matter for water. Interpretation of information in a graphical form might have been a hurdle in this question.

'Melting ice'

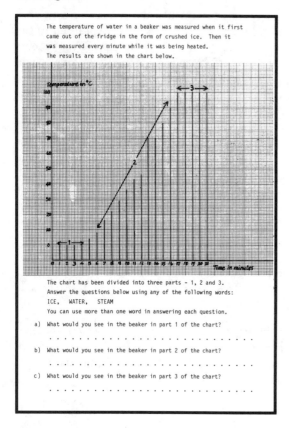

The temperature of water in a beaker was measured when it first came out of the fridge in the form of crushed ice. Then it was measured every minute while it was being heated. The results are shown in the chart below.

The chart has been divided into three parts - 1, 2 and 3. Answer the questions below using any of the following words: ICE, WATER, STEAM
You can use more than one word in answering each question.

a) What would you see in the beaker in part 1 of the chart?

b) What would you see in the beaker in part 2 of the chart?

c) What would you see in the beaker in part 3 of the chart?

Mark scheme

a)	Ice	1
	Water	1
b)	Water	1
c)	Water	1
	Steam	1
	Total ⑤	

In part b) accept water and steam　　1

No marks given if all three are listed

Comment

In this section the word 'STEAM' was chosen after trials as being the term understood by most 13 year olds to mean condensed water vapour.

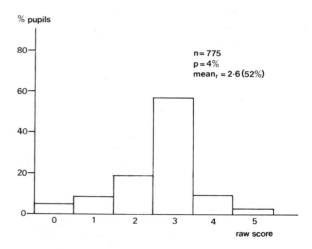

n = 775
p = 4%
$mean_r = 2.6$ (52%)

The performance of the boys was higher than that of the girls. This was the case for most of the questions set in this section. There was considerable variation in the performance levels on the questions in this section, the mean scores ranging from 17 per cent to 57 per cent of the maximum.

Table 4.14   *Categories of response: 'Melting ice'*

Nature of response			% of pupils
part (a)	part (b)	part (c)	
Ice and water	Water	Water and steam	2
Ice and water	Water and steam	Water and steam	1
Ice and water	Water and steam	Steam	2
Ice	Water and steam	Water and steam	8
Ice	Water and steam	Steam	48
Reverse response			
Steam	Water	Ice	3
Responses which indicate a progression			
Ice	Ice	Water	1
Ice and water	Ice and lots of water	Water	1
Ice	Ice and water	Water	2
Ice	Water	Water	2
Ice	Ice and water	Steam	1
Ice	Ice and water	Water and steam	3
Responses which indicate no progression			
Ice	Steam	Water	8
Water	Steam	Ice	3
Water	Ice	Steam	3
Writes everything at each part			1
Irrelevant response			8
No response			4

Metals and Non-metals   The pupils' performance on questions within this section was more consistent than for any other section of chemical concepts. This might reflect the relative homogeneity of the concepts listed and the fact that they were largely descriptive rather than abstract.

An example of one of the questions, 'Heating elements', is given with a description of pupil responses in Table 4.15.

Thirty-four per cent of the pupils gave responses which indicated that they had used the information in the table. This question further demonstrates that while about half of the pupils could state a correct inference based on their interpretation of the information, a large proportion of these pupils (56 per cent) were unable to say how they interpreted the information. They appeared to be unable to state the generalisation upon which the inference is based and referred only to specific aspects of the generalisation.

'Heating elements'

A pupil carried out an investigation of several different elements, both metals and non-metals. She heated each element on flameproof paper and found the mass before and after heating. She wrote down her results in the table.

Element	Mass before heating	Mass after heating
Iron	2.00 g	2.03 g
Carbon	2.00 g	0.20 g
Sulphur	2.00 g	0.00 g
Aluminium	2.00 g	2.02 g
Copper	2.00 g	2.03 g
Iodine	2.00 g	0.03 g
Magnesium	2.00 g	2.83 g

a) If the pupil now heated the element zinc, what would you expect to happen to its mass?

. . . .

. . . .

b) How did you work this out?

. . . .

. . . .

. . . .

. . . .

Mark scheme

Mark scheme

Heating elements

a) Zinc is a metal so its mass   1
   will increase on heating   1

b) Metals gain weight on heating   1
   Non-metals lose weight on heating   1

Total ④

Give the mark for the statement zinc is a metal whether it occurs in part (a) or (b)

Comments

In order to answer this question pupils have to know which elements are metals and which are non-metals and that each group has common properties from which generalisations can be made.

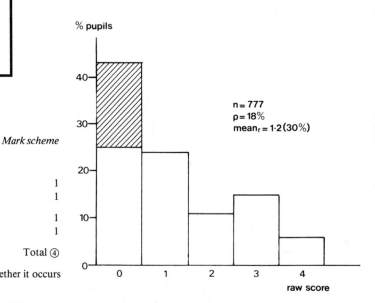

% pupils

n = 777
p = 18%
mean$_r$ = 1·2 (30%)

raw score

Girls achieved a higher mean score on this question than the boys. Two per cent more girls than boys scored full marks and four per cent more boys than girls gave an explanation in terms of expansion of the metal.

Some chemical reactions In this section questions depended upon the understanding of some chemical reactions. Pupil performance varied depending on the reaction involved and the type of question asked about it. Three questions — 'Nail', 'Rust' and 'Heating compounds' — are included to illustrate pupil performance.

Table 4.15 *Categories of response: 'Heating elements'*

Nature of response	% of pupils	score
Responses gaining one or more marks		
Mass increase because zinc is a metal. The information shows that metals gain mass on heating and non-metals lose mass	6	4
Mass increases because zinc is a metal. The information shows that metals gain mass on heating	15	3
Zinc is a metal and its mass increases — specifies amount eg 2.46 g	11	2
The mass increases — explanation given in terms of specific observations eg because it shrivels up/ash formed on the zinc, etc	16	1
The mass increases because it is heated	2	1
Increases in mass — no explanation	6	1
Responses gaining no marks		
The zinc will expand — no reference to mass	8	0
No change in mass will occur	4	0
Decrease in mass — the zinc burns/melts, etc	2	0
Decrease in mass — zinc is not a metal	2	0
Decrease in mass — no explanation	3	0
Irrelevant response	7	0
No response	18	0

In the first example, 'Nail', the pupils had to select a prediction and explain the reason for their choice.

From the score distribution it can be seen that 51 per cent of the pupils selected the correct prediction. Of these pupils 80 per cent were able to explain that at the interface the iron was in contact with both water and air. Thirty-six per cent of the pupils opted for distractor C which suggests that they associate the rusting of iron with water more than oxygen or air. Ten more boys than girls chose Key B and 12 per cent more girls than boys selected distractor C.

Another question, 'Rust', in this section, which also concerned the rusting of iron, showed no difference in the performance of boys and girls. The mean score on this question was 37 per cent of the maximum. The question differed from 'Nail' in that the pupils were presented with three different situations: iron in a bowl of water, in a fridge and in a freezer. The pupils had to say whether the iron would rust in each situation and explain their answer. This question also required pupils to know what conditions were necessary in order for iron to rust but they

'Nail'

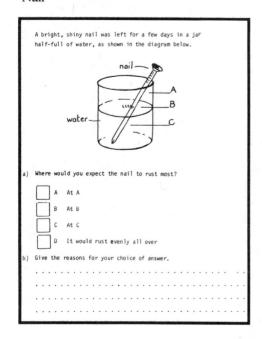

A bright, shiny nail was left for a few days in a jar half-full of water, as shown in the diagram below.

nail

A
B
water
C

a) Where would you expect the nail to rust most?

☐ A At A
☐ B At B
☐ C At C
☐ D It would rust evenly all over

b) Give the reasons for your choice of answer.

. . . .
. . . .
. . . .
. . . .

Comment

In order to score marks the pupils have to know what conditions are necessary in order for iron to rust and in the given situation where the conditions are most favourable.

Mark scheme

a) Key B   1

b) At B the nail is in contact with most air and water   1

Total ②

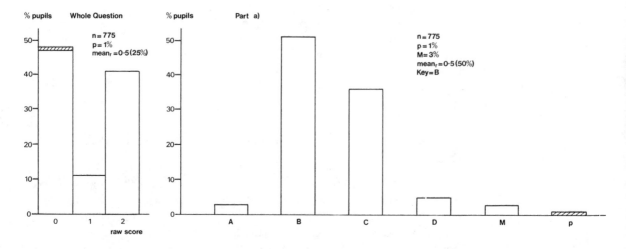

% pupils   Whole Question

n = 775
p = 1%
mean$_r$ = 0·5 (25%)

raw score

% pupils   Part a)

n = 775
p = 1%
M = 3%
mean$_r$ = 0·5 (50%)
Key = B

had to assess the three situations to see if the conditions were satisfied, as opposed to deciding which conditions were the most favourable.

From the score distribution for the question 'Heating compounds' it can be seen that a large proportion of the pupils (60 per cent) selected the correct response in both part (a) and part (b). Both parts had similar mean scores and the most common error for both was that the pupils made a multiple response (11 per cent). Eleven per cent of the pupils getting the correct response to part (a) failed

'Heating compounds'

Four compounds P, Q, R and S were heated gently in separate test tubes. The changes that were observed are written down in the table below:

Compound	Colour before heating	Colour when hot	Colour when cold	Change in mass
P	White powder	Yellow powder	White powder	None
Q	Brown powder	Brown powder	Brown powder	None
R	White crystals	White crystals	White crystals	None
S	Green powder	Black powder	Black powder	Loss

a) Which compound changes on heating but re-forms on cooling?

- [ ] A   Compound P
- [ ] B   Compound Q
- [ ] C   Compound R
- [ ] D   Compound S

b) Which compound has reacted on heating?

- [ ] A   Compound P
- [ ] B   Compound Q
- [ ] C   Compound R
- [ ] D   Compound S

Comment

In this question pupils need to understand some of the characteristics of a physical and chemical change.

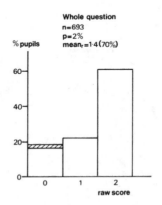

Whole question
n=693
p=2%
mean$_r$=1·4 (70%)

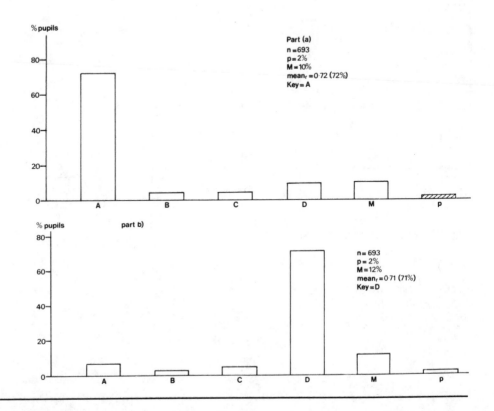

Part (a)
n=693
p=2%
M=10%
mean$_r$=0·72 (72%)
Key=A

part b)
n=693
p=2%
M=12%
mean$_r$=0·71 (71%)
Key=D

part (b). A similar proportion (14 per cent) of the pupils getting part (b) right failed part (a).

Properties of chemical reactions   Questions in this section were concerned with the general properties of chemical reactions rather than the understanding of specific reactions. Very few questions could be included in this section at age 13 as there were few concept statements listed.

The example 'Phosphorus' involved the concept of conservation of mass.

'Phosphorus'

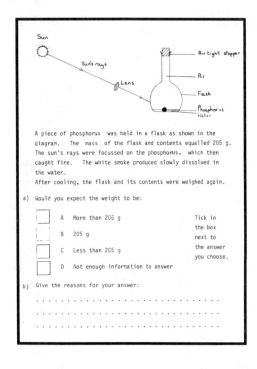

A piece of phosphorus was held in a flask as shown in the diagram. The mass of the flask and contents equalled 205 g. The sun's rays were focussed on the phosphorus, which then caught fire. The white smoke produced slowly dissolved in the water.
After cooling, the flask and its contents were weighed again.

a) Would you expect the weight to be:

   A   More than 205 g

   B   205 g

   C   Less than 205 g

   D   Not enough information to answer

Tick in the box next to the answer you choose.

b) Give the reasons for your answer:

. . . .
. . . .
. . . .

Comment

It is difficult to set a question involving this concept in a novel context which is one of the aims of the assessment. In order to overcome this slightly, a novel *reaction* set-up was used.

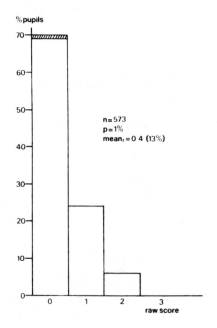

n = 573
p = 1%
mean$_r$ = 0 4 (13%)

Mark scheme

a) Key B   1

b) Matter cannot be created or destroyed   1
   Mass remains constant — product cannot escape   1

Total ③

The mean score on this question was low, being around 13 per cent of the maximum. The question was also included in the monitoring at age 15.

The different types of response given by pupils is shown in Table 4.16.

Table 4.16   *Categories of response: 'Phosphorus'*

Nature of response	% of pupils
Responses in which pupils opted for A in part (a) — mass will increase	
The size of the phosphorus increases on burning and thus its mass increases	5
The gas produced is heavier than air — or the gas dissolves in the water so the water is heavier or rises	7
Irrelevant response	3
No response to part (b)	1
Responses in which pupils opted for the key B in part (a) — mass will remain the same	
The airtight stopper prevents the product from escaping so the mass does not change	6
The phosphorus would lose weight but the product dissolves in water	2
The smoke produced is too light to weigh anything	16
Irrelevant response	6
Responses in which pupils opted for C in part (a) — mass decreases	
The burnt phosphorus or smoke weighs less/less dense than the solid	20
The phosphorus dissolves so only water is left	9
The water is lost/evaporates	9
The phosphorus melts and so it is lighter	1
The phosphorus took in oxygen and so becomes lighter	3
Irrelevant response	4
No response	1
Responses in which pupils opted for D in part (a) — not enough information	
No response to part (b)	7

Thirty per cent of the pupils opted for the correct answer in part (a). 80 per cent of these pupils, however, demonstrated no apparent understanding of the notion of conservation of mass.

The largest proportion of pupils (47 per cent) thought that the mass would decrease. The majority of this group gave responses which indicated that the effect of heating on the phosphorus caused a decrease in mass and the product of the reaction was not considered by them.

Boys achieved a higher mean score than girls on this question: the main differences in performance were that 35 per cent of the boys opted for Key B compared to 26 per cent of the girls, and more boys — 20 per cent compared to 12 per cent of the girls — gave the response that the smoke produced is too light to weigh anything.

Summary of results for sub-category $4\delta_{EF}$ Three of the various category 4 test packages contained nine $4\delta_{EF}$ questions each, alongside similar numbers of questions relating to one of 4α, $4\delta_{AB}$ or $4\delta_{CD}$. There were thus in total 27 questions representing this particular sub-category.

The three sub-test mark distributions were similar in shape to each other and to those of the other 4δ distributions, with more pupils achieving total marks in the lower half of the mark range than in the upper half. The mean marks were in each case about one-third along the mark scale. Again, a low one per cent of the 2 000 + pupils who attempted a $4\delta_{EF}$ sub-test failed to achieve at least one mark. The maximum score achieved was again about 75 per cent.

In this sub-category the questions selected were fairly evenly spread over eight different sections of chemical concepts. As a consequence there were few questions in any one section and so it was difficult to generalise about pupil performance within any one section or to make comparisons between sections.

What was clear from the data was the considerable variation in mean scores achieved for questions within any one concept section. Pupil performance was higher and less varied when the concepts involved in the questions were descriptive rather than abstract as, for example, in the section on metals and non-metals. Similarly the section in which questions were concerned with specific chemical reactions had a higher overall performance level, around 40 per cent of the maximum, compared to the section which involved generalisations about the properties of chemical reactions (23 per cent). A low performance level (23 per cent) was achieved in the section about acids and bases which required the understanding of neutralisation and pH number.

From individual question responses between 50 and 60 per cent of the pupils demonstrated an understanding that the changes of state went from solid to liquid to gas, and of the link between change of state and temperature.

Between 30 and 40 per cent of the pupils appreciated the connection between the colour of universal indicator and whether the substance was an acid or an alkali. Only a small proportion (20 per cent) of the pupils appeared to know about the process of neutralisation of acids and alkalis. Around 40−50 per cent of the pupils knew the major characteristic properties of metals, but fewer pupils (30 per cent) were able to group metals and non-metals by their specific properties.

Within the chemical concept region differences in performance due to question type were even less clear than in the physics region. The performance level on questions where explanations had to be generated was again lower (20 per cent) than where the correct one had to be selected (57 per cent), but the mean score achieved on the individual questions was affected by the nature of the concept involved.

If performance on questions of the same type but with different concept demands is considered, the variation in mean score decreases but is still considerable. The effects of question type are more noticeable if individual questions with similar concept demands are considered. In one question information was presented about groups of elements and their properties and the properties of two separate elements X and Y. The pupils had to predict to which group the elements X and Y belonged. The mean score achieved on this was 80 per cent of the maximum and the non-response rate was nine per cent. In another question with a similar concept demand information was presented about the group and the characteristic properties of the elements in the group. The pupils then had to predict some of the general properties of another member of the group that had not been listed. The mean score on this question was around 20 per cent of the maximum and the non-response rate was 30 per cent. What seemed to depress performance here was the open-endness of the response. Pupils appeared to be more confident about matching the properties rather than proposing them.

The performance level on questions set in the concept area 'Chemical interaction' was generally higher (about 41 per cent) than performance in the area 'The classification and structure of matter' (about one-third of the maximum).

4.9 Sub-category 4ε: generating alternative hypotheses

Range of questions used   In this sub-category, as in 4δ, pupils were required to apply science concepts. They had to suggest different possible explanations for the same set of observations or events. It was found in trials that responses to the questions depended on the particular event presented. This sub-category differs in that respect from 4δ and the questions are reported individually and no attempt was made to generalise from them.

Four questions are reported which involve some biological, physical and chemical concepts — 'Grasshoppers', 'Ivy', 'Electro-magnets' and 'Coal and oil'. The questions were concentrated in two packages and one of them, 'Ivy', was included in the survey at age 11 as well as at age 13.

The questions are reported in detail which includes the kinds of responses given and the scores achieved. Two marking systems were used in the questions: in one the response could score one or zero and in the second the response could score two, one or zero.

Results for questions in 4ε

'Grasshopper'

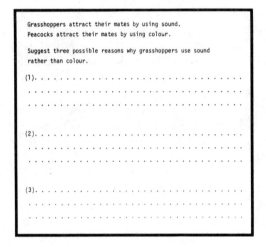

Grasshoppers attract their mates by using sound.
Peacocks attract their mates by using colour.

Suggest three possible reasons why grasshoppers use sound
rather than colour.

(1). . . . .
. . . .
. . . .

(2). . . . .
. . . .
. . . .

(3). . . . .
. . . .
. . . .

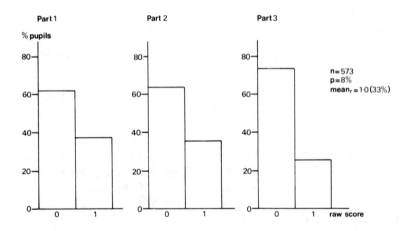

Part 1   Part 2   Part 3

% pupils

n= 573
p=8%
mean$_r$ =1·0 (33%)

raw score

The different responses given by the pupils to the question 'Grasshopper' are shown in Table 4.17.

The most common scoring response, given by 15 per cent of the pupils, referred to the need for grasshoppers to be camouflaged from their predators, hence the necessity for dull colours to blend in with the background grass, etc.

Table 4.17   *Categories of response: 'Grasshopper'*

Nature of response	% of pupils				
	overall	part (1)	part (2)	part (3)	score
Bright colours would make grass-hoppers more visible to their predators (dull colours for camouflage)	15	24	14	8	1
In the grasshoppers' environment (grass) sound can be detected at a greater distance than colours	6	7	6	4	1
Grasshoppers are colour blind/poor sighted/blind	5	5	5	5	1
Grasshoppers have well developed hearing mechanisms	3	1	3	4	1
Grasshoppers have mechanisms for making characteristic sounds	4	1	6	5	1
Grasshoppers mate only at night	1	—	1	1	1
Grasshoppers have no feathers	1	1	1		0
Grasshoppers are too small	8	12	7	6	0
Grasshoppers are not beautiful	1	1	1	1	0
Noise travels farther/grasshoppers are noisier than peacocks	8	5	13	7	0
Grasshoppers are not coloured/do not like to be seen/same colour/dull	14	29	9	4	0
Previous statement repeated	5	—	6	10	0
Meaningless response/irrelevant	21	13	23	28	0
No response	8	1	5	17	0

In all about a third of the responses given by the pupils explained the difference in terms of suitability with respect to the environment or the attributes of the grasshoppers. A similar proportion gave explanations which suggested that rather than the grasshoppers being adapted to their environment etc., they had to adapt to cope with their inherent inadequacies eg blindness, ugliness, within their environment. As one would expect, the non-response rate increased from one per cent in part (a) to 17 per cent in part (c).

'Ivy'

Walking along this footpath Thomas noticed that there was ivy growing on the trees but only round three-quarters of the trunks.   None of the trees had ivy growing on the side nearest to the path.

Think of <u>two</u> different reasons why the ivy might grow only on some sides of the trees.   Write the first at a) and the second at b)

a)   I think it might be because . . . .
. . . .
. . . .
. . . .

b)   Or it might be because . . . .
. . . .
. . . .

Comment

This question has only two parts, a) and b), as it was originally for 11 year olds. It was felt that to expect more than two alternative hypotheses from an 11 year old was unreasonable. Two marks were given for the hypothesis and explanation and one mark for the hypothesis alone. Hypotheses were accepted if they were consistent with the information given and with accepted science concepts.

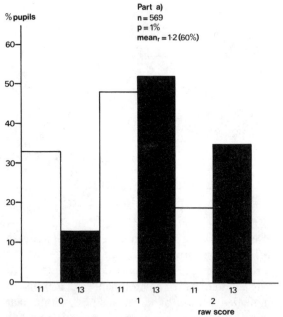

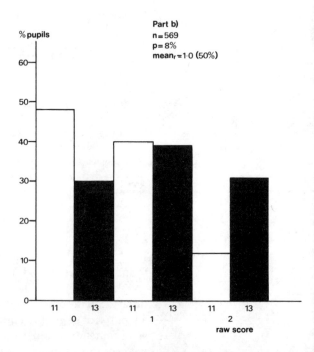

Table 4.18 *Categories of response: 'Ivy'*

Nature of response	% of pupils						possible score
	total		part (a)		part (b)		
	13	11	13	11	13	11	
Not so much light on the side shaded by the fence/because of the shade	12	8	16	10	7	6	1–2
Sun only shines on three sides of the trees/does not shine on the fourth side/because of the sunlight more on one side	19	14	27	22	10	6	1–2
Sun on the path side and would dry up the ivy/too much sun	3	2	3	2	2	2	1–2
People walking on the path pull/knock the ivy off	13	10	11	9	14	10	2
Cars and dogs are more likely to have scratched it off on the footpath side	1	1	—	—	1	1	2
Not enough water on one side because of shelter from fence/wind/damper on one side	10	6	10	5	10	6	1–2
Wind blows harder on the path side blows ivy back/because of the wind	4	5	6	5	2	5	0–2
May be a fungus on the trees on the path side which stops ivy growing/something which attracts the ivy to one side so it won't grow on the other	5	3	2	2	8	3	1–2
Vehicles on the road provide things the plant likes so it grows	5	2	5	2	4	2	1
The soil is poorer on one side	3	2	2	1	3	2	1
The ivy was only planted on one side	6	6	6	5	5	6	1
It hasn't had time to grow on the other side	2	4	—	3	4	4	1
Reasons in terms of coincidental features							
The presence of the road/path	1	1	1	1	1	1	0
The side by the road faces open & not a fence	0	0	—	—	—	0.5	0
The presence of the grass	1	1	1	1	1	1	0
Reasons for which there is no evidence or contradictory evidence							
Pollution by cars prevents growth/only grass on one side of the trees	0	2		2		2	0
Ivy does not grow on certain sides of trees	3	5	2	4	3	5	0
The trees are healthier on the road side	2	3	1	2	2	4	0
Irrelevant or tautological statements							
The trees' branches shade the trunks/roots grow underground/birds spread the seeds	0	6	—	5	1	6	0
The ivy is only growing on the sides of the trees	0	2	—	2	—	1	0
Meaningless or incomprehensible/repeat of previous statement	7	13	6	11	7	15	0
Non-response	5	0	1		8		

The performance of boys and girls differed on the question 'Grasshopper'. In each part five to seven per cent more boys than girls gave the response that grasshoppers need to be protected from their predators. More girls than boys gave the response that grasshoppers were not coloured and did not like to be seen. In part (a) and part (b) six per cent more girls gave a meaningless response, but in part (c) two per cent more boys did so. The non-response rate on part (a) and part (b) were similar, but in part (c) six per cent more girls than boys failed to suggest a third hypothesis.

The raw mean score achieved on the question 'Ivy' was 1.1 at age 13 and 0.75 at age 11.

The different responses given to part (a) and part (b) at the two ages are shown in Table 4.18.

Generally the responses given by the pupils at age 13 were concept-based and explained the event in terms of the conditions necessary for the plants to grow. The most frequent response referred to sunlight and the fact that the side without ivy lacked sunshine or light (19 per cent). The same notion, but stated in terms of the shade produced by the fence, was suggested by 12 per cent of the pupils at age 13. The next most popular response was not dependent on any taught science concept but reflected the pupils' commonsense view that people or vandals walking past would have knocked or pulled the ivy off. Ten per cent of the pupils thought that the shelter of the fence could have resulted in a lack of moisture and so prevented the growth of the ivy. A further three per cent also referred to the lack of water as the cause but explained that it arose because of excess sun on the path side. Similar proportions of pupils (five per cent) gave responses which indicated that the wind or fungal growth had inhibited the ivy's growth. Five per cent of the pupils suggested that car fumes actually encouraged the ivy to grow on the sides nearest the road.

At age 11, 22 per cent of the pupils compared with 31 per cent of 13 year olds gave answers which referred to the absence or presence of light and its effect on the ivy. Eight per cent of 11 year olds suggested that the lack of moisture due to various different factors caused the non-growth of the ivy: 13 per cent of 13 year olds responded in this way.

At age 11 slightly more hypotheses were suggested than at age 13 but they were generally irrelevant or based on no evidence or contradictory evidence. At age 13 the non-response rate increased from one per cent in part (a) to eight per cent in part (b).

There were some differences in the performance of boys and girls, more girls (ten per cent) than boys (six per cent) did not give an answer in part (b). On part (a) six per cent more girls than boys said that there was less light due to the shade of the fence and in part (a) and part (b) seven per cent more boys suggested that the sun shines only on three sides of the trees.

There were three parts to the question 'Electro-magnet' and a score of two, one or zero could be obtained on each part. The different kinds of response given by 13 year olds are shown in Table 4.19.

All the scoring responses to this question depended on taught science concepts

'Electro-magnet'

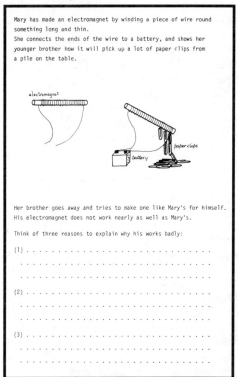

Mary has made an electromagnet by winding a piece of wire round something long and thin.
She connects the ends of the wire to a battery, and shows her younger brother how it will pick up a lot of paper clips from a pile on the table.

Her brother goes away and tries to make one like Mary's for himself. His electromagnet does not work nearly as well as Mary's.

Think of three reasons to explain why his works badly:

(1) . . . .
. . . .
. . . .

(2) . . . .
. . . .
. . . .

(3) . . . .
. . . .
. . . .

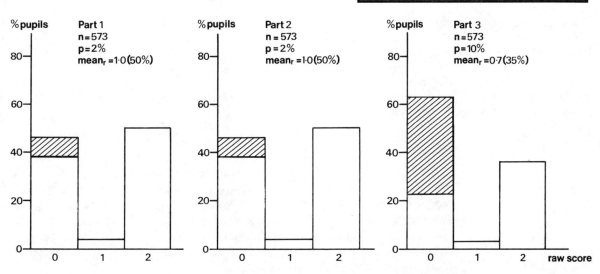

Part 1
n = 573
p = 2%
$mean_r$ = 1·0 (50%)

Part 2
n = 573
p = 2%
$mean_r$ = 1·0 (50%)

Part 3
n = 573
p = 10%
$mean_r$ = 0·7 (35%)

and yet the mean score was higher on this question than for the other two examples. The concepts involved in both 'Ivy' and this example are common to most general science courses. The context of this question was, however, a familiar school-based one compared to the more novel situation presented in 'Ivy'.

Table 4.19   *Categories of response: 'Electro-magnet'*

Nature of response	% of pupils				score
	total	part (1)	part (2)	part (3)	
Responses about circuit deficiencies					
Flat battery — weak battery or low voltage	22	26	27	14	2
Poor connections at the battery — no circuit	11	11	10	11	2
Connected wrongly	5	5	5	6	0
Responses about the wire					
A different wire was used which was a poorer conductor	2	1	3	2	2
A different wire which was too thick	2	1	2	2	1
Different wire — no explanation (wire not as good)	4	3	5	4	0
The wire was not magnetic	0		0.5	1	0
Responses about the core and coils					
Not enough wire used so too few coils or coils too far apart	6	9	5	4	2
Not enough wire/coils — no explanation	2	3	2	1	1
Wire not wound properly	6	8	4	5	0
The core was an insulator	2	2	2	2	2
The core took the charge away/not the right material	5	4	4	7	0
The core was too fat or not thin enough/the turns were larger/not coiled tight enough	2	3	3	1	2
Core too fat — no explanation	6	5	5	7	0
Core too long/short — no explanation	1	0.5	1	2	0
Paper clips were not made of magnetic material	1	—	0.5	2	2
Previous statement repeated	2	—	2	5	0
Irrelevant explanation eg he was too young — too many paper clips	15	17	14	13	0
Meaningless/incomprehensible statement	3	2	3	4	0
No response	5	2	2	10	0

The most frequently suggested hypothesis referred to the battery in the circuit and was given by 22 per cent of the pupils. Overall circuit deficiencies accounted for 38 per cent of the responses made. A wider variety of explanations was given with respect to the core and coils but by consistently small proportions of pupils for each part of the question. Quite a large number of pupils, 15 per cent, gave irrelevant explanations by trying to explain the situation in terms of extraneous factors eg the boy was too young.

The number of pupils repeating a previous statement increased from two per cent to five per cent and the non-response rate increased from two per cent in the first two parts of the question to ten per cent in part (c).

There were some differences in the responses given by the girls and boys which were most noticeable in parts (a) and (b) of the question. In part (a) 12 per cent more boys than girls referred to the battery being flat or with too low a voltage, whereas ten per cent more girls than boys suggested that there was no circuit due to poor connections at the battery. More boys (seven per cent) gave the response that there was insufficient wire and so too few coils. A higher proportion of girls gave an irrelevant explanation compared to the boys — 22 per cent compared with 13 per cent. In part (b) the same difference occurred in the responses about the battery and the circuit, but they were less magnified. Similarly seven per cent more girls than boys gave an irrelevant explanation. In part (c) the proportions of girls and boys giving different answers was very similar but three per cent more girls failed to respond in this part than boys.

'Coal and oil'

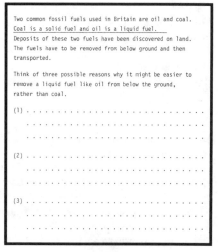

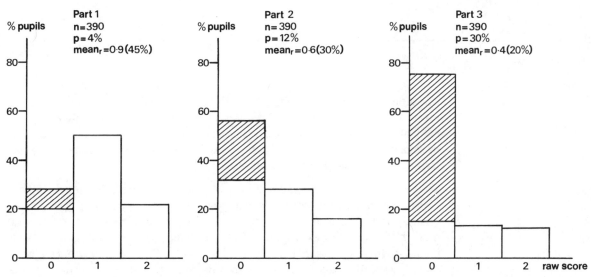

The overall mean score for the question 'Coal and oil' was 32 per cent.

Table 4.20   *Categories of response: 'Coal and oil'*

Nature of response	% of pupils				
	total	(1)	(2)	(3)	score
Liquid fuel can be pumped out so it is easier to get it to the surface	6	14	2	1	2
Oil can be sucked/pumped up	13	29	8	3	1
To remove coal you have to build a shaft etc — more work involved	3	4	4	2	2
Have to mine coal	8	12	8	3	1
More men are involved in the removal of coal — more expensive	1	1	2	—	2
More men needed	4	2	6	4	1
The removal of coal from underground is more hazardous — floods, cave-ins, gas etc	5	2	6	8	2
Solid fuel has to be dug out/blown out and then sorted from the debris	1	1	2	1	2
Liquid fuel can take any shape/less bulky	5	7	6	3	1
Repeats in different words a previous statement	6	—	7	10	0
Irrelevant response/meaningless	32	24	38	35	0
No response	15	4	12	30	0

The non-response rate again increased from part (1) to part (3), as did the proportion of pupils giving an irrelevant response. The most common responses highlighted the major mining difference ie that oil is pumped out and coal has to be mined. Difficulties or advantages associated with the different removal techniques were less frequently suggested.

The performance of boys and girls did differ in certain categories, for example in part (1) seven per cent more girls than boys gave an irrelevant response. In part (2) and part (3) this proportion decreased to five per cent. In part (2) four per cent more boys gave the explanation that the mining of coal was more labour-intensive. In part (3) more boys than girls explained that the mining of coal was a more hazardous process than the removal of oil. The other marked difference which was consistent for all the examples was that in part (3) more girls (35 per cent) failed to respond than boys (24 per cent).

5   Category 5 : design of investigations

5.1 Nature of the category

This chapter is concerned with the way pupils plan investigations on paper. Their *practical* response to an invitation to design and carry out an experiment to solve a given problem is the subject of category 6, 'Performance of investigations', the assessment of which was deferred, for age 13, until the 1981 survey.

Questions in category 5 were divided into three groups. In the first, sub-category α, they were designed to find out how far pupils could distinguish between statements which can be tested scientifically and those which, by their nature, cannot be subjected to such a test. In sub-category β pupils were asked to identify procedures which are appropriate for testing the given proposition, or to criticise suggested methods of testing them. It was often necessary for pupils to make judgements about which variables needed to be controlled and which varied. In the final sub-category γ, pupils were required to devise an investigation to solve a given problem, and then to describe it and explain how results would lead to a solution.

5.2 Sub-category 5α: identifying or proposing testable statements

The range of questions used   Three types of question were used: in the first two pupils were to consider a number of statements and decide which were testable and which were not; the third type required the reformulation of a general statement into two alternative statements which could be checked. There were 17 different questions.

Selecting testable statements   In this type of question pupils were given a set of five statements, only one of which could be tested in a scientific way.

The mean score for the question 'Doggy' (over) was 80 per cent and, as can be seen from the chart, more pupils failed to score through marking more than one box than through choosing any particular wrong option.

The response rate was high for all six questions of this type, and the mean score ranged from 40 to 80 per cent. In 'Doggy' success hinged on the recognition that the phrase 'is better' has no clearly defined and universally accepted meaning. In other questions, the corresponding untestable statements and mean scores were as follows:

Coffee tastes better than tea (70 per cent)

Fat people lead better lives than thin ones (50 per cent)

'Washo' makes wash-day a pleasure (70 per cent)

It is more pleasant to live in Europe than in America (60 per cent)

Fluoropaste makes teeth more attractive than brand X (40 per cent)

A possible source of error is that pupils may consider that it is possible to check the correctness of a statement by taking an opinion poll. This may have

'Doggy

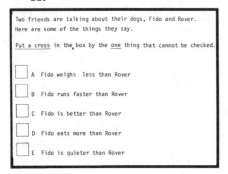

Two friends are talking about their dogs, Fido and Rover.
Here are some of the things they say.

<u>Put a cross</u> in the box by the <u>one</u> thing that cannot be checked.

☐ A Fido weighs less than Rover

☐ B Fido runs faster than Rover

☐ C Fido is better than Rover

☐ D Fido eats more than Rover

☐ E Fido is quieter than Rover

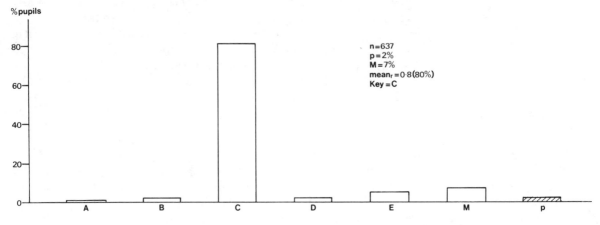

%pupils

n=637
p=2%
M=7%
mean$_r$=0·8(80%)
Key=C

happened in the question about toothpaste. Indeed, had the statement been worded slightly differently — for example "Nine out of ten people say Fluoropaste makes teeth more attractive than brand X" — it would in fact have been testable.

However, the pattern of response depends not only on how easy it is for pupils to see that the correct response cannot be checked, but also on how easy it is for them to imagine a way of checking the incorrect responses — the ones that are, in fact testable.

Few pupils were misled into choosing incorrect responses in 'Doggy'; it was easy to imagine ways of checking each of them. This may not have been the case for the incorrect response 'Fat people earn more than thin ones' in another question.

Identifying testable and relevant statements In a second type of question, pupils were given a set of five statements each of which was suggested as a substitute for the quoted non-testable opinion. They were required to identify the statement which was not only testable but also relevant.

It is interesting to speculate on the reasons why so many pupils failed to select the correct response, E, in 'Margarine'. Some may have thought that it would not be

'Margarine'

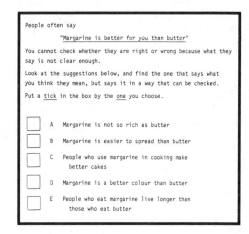

People often say

   "Margarine is better for you than butter"

You cannot check whether they are right or wrong because what they say is not clear enough.

Look at the suggestions below, and find the one that says what you think they mean, but says it in a way that can be checked.

Put a tick in the box by the one you choose.

☐   A   Margarine is not so rich as butter

☐   B   Margarine is easier to spread than butter

☐   C   People who use margarine in cooking make
             better cakes

☐   D   Margarine is a better colour than butter

☐   E   People who eat margarine live longer than
             those who eat butter

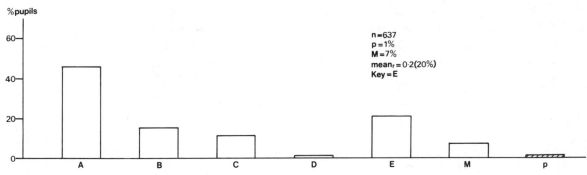

% pupils

n = 637
p = 1%
M = 7%
mean$_r$ = 0.2(20%)
Key = E

possible to check the statement; the kind of retrospective or extended investigation necessary for such a test may not be within the experience of some 13 year old pupils. Others may have considered it to be untrue, and although this would not in fact have been a good reason for rejecting it, pupils may have been reluctant to tick a statement they saw as 'wrong'. Some may have been looking for a *reason* for the original statement and therefore selected response A (even though it is not testable); they are so often required to do that that it perhaps becomes an automatic reaction. Finally seven per cent of the pupils failed to follow the instructions and ticked more than one box.

Mean scores for this type of question ranged from 20 to 60 per cent, but only one per cent of the pupils failed to respond in some way.

Reformulating general statements   Questions in the third type in sub-category 5α required pupils to reformulate a general statement so as to turn it into one which could be checked. It proved very difficult to word the questions in such a way that 13 year old pupils understood what was required of them. During small-scale trials a number of alternative ways of asking the question were investigated. One difficulty was that in order to make the matter clear to pupils of this age, a great many words were necessary; so that in removing one difficulty another was

'Footbridge'

```
Some people say
        It is better to cross a main road by a footbridge

You would have a job to tell whether they are right or wrong
because what they say is not clear enough to be checked.

Think of two different things they might mean, which could both
be checked.

They might mean:
(1) . . . . . . . . . . . . . . . . . . . . . . . . . . . .
. . . . . . . . . . . . . . . . . . . . . . . . . . . . . .
. . . . . . . . . . . . . . . . . . . . . . . . . . . . . .

or they might mean:
(2) . . . . . . . . . . . . . . . . . . . . . . . . . . . .
. . . . . . . . . . . . . . . . . . . . . . . . . . . . . .
. . . . . . . . . . . . . . . . . . . . . . . . . . . . . .
```

'Molten metal'

```
Someone says
    "I can't get this lump of metal to melt however much I heat it"

You would have a job to check whether the person is right or
wrong because what is said is not clear enough.

Think of two different things that might be meant by the words
underlined, which could   both be checked.

The words might mean:
(1) . . . . . . . . . . . . . . . . . . . . . . . . . . . .
. . . . . . . . . . . . . . . . . . . . . . . . . . . . . .

or they might mean:
(2) . . . . . . . . . . . . . . . . . . . . . . . . . . . .
. . . . . . . . . . . . . . . . . . . . . . . . . . . . . .
. . . . . . . . . . . . . . . . . . . . . . . . . . . . . .
```

Table 5.1   *'Footbridge' : examples of types of suggestion made*   *(n = 637)*

Type of statement	% of pupils making it:	
	in (1)	in (2)
Relevant and testable (not necessarily true)		
About pedestrians:		
Fewer pedestrians killed or injured	10	3
Pedestrians need not hurry	0	1
Pedestrians need not wait to cross	2	10
About traffic:		
Traffic flows faster	0	2
Other:		
eg It's a shorter distance by footbridge	0	1
Relevant but not testable		
eg It's safer	62	49
Testable but not relevant		
eg Cars will slow down when drivers see a bridge	2	1
Neither testable nor relevant		
(Usually meaningless)	11	19
Special cases		
Opposite of original statement	1	2
Repetition of original statement	5	3
No response	5	10

Table 5.2   *'Molten metal' : examples of types of suggestion made*   *(n = 637)*

Type of statement	% of pupils making it:	
	in (1)	in (2)
Relevant and testable, referring to:		
Time (eg however long I heat it)	8	7
Quantity of heat (no. of Bunsen burners)	3	2
Temperature	10	14
Limitations of equipment	0	1
Incorrect use of equipment	1	1
Relevant but not testable	23	16
Neither relevant nor testable	26	32
Special cases		
An attempt to give a reason in terms of properties of the metal	3	4
Repetition of original statement	8	4
No response	10	17

introduced. Eventually a compromise was reached, illustrated by the two examples shown. In each case the responses were assigned to a number of categories.

The difficulty pupils had in grasping what the question demanded of them was apparent in the kinds of responses they made. Often they simply copied the original statement, or wrote the exact opposite. Most responses, however, were harder to describe. Some were not relevant, some were not testable, and they were remarkably varied.

Summary of results in sub-category 5α   Three category 5 test packages contained equal numbers of 5α and 5β questions (nine each per package). Sub-category 5α was represented by a total of 27 questions with some repetition across packages. All three sub-test distributions used the full mark range, and the mean scores fell about half-way along the scale. About two per cent of the 2 000-plus pupils who took one or other of these packages failed to achieve at least one mark for 5α performance.

The rate of non-response was high in the open-ended question type where pupils were required to propose statements that could be checked. In questions where pupils were required to distinguish between statements presented to them with regard to whether they could be checked, the non-response rate was lower, and the mean score higher. In five of the eight open-ended questions, girls had a higher mean score than boys.

5.3 Sub-category 5β: assessing experimental procedures

Range of questions used   Twenty-four different questions were used to test pupil performance in this sub-category. They were of five different types, requiring procedures to be considered in relation to practical problems.

Selecting suitable procedures   In the first type to be illustrated, a problem was posed and pupils were asked to select the most suitable procedure for its solution from four or five alternative suggestions. The choice of suggestion was designed to test pupils' ability to decide which factors should be varied and which controlled in solving the problem. 'Acceleration' is one example of this type: in it, pupils have to locate the option in which the size of the ball is varied while the mass and height are held constant. The chart shows that 48 per cent of the pupils succeeded in doing this.

The next most popular choice was option A, in which mass is varied while size

'Acceleration'

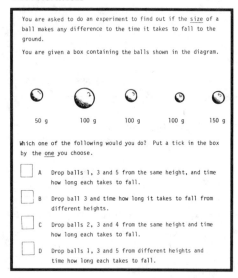

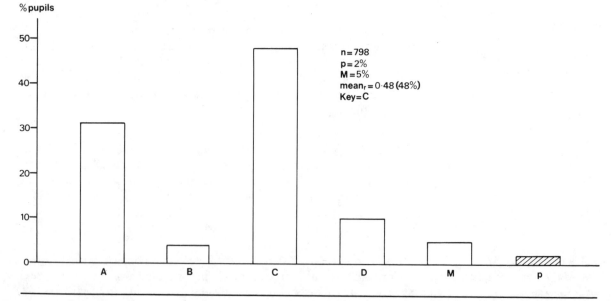

and height are held constant. Perhaps some pupils mistakenly related mass to size although the use of drawings to describe size, rather than figures indicating volume or diameter was intended to minimise such confusion.

The second example of this type of question, 'Light and death', called for rather more judgement since the variables to be considered were not stated so explicitly as in 'Acceleration'.

'Light and death'

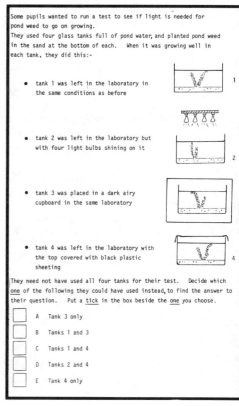

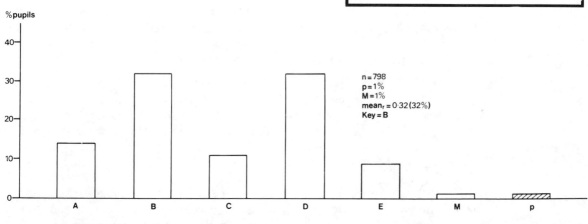

Of the five suggestions offered, D (tanks 2 and 4) was selected by as many pupils as B (tanks 1 and 3). Those who chose D failed to take account of some drawbacks in their choice; for example the possible heating effects in tank 2, and lack of air and complete darkness in tank 4. Pupils who chose A and E may have done so because they did not appreciate the need for a control experiment; or they may have misunderstood the instructions and been wrongly influenced by the word *one* which appears in the sentence before the list of options.

In questions of the type illustrated above, the mean scores were in the range 30 to 60 per cent of the maximum; that is, between 30 and 60 per cent of the pupils chose the correct option. The non-response rate was low; usually less than one per cent of the pupils failed to attempt the question.

Suggesting variables to be controlled   The second type of question differed from that already discussed in this way: a problem was described, as before, but this was followed by an account of the general method to be used to solve it. The way in which the main independent variable was to be changed was indicated, but pupils were then asked to suggest three variables which ought to be kept constant during the investigation.

'Cabbage' illustrates the general format of these questions, and the way in which they were phrased.

A mean score of 70 per cent or more was achieved for all three questions of this type, between three and four per cent of the pupils failing to respond. The mean score for girls was consistently higher than that for boys.

Sequencing procedures   In a third type of question, stages in an investigation were described, but listed in the wrong order. Pupils were asked to decide on the sequence in which the stages of the operation should be carried out.

'Rose petals' (page 134) illustrates the type, although one question is slightly different in that redundant stages were included; pupils were warned of this and asked to select the appropriate stages and then decide on their correct sequence.

The pattern of response was similar for all three questions: that is, more pupils scored low or high than in between. Mean scores were between 30 per cent (for 'Rose petals') and 55 per cent (for a question about finding the volume of a stone by displacing water from a can brimful of water).

Whereas success in 'Rose petals' depended on a knowledge of a particular technique, not likely to have been gained outside a school laboratory, it may be that pupils were able to work out the appropriate sequences for the other two questions by using common sense; this may have accounted for their higher mean scores.

Criticising procedures   In another type of question, pupils were asked to criticise a proposed method of carrying out an investigation. It had proved unproductive, in earlier trials, to ask directly for a criticism; so questions called

'Cabbage'

A farmer is trying to find out which soil would be best for his cabbage crop.
He decided to plant 10 cabbages in a section of acid soil, and 10 cabbages in alkaline soil.

acid
Soil

alkaline
soil

If he wants it to be a _fair_ test he will have to make sure that some things are the same for both patches of ground.

Suggest three things that should be the same:

(1) . . . .
. . . .
. . . .

(2) . . . .
. . . .
. . . .

(3) . . . .
. . . .
. . . .

Mark scheme

Give 1 mark for each different variable that would have to be controlled, up to a maximum of 3.

Examples are:

(1) Both patches get equal amounts of sunlight
(2) Both patches get equal amounts of water
(3) Both patches get equal amounts of fertilizer
(4) Cabbages should be equally spaced
(5) Cabbages should all be the same variety
(6) Both patches should be dug over in the same way   ③

N.B. Each different variable given can earn a mark, even if the pupil mentions them all in the same sentence.

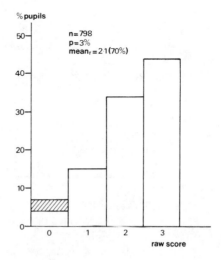

'Rose petals'

Bob has been asked to do a test to find out whether the colouring material in pink rose petals is a pure substance or a mixture.

He has been given this set of instructions for the test, which are not in the right order.

- [ ]   A   Crush sand, acetone and rose petals together
- [ ]   B   Pour off the liquid into a beaker
- [ ]   C   Add acetone, a drop at a time, to the middle of the coloured patch
- [ ]   D   Put a few drops of rose petal extract in the middle of a filter paper

Decide on the right order for this job.
Put 1 in the box by the side of the first thing Bob should do, 2 by the next thing, and so on.

Mark scheme

No marks are given once the pupil has deviated from the correct sequence.

Give marks for:

Start at A	1
Step A to B	1
Step B to D	1

(3)

N.B. The final step D to C is automatic and gets no marks.

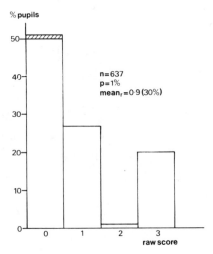

% pupils

n = 637
p = 1%
$mean_r = 0.9 \, (30\%)$

raw score

instead for suggestions for modification or improvement. This is illustrated in the example, 'Heat stores'.

The low mean score for this question is at least partly attributable to the fact that many pupils, failing to heed the instructions, introduced fresh apparatus in their answers to the first part. Others made suggestions which repeated some action that had already been carried out — for example "use the same amount of each metal".

'Heat stores'

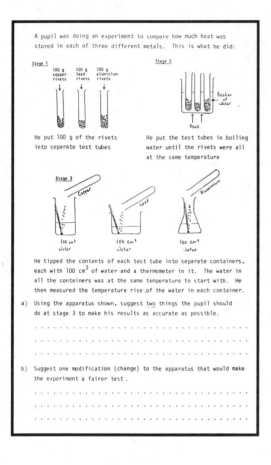

A pupil was doing an experiment to compare how much heat was stored in each of three different metals. This is what he did:

Stage 1

100 g copper rivets   100 g lead rivets   100 g aluminium rivets

He put 100 g of the rivets into separate test tubes

Stage 2

Beaker of water

Heat

He put the test tubes in boiling water until the rivets were all at the same temperature

Stage 3

Copper   Lead   Aluminium

100 cm³ water   100 cm³ water   100 cm³ water

He tipped the contents of each test tube into separate containers, each with 100 cm³ of water and a thermometer in it. The water in all the containers was at the same temperature to start with. He then measured the temperature rise of the water in each container.

a) Using the apparatus shown, suggest <u>two</u> things the pupil should do at stage 3 to make his results as accurate as possible.

. . . .
. . . .
. . . .

b) Suggest one modification (change) to the apparatus that would make the experiment a fairer test.

. . . .
. . . .
. . . .

Mark scheme

a) (1) Stir   1
    (2) Wait for maximum temperature rise 1
    (3) Make sure all containers were in   Max. Total (2)
         same ambient temperature, same
         surface, (no draught)   1

b) Possible modifications
    (1) Use similar containers   1   Max. Total (1)
    (2) Use lagging and lids for the
         containers   1

    1 mark for *one* suggestion

③

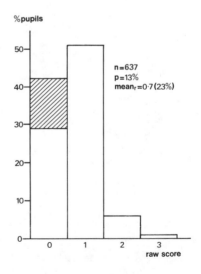

%**pupils**

n = 637
p = 13%
mean$_r$ = 0·7 (23%)

raw score

The mean score for this type of question was generally low, and the rate of non-response high.

Selecting the statement tested   The last kind of question required pupils to select propositions which a given procedure would test. An investigation was described in some detail, and this was followed by a list of propositions or questions on which the investigation might be thought to have some bearing. Pupils were to consider each suggestion in turn and tick or cross according to whether or not they decided that the proposition could be tested (or the question answered) by the procedure described.

'Stamped' was one of five questions of this type.

'Stamped'

Margaret decided to find out how efficient the postal service was. This is what she did:

(1) She addressed 16 identical envelopes to herself and marked them with the numbers 1 to 16.

(2) She put first class stamps on 8 envelopes and second class stamps on the other 8.

(3) On Monday at ten o'clock in the morning, she put two of the first class and two of the second class envelopes into the nearest post box.

(4) She did the same again on Tuesday, Wednesday and Thursday.

(5) She kept a record of the posting and arrival time of each envelope.

Which of the following things could she find out about from her results? Put a tick in the box by those you choose, and a cross by those that she could not find out about.

A How regularly the letters were collected from the local post box.

B How long it took to deliver letters in her area.

C The difference between the time it takes for first and second class letters to arrive.

D The difference between the way letters and parcels are treated.

E Whether different postmen work at different speeds.

Mark scheme

A	×	1
B	✔	1
C	✔	1
D	×	1
E	×	1

% pupils

n=637
p=2%
mean$_r$=3·3(67%)
mean$_t$=50%

For this question the mean score after transformation was 50 per cent of the maximum. For the other four questions of this type it was between 20 and 40 per cent.

Summary of results for sub-category 5β   Sub-category 5β performance was assessed using a total of 27 questions, nine in each of the category 5 test packages described previously (three questions occurred in more than one package). The mean marks for the three sub-test distributions fell about half-way along the mark scale; approximately one per cent of the 2 000-plus pupils who attempted a 5β sub-test failed to achieve a mark.

In sub-category 5β as a whole, variation of non-response rate with question type was marked. It was highest — in double figures — for the most open-ended type, in which procedures were to be criticised and improvements suggested. Next came the type of which 'Cabbage' is an example, in which pupils had to propose three variables which needed to be controlled; for these it was running at about three per cent. But for all coded answer questions, whether the mean score was high or low, the response was good, with only about one per cent of the pupils failing to answer.

The relationship between performance level and question type was less clear cut. Mean scores appear to be related as much to properties of individual questions — specific concepts or contexts — as to common demands of questions of a given type.

A difference of performance of boys and girls is only apparent in questions of the 'Cabbage' type, in whch girls have a higher mean score than boys. It may therefore be connected with girls' greater facility for verbal expression. This superiority did not, however, extend to the *most* open-ended type of question, of which 'Heat stores' was an example.

5.4 Sub-category 5γ: devising and describing investigations

Range of questions asked   Six hundred and seventy-seven pupils were asked to answer four questions from this sub-category. In each question a situation was described and a problem posed which could be solved by an experimental method. Pupils were required to design and describe a suitable procedure for the solution of the problem.

In 'Fur kettle' (over) pupils were required to design an investigation to see which of two different propositions was better supported by experimental evidence.

The number of pupils for whom no entries were made on the marking grid was very high: 59 per cent of the 677 pupils concerned failed to make any of the statements listed on the marking scheme. However, 27 per cent of the pupils suggested a test involving changing the material of the element or boiling water without the element, while 11 per cent suggested boiling something other than the water used in the first place.

Nearly all pupils who chose the first method described a satisfactory procedure by which water was to be boiled in the absence of the element (or with a different kind of element) and about half of them went on to explain that if there was then no fur to be seen this would indicate that it had previously been due to something in the element. However very few of them stated that the type of water used should be controlled. In contrast to this, nearly all of those pupils who suggested the alternative method of varying the type of water used made the point that the material of the element should be controlled. About a third of this group of pupils did not explain what they meant by ''using a different kind of water'', and some of the suggestions that *were* made may not in practice have yielded very

'Fur kettle'

After using a new electric kettle for several weeks, Simon noticed that the inside of the kettle was coated with a layer of whitish "fur".

His brother, Christopher, thought the "fur" had come from the heating element in the kettle.   Simon said it came from the water.

Describe an experiment you would do to test which of these is the better explanation. Be sure to write about:

● the equipment you would use and how you would use it

● the things you would do to make it a fair test

● how to work out your results

Mark scheme

This question is to be marked by ticking columns on a grid. The idea is to record the way the pupil responds, rather than to arrive at a numerical score.

Two different strategies are suggested by pupils:

a) keep the water source the same but effectively remove the element.

b) use the same or similar element, but vary the source of the water.

Interesting variations that are not allowed for on the grid should be noted under 'Comments'.

The brief headings of the columns are expanded below.

Tick in the appropriate column if the pupil indicates:

Either		
	1)	water from the same source is boiled.
	2)	without the original element.
	3)	in saucepan, or beaker, or in the kettle with the element removed, etc
	4)	look for fur.
	5)	if no fur now, original due to something in the element.
Or	6)	keep element same.
	7)	but clean fur off before use (or use similar, but new, element)
	8)	use water from different source.
	9)	distilled, boiled, rain, etc. — even orange squash
	10)	look for fur.
	11)	if none present, original due to something in the water.

Marking grid

Script No.	1 Same water	2 Change element	3 how	4 Any fur	5 Analysis	6 Same element	7 how	8 Change water	9 how	0 Any fur	Analysis	Comments

helpful results, since they included the use of milk, vinegar and petrol. About a third of the group explained how to use any results that might be obtained to solve the problem posed.

The points made by the two groups of pupils referred to in the paragraph above are summarised in Tables 5.3 and 5.4. The percentages of pupils making the point, or combination of points, indicated are given at the foot of the relevant columns. It is clear from the tables that the percentage of pupils making useful combinations of points is very much lower than that for those giving correct, but isolated, suggestions.

General strategy: vary material of element, control type of water
Points made in the response:

Table 5.3 *Categories of response: 'Fur kettle' (method 1)* $n = 677$

No element, or element of different material	✓	✓	✓	✓	✓	✓
Water from same source				✓	✓	✓
Method of 'varying' element			✓	✓	✓	✓
What observation is to be made				✓		✓
Interpreting the results				✓		✓
% of pupils making the points indicated	27	25	14	3	3	2

General strategy: vary type of water, control material of element
Points made in the response:

Table 5.4 *Categories of response: 'Fur kettle' (method 2)* $n = 677$

Different water	✓		✓	✓	✓
Material of element the same		✓		✓	✓
Method of changing the type of water			✓	✓	✓
Method of control of element		✓		✓	✓
What observation to be made					✓
Interpreting the results					✓
% of pupils making the points indicated	11	9	7	6	4

There were some alternatives to the methods already indicated. About five per cent of the pupils proposed to 'boil' the kettle without water, their argument being that if the fur still appeared it must have been due to the element. A few pupils thought that the appropriate move would be to check up with the Water Board, though this would hardly count as an experiment; while a few attempted to explain the problem of the fur by identifying it with a fungus, or minute animals visible through a microscope, or with a deposit caused by the use of tea bags.

'Indicator'

Sandra has been given 5 bottles labelled P, Q, R, S and T, with colourless liquids in them. She is told that two of the liquids are dilute acids, one is an alkali and the other two are water. She also has a liquid indicator (called phenophthalein). This goes colourless in acid
        red in alkali
        colourless in water

Write some instructions for Sandra so that she can find out whether the liquid in each bottle is an acid, or an alkali or just water. She is allowed to use a rack of test tubes, the indicator, and the liquids from the bottles P, Q, R, S and T.

Make sure you say exactly what she must do so that when she has finished she can label the bottles 'acid', 'alkali' or 'water'.

You may draw if you think it might help.

. . . .
. . . .
. . . .
. . . .
. . . .
. . . .
. . . .
. . . .
. . . .
. . . .
. . . .
. . . .
. . . .

Mark scheme

This question is to be marked by ticking columns on a grid. The idea is to record the way the pupil responds, rather than to arrive at a numerical score.

Noteworthy variations not catered for by the columns on the grid should be recorded under 'Comments'.

The brief headings of the columns are expanded below.

Tick in the appropriate column if the pupil indicates:

1. The 5 liquids are put into separate test tubes.
2. Phenolphthalein solution is added to each.
3. The liquid which turns red is the alkali.
4. Some other indicator should now be used to distinguish between water and acid (in spite of the prohibition in the question).
5. The alkali identified in 3. is added to the 4 other unidentified liquids in test tubes (or fresh alkali and fresh liquids).
6. Phenolphthalein is still present, by implication, or is added if needed.
7. Alkali should be added drop by drop to avoid 'overpowering' the acid.
8. The two liquids which turn red first are water.
9. Because they are now alkaline.
10. The two which remain colourless are the acids.

Marking grid

Script No.	1 Liquids in t.t.	2 Add phth.	3 Red = alkali	4 Other indic.	5 Add alkali	6 Phth. present	7 Drop by drop	8 2 red = water	9 Because alkali	10 2 col. = acid	Comments

In 'Indicator' pupils were required to apply their knowledge of the behaviour of a chemical indicator to suggest an investigation by means of which each of five colourless liquids could be identified as acid, alkali, or water. The percentage of pupils for whom no entry was made on the marking grid was 27 per cent.

The question indicates which reagents and pieces of apparatus are available but does not prohibit the use of other items except by implication. Consequently many pupils suggested the use of other pieces of equipment. These included test papers of various kinds and degrees of usefulness — litmus paper, universal indicator paper, cobalt chloride paper and 'science' paper — thermometers, and means of heating the liquids.

By the method indicated in the mark scheme, very few pupils got further than the identification of the alkali, as Table 5.5 shows. Of the 44 per cent who explained how the alkali could be located, over half either stated or implied by default that the indicator should be added to the bottles rather than to samples of the liquids in test tubes. Only two per cent of the pupils described a suitable procedure and explained what results to look for and how to use them to solve the problem posed.

Table 5.5   *Categories of response: 'Indicator'*   *n = 677*

Points made in the response					
Liquid with separate test tubes			✔	✔	✔
Indicator added to each	✔	✔	✔	✔	✔
Liquid turning red is the alkali		✔	✔	✔	✔
This liquid added to the other four				✔	✔
The two which turn red are water				✔	✔
The remaining two are acid					✔
% of pupils making the points indicated	66	44	27	3	2

However, seven per cent of the pupils suggested identifying the water by measuring the boiling point of the four liquids left once the alkali was found; two per cent thought that it would be possible to distinguish between acid and water by smell, and a few suggested that they should all be tasted. Other pupils thought of detecting the acid by its corrosive effect on the fingers, on cloth, or on the floor. Fortunately only one proposed adding a fish to each of the four unidentified liquids — "if it dies, it was acid"!

In 'Ping-pong' (over) 24 per cent of the pupils failed to make a statement corresponding to a tick on the marking grid. The majority of sensible suggestions related to one or other of the strategies anticipated in the mark scheme, although a third common method, proposed by four per cent of the pupils, was to compare the times taken for the ball to stop bouncing on the different surfaces.

Forty-eight per cent of the pupils suggested comparing the rebound heights of the ball from different surfaces. Less than half of this group mentioned the need

'Ping-pong'

When a table tennis ball is dropped onto a table top, the
height of the ball gets less at each bounce.   This means
the ball loses energy at each bounce.

Describe how you would do an experiment to find out whether
different surfaces (like wood, glass and metal) on which the
ball bounces make the ball lose different amounts of energy.

You must say ● what you would use
              ● what you would measure
              ● how you would measure it
              ● how you would use the results
              ● what you think would be most likely
                 to make your results inaccurate

. . . .
. . . .
. . . .
. . . .
. . . .
. . . .
. . . .
. . . .
. . . .
. . . .
. . . .
. . . .
. . . .
. . . .
. . . .

Mark scheme

This question is to be marked by ticking columns on a grid. The idea is to
record the way the pupil responds, rather than to arrive at a numerical
score for the answer.

Pupils usually suggest one of two strategies:

a)   measure the height to which the ball rebounds after one
      bounce.

b)   count the total number of bounces.

Any other variations should be recorded under 'Comments'. The brief
headings of the columns on the grid are expanded below.

Tick in the appropriate column if the pupil indicates:

1)   that the initial height of the ball must be the same for all
      surfaces.

2)   how this condition can be ensured.

3)   that several different surfaces are used in turn.

Either   4)   that the rebound heights for different surfaces are to be
                  compared.

5)   how this is to be done (by measuring, marking on card, etc)

6)   how the results can be analysed: the higher the rebound, the
      less energy is lost.

7)   the major errors or difficulties likely to arise:
      (a) parallax errors if the observers' eye is not at the level of ball
      (b) difficulty of judging just when the ball is at its maximum
      height.

Or   8)   that the total number of bounces should be counted.

9)   how the results can then be analysed: the more bounces, the
      less the loss of energy.

10)   the major errors or difficulties likely to arise:
      (a) separate bounces are hard to distinguish towards the end
      (b) the ball tends to bounce off the surface.

And   11)   that each result should be checked by repetition.

Marking grid

Script No.	Initial height surfaces			Rebound heights				No. of bounces			Repeats	Comments
	1 same	2 how	3 vary	4 compare	5 how	6 analysis	7 errors	8 count	9 analysis	10 errors	11 ?	

to control the initial height of the ball, and a very few explained how to relate the results obtained to the problem posed.

Table 5.6 shows the percentages of pupils making the points, or combination of points, indicated.

Table 5.6   *Categories of response: 'Ping-pong' (method 1)*   *n = 677*

Points made in the response			
Control initial height		✔	✔
Vary the surface	✔	✔	✔
Compare rebound heights	✔	✔	✔
Use of results			✔
% of pupils	48	21	3

Most of the pupils were able to say how the rebound height could be measured, but only four per cent of the total number mentioned possible sources of error.

The second most common method suggested was to count the number of bounces made by the ball on the different surfaces, having, presumably, been dropped from the same initial height. Thirteen per cent of the pupils favoured this method, but very few related possible results to the problem, as can be seen from Table 5.7.

Table 5.7   *Categories of response: 'Ping-pong' (method 2)*   *n = 677*

Points made in the response			
Control initial height		✔	
Vary the surface	✔	✔	✔
Count number of bounces	✔	✔	✔
Use of results			✔
% of pupils	13	8	2

Very few pupils (less than one per cent of the total number) mentioned any possible source of error, and only two per cent of the pupils suggested repeating any part of the procedure for any reason, either in this method or the first.

About one per cent of the pupils suggested the use of a camera to help in comparing the height of the ball after rebound, some of them using the term 'multiflash photography'. About the same number of pupils suggested finding the time between bounces, though they did not explain how this was to be done. Only half of the pupils who made otherwise sensible suggestions, of whatever kind, stated that the initial height of the ball should be the same for each surface.

'Gas cooker'

The tap to each burner on a gas ring has two 'on' positions marked HALF and FULL ON.
A housewife wants to find if the amount of heat given on the HALF setting is half the heat given on the FULL setting.

Think out an experiment she could do to test this.
Write out a plan of what she should do. Make your instructions clear and easy to follow. Be sure to write about:

- the things she should measure
- the things she should do to make it a fair test
- the equipment she should use and how she should use it
- how she should work out her results
- the things (apart from careless slips) that would be most likely to make her results inaccurate

Mark scheme

This question is to be marked by ticking columns on a grid. The idea is to record the way the pupil responds, rather than to arrive at a numerical score.

At least three different strategies occur among pupils' responses:

a) heat equal volumes of water for the same time on each setting and note final temperature.

b) heat equal volumes until they reach the same temperature (often boiling) and note time taken.

c) heat $\frac{1}{2}$ volume at $\frac{1}{2}$ setting to same temperature and note time.

Any other variations should be noted under 'Comments'. The brief headings on the graph are expanded below:

Tick in the appropriate column if the pupil indicates:

1) that similar containers should be used on both settings (or the same, suitably cooled).
2) that the water should be at the same initial temperature.
3) how to ensure this.
4) same volume of water used for both settings.
5) $\frac{1}{2}$ volume of water used for $\frac{1}{2}$ setting.
6) how to ensure 4 or 5.
7) same time of heating for both settings.
8) measure final temperature for both settings (or see how hot it gets).
9) with thermometer (use of word temperature in 8 can be taken to imply use of thermometer in 9).
10) same final temperature for both settings.
11) how to ensure this (thermometer or till boiling).
12) measure time taken.
13) for method a), *rise* in temperature should be double on full setting.
for method b), time taken should be half on full setting.
for method c), time taken should be same on both settings.
14) reasoning reversed — eg $\frac{1}{2}$ setting takes $\frac{1}{2}$ time.
15) error because heat loss to surroundings is not accounted for.

Marking grid

	1	2	3	4	5	6	7	8	9	10	11	12	13	14	15	16	
Script No.	Sim. com.	Initial temp.		Vol. of water			Same time	Final temp.		Final temp		Meas. time	Analysis			Errors	Comments
		same	how	same	½	how		meas.	how	same	how		Yes	Wrong	None		

In 'Gas cooker', of the three strategies anticipated in the mark scheme as a result of question trials, (b) (time how long equal volumes of water take to reach boiling point on each setting of the tap) was the most often suggested. Forty-six per cent of the pupils failed to make any statement which could be ticked on the marking grid. However, some of this group suggested other types of investigation.

Although 24 per cent of the pupils proposed finding the time taken for equal volumes of water (or other liquid) to reach boiling point on the HALF and FULL settings in turn, only a sixth of this group mentioned the need to control the initial temperature of the water. Almost a third of them correctly explained how to use the result to solve the problem, but a sixth of them got the explanation reversed; they said that if the time taken on the HALF setting was half the time taken on the FULL setting, the labelling was correct. This error is indicated by the letters Rev. on Table 5.8.

Table 5.8   *Categories of response: 'Gas cooker' (method 1)*   *n = 677*

Points made					
Same volume of water/liquid	✔	✔	✔	✔	✔
Control container		✔	✔	✔	✔
Control initial temperature			✔		
Same final temp. (ie boiling point)	✔	✔	✔	✔	✔
Measure time taken	✔	✔	✔	✔	✔
Use made of results				✔	Rev.
% of pupils making the points indicated	24	18	4	9	4

A smaller group of pupils (eight per cent) suggested heating equal volumes of water for the same time on each setting, and measuring the temperature reached. Three-quarters of these pupils mentioned the need to use a similar container, but very few the need to start with water at the same initial temperature. Since they wrote in terms of temperature reached, and not rise in temperature, this was essential. Less than a third of the group explained the use of results.

Only one per cent of the pupils suggested the third method anticipated on the mark scheme, that is using half the volume of water on the HALF setting and checking to see if the time till boiling was the same as for the full amount on the FULL setting. None of the pupils made any sensible statement about likely sources of error, whichever of the three methods they described.

A number of other suggestions were made. About four per cent of the pupils recommended comparing the temperature of the flames with a thermometer (though one did mention the need to wear gloves for this operation) and two per cent suggested comparing the height of the flame. Some thought in terms of a pressure machine fixed to the burner; others of an evacuated container which was to be weighed after a given time on each of the settings. Some pupils thought the housewife should compare how long it took to cook something on the two settings in turn; suggestions included soup, eggs, milk, potatoes, and cake. Some thought of timing how long it would take to melt butter, or chocolate; and others of how long it would take to evaporate a given quantity of water. Half a dozen attacked the problem from a quite different angle; their suggestion was to read the gas meter before and after using the gas ring with the tap on each setting in turn for a given time.

Summary of results for sub-category 5γ   One characteristic of the responses in the four questions was the variety of methods suggested by pupils; some (like throwing a fish into an unknown liquid to see if it dies) are not to be recommended, even though they might work; others (like timing the interval between the bounces of a ball) are theoretically acceptable but difficult in practice.

A second characteristic is the low proportion of pupils who wrote down more than one or two of the set of statements which would constitute a minimum for a satisfactory response. Taken in isolation, all the statements are made by a fair percentage of pupils; but meaningful combinations are made by a much smaller proportion. In particular, pupils often fail to mention the need to control variables, or to explain how a conclusion is to be inferred from a hypothetical result.

5.5 General impression of category 5 tests

The interaction between questions, responses, and the individual pupil's command of the language was noticeable in all three sub-categories. In the first, 5α, the problem lay in making clear to 13 year old pupils exactly what was required of them. In the second, 5β, this was comparatively easy except that the resulting questions were then of necessity very long. Simply reading the question and remembering the alternatives may have been difficult for some pupils and this may have adversely affected their performance. The problem is not, of course, peculiar to this sub-category. In the third sub-category, 5γ, the difficulty was that some pupils may have been barred from answering a question because of their inability to express themselves in writing, rather than their inability to plan an investigation. The 1981 survey, which will include practical tasks from the category 6 'performance of investigations', will provide information about the extent to which these two inabilities differ from one another, since performance will be measured by observing pupil behaviours rather than by reading their written responses.

6   The assessment framework

6.1 Introduction

The background information in this chapter falls into four sections. First, the choice of categories for use in the assessment is explained, and then their distinguishing characteristics are discussed in detail. In the next section the types of question found suitable to represent the various sub-categories of the framework are listed. Finally the list of science concepts, which has particular significance for the sub-categories of 4δ, is presented.

6.2 The choice of categories

The purpose of the survey, as explained in the Introduction to this report, was to provide information about aspects of performance of 13 year old pupils which would be of use to those concerned with science education. The assessment was to relate to a representative sample of these pupils, rather than to any individual pupil, so the aim was to draw up a profile report of that population and then to relate some of the facets of the profile to a number of factors such as sex of pupil or type of school. The framework for assessment must match this purpose; its use must ensure that questions reflect the great variety of activities which contribute to performance in science and must enable performance on different kinds of activity to be reported separately in so far as this is possible. The first step in the construction of the framework was therefore the identification of the activities to be reported.

The policy determined by the Science Working Group of the APU was to focus on those skills and techniques which contribute to scientific performance. Some of these are not exclusive to science and it was proposed, in such cases, to measure levels and patterns of performance outside the framework of science as well as within it. The translation of this policy into operational terms by the monitoring teams was accompanied by extended discussions with the Working Group, which had by now become the Science Steering Group. The process was far from being a simple linear one, and the categories proposed were continually modified in the light of discussions and trials. Reactions to the consultative document published by the Department of Education and Science in October 1977 were also taken into account. The system of categories and sub-categories finally agreed has been summarised in the Introduction (page 3) and is discussed in detail below.

6.3 A description of the categories

Category 1: using symbolic representations   Questions designed to test a specific ability are often criticised when they present pupils with reading difficulties which may in themselves prevent the exercise of that ability. A comparable problem occurs when communication with the pupil involves symbolic representations of one kind or another, although the magnitude of this difficulty is less often discussed. Poor performance on questions designed to test, say, ability to make predictions may be due just as much to lack of understanding of tabulated information as to any failure to predict. Practical work is sometimes judged almost wholly by the smoothness of the graph drawn to relate the results, so that those with difficulties in this respect may actually be labelled as poor at practical work. Some investigations may fail to get off the ground at all simply because they depend on a pupil setting out apparatus in accordance with a conventionally drawn diagram. Questions in category 1 are designed to throw some light on the extent to which the use of symbolic representations constitutes a barrier to communication and therefore a hurdle to success in more complex activities.

The category has been divided into three sub-categories, as follows:

1 α Reading information from graphs, tables and charts. Pupils are required simply to 'translate' the information; the amount of reading, writing and interpretation necessary has been reduced to a minimum.

1 β Expressing information as graphs, tables and charts. Pupils are required to put information given in words or numbers into various symbolic forms; in some cases no help is given, and in others graphs or tables are partially completed. For example, the outlines of pie-charts may be drawn, or axes may be drawn and labelled.

1γ Using scientific symbols and conventions. At age 13, conventions are confined to those used in drawing simple circuits and arrangements of general laboratory apparatus. In some questions pupils are asked to identify pieces of equipment, either in isolation or when forming part of an experimental set-up, and in others they are required to draw conventional diagrams.

Category two: using apparatus and measuring instruments In this category, practical tasks have been designed to indicate what difficulties pupils encounter in using measuring instruments, handling equipment and following instructions, which might contribute to failure with more complex activities.

It is not difficult to think of tasks which will test these skills; but it *is* difficult to set them in such a way that they can be assessed from a pupil's written response, free from interference from problems of recording results. This difficulty is of course almost always present in practical tasks and so performance levels usually reflect a combination of abilities. Some methods of judging performance other than from the written record have been developed for use in tasks in this category, and these are discussed in detail in Appendix 2.

The category has three sub-divisions:

2α Using measuring instruments. Pupils are required to read scales, using appropriate units and to use measuring instruments and other laboratory apparatus in a clearly defined situation; there is no element of 'designing an investigation' in this sub-category.

2β Estimating quantities. This is tested in two contrasting ways. In one pupils are confronted with pre-determined amounts of material and asked to estimate the quantity present — the volume of a liquid, or the length of wire, for example; in the other, they are given a considerable surplus of material and asked to measure out a specified quantity. Estimating is a skill that is not often tested, although familiarity with quantities and units is an important aid to the understanding of the relevant concepts.

2γ Following instructions for practical work. The reason for the inclusion of this sub-category is that pupils' lack of ability to follow instructions confuses the interpretation of results of tests of so many other activities. Instructions of various kinds are included: some are written, some diagrammatic. In some cases they could be followed only by pupils who had learned the necessary techniques in a science laboratory, but in others they are complete in themselves. Since motivation may affect performance, pupils are offered a carrot: they may be invited to identify an unknown liquid, or make a model.

Category 3: using observation Most teachers would agree that use of observation is important in scientific performance; but it is seldom tested as a separate activity. Paper and pencil tests provide very limited opportunities for testing; for one thing, sight is the only sense that can be brought into play. And if an event or situation is described or drawn on paper, the relevant observations have already been picked out, to some extent, from the mass of background detail that normally surrounds them. For this reason, use of observation is tested by a variety of practical tasks: many of them demand the examination of real objects, some involve careful study and comparison of photographs; and others require pupils to use simple laboratory apparatus and observe changes over a short period of time.

There are three sub-divisions within the category:

3α Using a branching key. Pupils are required to identify objects, either real or by means of photographs, with the help of a branching key.

3β Observing similarities and differences. Pupils are required to make comparisons either between two or more objects, photographs or events, or between successive stages of an event. They may have to decide what is important and relevant in the comparisons and record their decisions in a variety of ways.

3γ Interpreting observations. Pupils are required to collect information by observation, often by making comparisons or noting changes, and then use what they take to be relevant to go beyond their observations to find patterns, explain what they observe or make predictions.

Category 4: interpretation and application There are two major divisions in this category; each is concerned with the ability of the pupil to interpret information and each contains questions making similar demands, such as the ability to generalise. The distinction between them lies in the degree to which such operations depend upon an understanding of scientific concepts. Performance levels and patterns may very well be influenced by the kinds of concepts involved, and the extent of this influence can only be determined by arranging for similar questions to be asked in circumstances which demand understanding of a variety of concepts: some within the everyday experience of pupils and some likely to have been met in science lessons.

In order to write appropriate questions, and to make sense of the results, a list of appropriate concepts has been developed.

The concept list   The very wide range of science courses which exist, even for pupils aged 13, presents serious problems if an attempt is made to draw up a suitable list of specific items of content. However, the problem is reduced if attention is focussed on more generalised statements of concepts; since understanding of these could have been reached by pupils with a variety of different content backgrounds. The fact that organisms undergo a repetitive pattern of life cycles is an example of such a statement. A list of this kind, referring to concepts to which a large proportion of pupils might be expected to have been exposed, has been prepared by the monitoring teams. During its development, teachers from many schools were consulted, and the advice offered by the Science Steering Group and others interested in science education was taken into account. Many school syllabuses, and those published by the various examination boards, were studied. However, the resulting lists of concepts is not intended to be used as either a teaching or an examination syllabus. Its functions are to help in providing a spread of questions across concept areas, and to form part of a complex labelling system for use in controlling the selection of questions from the bank, which is described in Appendix 1.

The complete list, which was originally published as an Appendix to the Science Progress Report in 1978, related to all three ages at which scientific performance is to be assessed. The subset of statements which is applicable to pupils aged thirteen is to be found in Section 6.5 of this report.

Category 4 has five sub-categories, which are described below. In the first three there are questions for which the information or concepts needed are either assumed to be within the everyday experience of the pupil, or given in the question itself.

4α Describing and using patterns in information.   Pupils are required to describe, select or use patterns derived from information given or to use generalisations stated in the question. This information may be presented in pictorial, graphical, tabular or written form.

4β Judging the applicability of a given generalisation.   Pupils are required to judge the extent to which a suggested generalisation or hypothesis applies to a given situation(s).

4γ Distinguishing degrees of inference.   Pupils are required to select a statement which makes the fewest additional assumptions about a verbal or pictorial account of an event.

In the last two sub-categories there are questions in which pupils are required to make use of prior knowledge of science concepts.

4δ Making sense of information using science concepts.   As in the case of sub-categories 4α, 4β and 4γ, information may be presented in diagrammatic, tabular or written form. Pupils are required to apply science concepts to make or select predictions, to give explanations, or to assess explanations or hypotheses in relation to that information.

If performance in these activities is indeed affected by the introduction of the need to use science concepts, then it is also probable that the effect is different for different concepts. A very wide range has been met by pupils by the time they reach the age of 13, so in order to help in the interpretation of results in this sub-category, 4δ, the complete list of concepts has been split into three regions: biological, physical and chemical. These are further sub-divided: first into concept areas (labelled A to F) and then into numbered sections each containing a set of related statements. The three concept regions of 4δ are reported separately, in order that performance in them can be separately related to school and other variables.

4ε Generating alternative hypotheses.   Pupils are required to generate alter-native hypotheses each of which must be consistent with information given and with science concepts.

Category 5: design of investigations   In this category, questions have been planned to test various different aspects of planning investigations on paper. It seems probable that pupil response will differ from that made in corresponding practical situations. Pupils may be able to describe a procedure without being able to execute it; or they may, in practice, control variables, while assuming the matter to be too obvious to mention in a written plan of action.

There are three sub-categories:

5α Identifying or proposing testable statements.   Claims and propositions are often made which cannot be subjected to scientific investigation, either because of their nature or because they are not expressed with sufficient clarity and precision. Questions in 5α are intended to test the ability of pupils to distinguish between testable and non-testable statements, and to reformulate a general proposition in such a way that it can be checked scientifically.

5β Assessing experimental procedures.   In some questions representing this category, procedures relating to a given proposition are described. Pupils then have to select the most suitable, or to criticse, explain or complete the one procedure suggested. In other cases, pupils are required to distinguish between questions which could be answered by a given procedure, and those which cannot.

5γ Devising and describing investigations. It is quite common in schools for pupils to write a description of an investigation which they or their teachers have just made. It is probably less common for them to be asked to plan the investigation for themselves and then describe it on paper before carrying it out. This is what is required in questions in this sub-category. A problem is presented, for the solution of which a test has to be devised; pupils then write an account of this test and explain how the results could be used to solve the problem.

Category 6: performance of investigations The actual performance of an investigation involves many of the abilities referred to in discussions of the earlier categories; different investigations will have the emphasis on different selections of the component activities. It is likely that when pupils are required to find a practical solution of a real problem the pattern of performance differs from that represented by the sum of performance in the contributory activities taken in isolation. Although no assessment of performance in this category was made in the 1980 survey at age 13, it is planned for 1981. A detailed check-list will be used by trained administrators while observing the actions of an individual pupil while carrying out the investigation.

The validity of the framework of science performance categories The discussion above is intended only as a general description of the approach adopted. Alternative approaches could have been adopted and the choice between these would have to be based on general beliefs and values about education. It is not claimed that the approach described here rests on any particular empirical or theoretical basis; in particular it is not claimed that the various categories and sub-categories are fully validated constructs.

The description does make clear that where, as in some sub-categories, the test questions cover a wide range of contexts, this has been done for the educational reasons explained. It may be the case, for example, in the category concerned with "observation" that the implied notion of there being a single skill that a pupil can be said to possess and so apply in many contexts is open to question. The extent to which such a notion is not contradicted within the range of test questions employed here can be tested empirically by analysis of the consistency of pupil scores within and between the various sub-categories. Whilst the first results of question trials showed that the question groups behaved adequately in this respect, a full analysis of the monitoring data will have to be conducted at a later stage to provide more substantial and detailed evidence.

6.4 Types of question used in the survey

The question descriptors listed below are those currently applicable to the age 13 item bank. The sub-categories for which no overall measures of performance have been calculated are indicated by the letter Q. In such cases most questions are reported in detail.

Category 1: using symbolic representations (written tests)

Table 6.1 *Sub-category 1α: reading information from graphs, tables and charts*

Given	Demand
A table of a) figures, b) representative symbols, c)non-representative symbols, d)a short paragraph	Read off information as directed
A schematic representation of a process or series of linked events or relationships	Read off information as directed
Vertical or horizontal bar chart	Read off information as directed
Pie chart	Read off information as directed
Graph	Read off information as directed
Graph and statement of what it represents	Read off information as directed
a) line graph b) points located by co-ordinates	Read co-ordinates of a designated point

Table 6.2 *Sub-category 1β: expressing information as graphs, tables and charts*

Data and a partially completed table	Add further data to complete table
A partially complete schematic representation of a process, series of linked events or relationships and data to add	Add given data to complete schematic representation
Data and a partially completed bar chart	Add further data to complete chart
Data and a partially completed pie chart	Add further data to complete chart
Data and a partially completed line graph	Add further data to complete graph
Data in the form of pairs of related quantities	Draw axes, select scale and construct a bar chart
Data in the form of continuously varying quantities or pairs of related quantities	Draw axes, select scale and plot points and draw line graph
A pair of labelled axes and a) data, b)points to plot, c) data	Construct a) bar chart representing data, b) points, c) line graph — as directed
Data represented in four–five different graphical representations	Select the most appropriate representation

Table 6.3   *Sub-category 1γ: using scientific symbols and conventions*

Given	Demand
Section diagram of assorted objects and a list of names with some redundancy	Identify the objects by matching names to objects
A 3-D drawing of an experimental set-up using general laboratory apparatus	Make a conventional section drawing
A conventional section drawing of a set-up using general laboratory apparatus	Propose names for the components of the set-up
A 3-D drawing of a circuit	Draw a conventional circuit diagram
A conventional circuit diagram	Propose names for the components of the circuit

Category 2: using apparatus and measuring instruments (practical tests)

Table 6.4   *Sub-category 2α: using measuring instruments*

Physical quantity measured by instrument already set up	Give a value with appropriate units
Physical quantity, object, or event, and instrument(s) for measuring or observing it	Employ appropriate instrument(s) to give an answer or give a value with units or leave a measured quantity

Table 6.5   *Sub-category 2β: estimating quantities*

Objects or events and units of physical quantities	Give a value
Supply of material and an amount specified	Leave or indicate the right amount of material

Table 6.6   *Sub-category 2γ: following instructions for practical work* (Q)

Instructions, in the form of a conventional diagram, for setting up apparatus for a stated purpose	Set up apparatus
Detailed instructions for completing an unfamiliar task	Comply exactly with instructions in order to complete the task
Detailed instructions for completing an unfamiliar task	Comply exactly with instructions in order to leave a product
Instructions for task that explicitly refer to standard techniques used in laboratories	Follow instructions, using the correct procedures, in order to complete the task
Instructions for task that require standard techniques used in laboratories. Reference to these is implicit	Follow instructions, recalling and using the correct procedures, in order to complete the task

Category 3: using observation (practical tests)

Table 6.7   *Sub-category 3α: using a branching key* (Q)

Given	Demand
Objects (or photographs of objects)	Identify objects

Table 6.8   *Sub-category 3β: observing similarities and differences*

Given	Demand
Objects (or photographs or drawings of objects)	Identify rules used to classify the objects and/or sort objects into an alternative set of groups
At least two objects (or photographs)	State as many differences as possible
At least two objects, photographs or events	State a specified number of similarities and differences
Event	Make a record of change
Objects (or photographs of objects) and drawings	Select the matching drawing
Object	Make a scientific drawing
Object (or photographs or diagrams of the object) and a written description	Select that object which matches the written description
Object (or photograph) and another photograph which is part of the object (or first photograph)	Identify where the part comes from
Set of photographs or drawings forming a sequence	Arrange the remainder in the correct order

Table 6.9   *Sub-category 3γ: interpreting observations*

Given	Demand
Event	Make a record of observations and create an hypothesis
Event and a list of explanations	Make a record of changes and select the appropriate explanation(s)
Event	Make a record of changes and make a prediction consistent with the data
a) At least two events, objects, photographs or drawings b) At least two events, objects, photographs or drawings, and a list of predictions	a) Note the difference and make a prediction consistent with the data b) Note differences and select a prediction consistent with the data
Event	Make a record of changes and identify a pattern in the observed changes

Category 4: interpretation and application (written tests)

Table 6.10   *Sub-category 4α: describing and/or using patterns in information*

Given	Demand
Data (to be sufficient to answer question without prior knowledge) in pictorial, tabular or graphical form	Describe pattern based on data alone (could involve pupils in drawing sketch graphs to determine pattern)
Data (to be sufficient to answer question without prior knowledge) in pictorial, tabular or graphical form	a) Describe pattern and use to make prediction, or b) make prediction giving reasons based on pattern
Data (to be sufficient to answer question without prior knowledge) and a minimum of four predictions	a) Describe pattern and use to select prediction or b) select prediction and give reason for choice
Data (to be sufficient to answer question without prior knowledge)	Make predictions/explanations based on data alone
Data and a minimum of four predictions	Select prediction consistent with data
Data sufficient to make required prediction plus a minimum of four patterns and four predictions	Select pattern and use to select prediction consistent with data

Table 6.11   *Sub-category 4β: judging the applicability of a given generalisation (Q)*

Data and hypothesis/explanation	Assess validity of presented hypothesis/explanation in relation to data

Table 6.12   *Sub-category 4γ: distinguishing degrees of inference (Q)*

A ''snapshot'' of an event (in words or line drawing) and five possible accounts of the event	Select the one which demands the fewest additional assumptions

Table 6.13   *Sub-category 4δ: making sense of information using science concepts[1]*

Given	Demand
Data	a) Describe pattern based on data *and* accepted concepts and use it to make predictions, or b) make predictions giving reasons
Data	Make predictions based on data and accepted concepts
Data and a minimum of four predictions	Select prediction and give reason based on data and accepted concepts
Data and a minimum of four predictions	Select predictions based on data and accepted concepts
Data and a description of an event or situation	Give an explanation consistent with the data and accepted concepts
Data, description of an event or situation, and hypothesis/explanation	Assess validity of hypothesis/explanation in relation to data and accepted concepts
Data, description of event or situation and a minimum of four hypotheses/explanations	Select the best hypothesis/explanation in relation to data *and* accepted concepts
Data, description of event or situation and a minimum of four hypotheses/explanations	Select all the hypotheses/explanations which are consistent with the data *and* accepted concepts

Table 6.14   *Sub-category 4ε: generating alternative hypotheses* (Q)

Given	Demand
Data, description of event or situation where there is no single obvious explanation	Generate alternative hypotheses/explanations consistent with data *and* accepted concepts

[1] See section 6.5

Category 5:   design of investigations (written tests)

Table 6.15   *Sub-category 5α: identifying or proposing testable statements*

Given	Demand
Four or five statements, one of which: a) can be tested scientifically b) cannot be tested scientifically	Select the statement which can be tested scientifically Select the one which cannot be tested scientifically
A general statement and four or five reformulations	Select the reformulation which is both testable and relevant
A general statement or opinion	Rewrite as a (number of) statement(s) each of which can be tested

Table 6.16   *Sub-category 5β: assessing experimental procedures*

Given	Demand
A proposition in a testable form and at least four specified variables (or procedures relating to specified variables)	Select which variables must be varied or controlled (or which procedures must be followed) to allow for testing
A proposition in a testable form and no specified variables	State variables to be controlled to allow testing
A proposition in a testable form and a procedure to test it	State the functions of the component parts of the procedure
A proposition in a testable form and at least four component procedures	Propose the best sequence
A proposition in a testable form and a procedure to test it	Criticise the procedure
A proposition in a testable form and a procedure to test it	Select the functions of the component parts of the procedure
A procedure and at least four statements about what it might test	Select the statement(s) which the procedure would test

Table 6.17   *Sub-category 5γ: devising and describing investigations* (Q)

Given	Demand
A proposition in a testable form	Plan a procedure to test, resolve or determine the point at issue (taking into account control of variables and selection of equipment)
Two propositions fitting the same data	Plan a procedure to distinguish between the two propositions

Category 6: performance of investigations (practical tests) No separate question types have been defined for this category and therefore no question descriptors are listed.

6.5 The list of science concepts

The purpose for which this list was drawn up is discussed in Section 6.2. The pages that follow contain statements applicable to pupils aged 13. They form a subset of the complete list which was published by the Department of Education and Science in 1977–78 as an Appendix to the Science Progress Report of the APU.

The statements in the list refer to concepts and knowledge on which the questions for the assessment of performance in science may be based, and represents a consensus as to what is a reasonable concept for the assessment.

For the sake of brevity and clarity, in some statements use has been made of words with which the pupils would not necessarily be familiar. Such words are indicated by the use of quotation marks. In addition, certain qualifying statements, which it might not be appropriate to stress to pupils of the age in question, have been included in parentheses.

The six main concept areas are as follows:
A. Interaction of living things with their environment.
B. Living things and their life processes
C. Force and field
D. Transfer of energy
E. The classification and structure of matter
F. Chemical interactions

These six divisions have been further sub-divided into sub-groups of related concept statements. It is emphasised that these groupings were made for purposes of classifying questions and to ensure that questions in any test are spread with respect to these concept areas as well as to science activity category and to context (science teaching, teaching in other subjects, everyday or out-of-school situations). They are in no way intended to indicate a teaching syllabus.

Table 6.18   *Index to concept areas*

Concept Areas	Sectors: sets of related statements	Concept Regions
A. Interaction of living things with their environment	1. Interdependence of living things 2. The physical and chemical environment 3. Classification of living things 4. Physical and chemical principles needed to interpret life phenomena	
		Biological region
B. Living things and their life processes	1. The cell 2. Nutrition 3. Respiration 4. Reproduction 5. Sensitivity and movement	

C.
Force and field

1. Movement and deformation
2. Properties of matter
3. Forces at a distance
4. The Earth in space

Physical region

D.
Transfer of energy

1. Work and energy
2. Current electricity
3. "Waves"[1]

E.
The classification and structure of matter

1. States of matter
2. Pure substance
3. Metals and non-metals
4. Acids and bases
5. Periodic table
6. Atomic model

Chemical region

F.
Chemical interactions

1. Solutions
2. Reactivity
3. Properties of a chemical reaction
4. Some chemical reactions

[1] The quotation marks here and elsewhere in the list denote words used for convenience. They would probably not be used in teaching.

A INTERACTION OF LIVING THINGS WITH THEIR ENVIRONMENT

A1 Interdependence of living things

Virtually all organisms are dependent on the presence and activities of other organisms for their survival.

Green plants use energy from the sun to make food by "photosynthesis". During this process the oxygen that is used by animals and plants is produced.

Some animals eat plants and some eat other animals, but all animals ultimately depend on green plants for food.

A2 The physical and chemical environment

Air fills the space around or near the earth's surface.

Water makes up a large proportion of all living things.

Soil is a mixture that includes rock particles, humus, water and air.

Plants take substances from both the air and the soil.

Substances taken from the soil must be replaced to maintain fertility.

Changes in the physical environment due to seasonal cycles are often matched by changes or events in the living world, such as fruiting or mating.

A3 Classification of living things

There are many different plants and animals which between them show a variety of ways of carrying out life processes.

There are many different ways of grouping living things.

Plants may be distinguished from animals by the way they obtain food and by their cell structure.

Animals are classified into two major groups — invertebrates and vertebrates.

There are five main groups of vertebrates: fish, amphibia, reptiles, birds and mammals.

A4 Physical and chemical principles needed to interpret life phenomena

The area of its surface affects the gain or loss of energy and matter from an organism or cell.

The ratio of surface area to the mass of an organism is critical for its survival and will reflect its relationship with its environment.

Animals that have a stable body temperature have a number of mechanisms for the control of loss of energy.

B LIVING THINGS AND THEIR LIFE PROCESSES

B1 The cell

The cell is the basic unit of most living things.

Cells have a nucleus and cell membrane.

Plant cells differ from animal cells in characteristic ways.

An organism may be formed from one or many cells.

Most cells reproduce themselves by division, which leads to growth or, in single-celled organisms, to new individuals.

B2 Nutrition

All living things need food as a source of energy and of raw materials for growth and reproduction.

Green plants use simple substances from their environment to make thir own food.

Animals require protein, fat, carbohydrates, minerals, vitamins and water.

Surplus food is stored as fat or carbohydrate.

All organisms are "structurally adapted" to the kind of food they need.

All living things produce waste materials in carrying out life processes.

B3 Respiration

Most living things take in oxygen from their surroundings to be used in the process of respiration.

All living things respire in order to make use of energy stored in food.

In respiration, energy is transferred from food with the release of carbon dioxide.

B4 Reproduction

Living things produce offspring of the same ''species'' as themselves.

Sexual reproduction involves two parents and the offspring will differ from their parents and generally from each other.

Sexual reproduction involves the fusion of two special sex cells, ova (eggs) and sperm or pollen; one cell from each parent.

The life cycle of an organism varies and is adapted to the circumstances in which the organism lives.

B5 Sensitivity and movement

All living organisms have means of receiving information from their environment.

In higher animals special organs are concerned with receiving different kinds of ''stimuli''. These are called sense organs.

In humans the senses include sight, touch, hearing, taste and smell.

The response to a ''stimulus'' often results in movement.

Voluntary movement in many animals is brought about by contraction of muscles attached to a skeleton.

C FORCE AND FIELD

C1 Movement and deformation

The average speed of an object is found by dividing the distance moved by the time taken.

Forces are necessary to change the motion of an object.

The turning effect of a force about a point is larger when the line of action of the force is further from the point.

Forces are needed to change the shape of an object. The force which an object can stand before breaking depends on its shape as well as the material from which it is made.

If materials recover their original shape after the applied force has been removed, the material is called elastic.

C2 Properties of matter

Different substances have different masses for equal volume; the mass of a unit volume of a substance is its density.

If the volume of a given mass increases, its density decreases.

Pressure can be decreased by spreading the same force over a larger surface area.

Water tends to flow until its surface reaches a common level.

Particles of a substance are in constant motion. Diffusion of a substance is due to the random motion of individual particles.

Most substances expand as their temperature increases.

Objects completely immersed in a liquid displace a volume of liquid equal to their own volume.

Most liquids rise up into narrow tubes or crevices above the level of an open surface.

C3 Forces at a distance

Magnets attract and repel other magnets and attract magnetic substances.

The region in which a magnetic effect can be detected is called a magnetic field.

There is a magnetic field surrounding the Earth.

Magnetism is induced in some materials when they are placed in a magnetic field.

An electric current in a coil of wire produces a magnetic field round it.

Some materials can be electrically charged by rubbing them with a different material.

Similarly charged objects repel each other, and oppositely charged objects attract each other. The force between such objects is stronger when the objects are close.

C4 The Earth in space

The weight of an object on the Earth is the force with which it is attracted to the Earth.

The weight of an object may vary from place to place, but its mass does not change.

The apparent movements of the sun, moon and stars follow a regular pattern.

The Earth spins on its axis; this gives rise to night and day.

The Earth revolves in an orbit around the sun with its axis tilted with respect to this orbit; this accounts for seasonal changes.

The moon orbits the Earth as a natural satellite.

D TRANSFER OF ENERGY

D1 Work and energy

There is a variety of sources of energy such as fuels (including food), other chemicals, deformed springs, capacitors and objects at a height.

Energy can be changed from one form to another but can never be created or destroyed.

Moving objects have energy which is transferred elsewhere when they are stopped.

The hotter a substance is, the more energy its particles have.

Different substances conduct heat at different rates.

D2 Current electricity

A complete circuit of conducting material is needed for a steady current to flow between the terminals of a battery or a d.c. power supply.

Some materials conduct electricity better than others. Bad conductors are known as insulators.

D3 Waves

Objects are seen because of the light they give out or reflect.

Light travels (in a uniform medium) in straight paths or rays.

Sound can be heard when objects vibrate in a "medium".

Sound requires a medium for its transmission.

E THE CLASSIFICATION AND STRUCTURE OF MATTER

E1 States of matter

In general a substance can be classified either as a solid or a liquid or a gas.

The behaviour of substances can be explained if it is assumed that matter is made of minute particles.

Solids have a definite shape and volume. They behave as if their particles are closely packed and held together.

Liquids have a definite volume and surface but no fixed shape. They behave as if their particles are closely packed but free to move.

Gases have no definite volume or shape. They behave as if their particles are free to move independently of each other.

A change in state does not involve a change in the chemical composition of the substance.

Changes of state caused by heating can be reversed by cooling and vice-versa.

Changes of state always involve a transfer of energy.

E2 Pure substance

A pure substance may be obtained from a mixture using one of several techniques, including evaporation, distillation, chromatography and filtration.

A pure substance is recognised by its characteristic chemical and physical properties (at STP) eg m.p., b.p., density and behaviour with other substances.

Pure substances may be classified into elements and compounds.

E3 Metals and non-metals

Materials can be classified into groups in many different ways. One way is by sorting into metals and non-metals.

In general, metals can be distinguished from non-metals by their characteristic physical properties. These include high m.p., b.p., shiny appearance and conduction of heat and electricity.

Another way of distinguishing metals from non-metals is by their characterisitc chemical properties. These may include the nature of the oxide.

Some metals do not exhibit all these characteristic properties.

E4 Acids and bases

Compounds can be classified into groups by their different properties. Acids and bases are two such groups.

Acids and bases have a characteristic effect on the colour of indicators.

Bases which are soluble in water are called alkalis.

In aqueous solution the degree of acidity depends on the substance.

The degree of acidity is expressed on a pH scale from 0 to 14.

A neutral solution has a pH value of 7; acidic solutions have pH values less than 7 and alkaline solutions pH values above 7.

E5 Periodic table

Families of elements with similar chemical behaviour can be identified.

E6 Atomic model
The atom is the smallest characteristic uncharged particle of an element.

F CHEMICAL INTERACTIONS

F1 Solutions

Some substances dissolve in water; others do not, but may dissolve in other liquids.

A liquid which will dissolve a substance to form a solution is called a solvent.

The substance which dissolves in the liquid is called a solute.

At a given temperature and pressure, the mass of solute which will dissolve in a given volume of solvent is limited and fixed.

For most solids solubility increases with increasing temperature.

F2 Reactivity

A more reactive element can be used to extract a less reactive element from one of its ores or compounds.

The reactions of metals with water or dilute acid may be used to place them in a reactivity series.

F3 Properties of a chemical reaction

A chemical reaction occurs when one or more different substances are formed from one or more original substances.

Most chemical reactions are initiated by an input of energy.

The total mass of reacting substances in any chemical reaction is the same as the total mass of products.

F4 Some chemical reactions

On heating, some compounds change colour due to loss of water. Often these changes are easily reversed.

When elements react with oxygen only they usually form oxides; this is an example of an oxidation reaction.

When a compound changes by losing oxygen, this is an example of a reduction reaction.

The oxidation of a metal by atmospheric oxygen is an example of corrosion.

Fuels such as coal and oil are formed by the gradual decay of plant and animal remains under high pressure.

Large amounts of energy can be transferred from these fuels when they react with oxygen. This is an example of a combustion reaction.

7.   Science provision in the survey schools

7.1 Introduction

The performances of the pupils who attempted the various tests used in this survey are the main focus of this report. It will be useful to be able to reflect on these performances in the light of knowledge about the kinds of schools from which the pupils were drawn, and, in particular, about the resources for science work which these schools had available. In order to collect such information, every school which participated in the survey was asked to complete a questionnaire concerning the human, physical and financial resources available to that school for work in science, and requesting information about the organisation of such work (90 per cent of the schools completed the questionnaire, which is reproduced as Appendix 4). In addition, the schools were asked to provide details of the science courses being taken by each of the pupils selected to take a survey test (93 per cent of the schools complied with this request).

This chapter presents a description of the 448 survey schools on the basis of the information provided by the school questionnaire and that already available from existing records.

The method by which the schools and pupils were selected is outlined in Appendix 3. The composition of the participating school sample fairly closely reflects that of the school population as a whole, and one or two features of this composition should be borne in mind when considering the findings presented throughout this and previous chapters.

Figure 7.1 (over) details the way in which England was sub-divided into the three regions of north, midlands and south, and indicates which counties were designated metropolitan or non-metropolitan within each of these regions.

The first feature to note is the clear imbalance in terms of this school location variable between the north region and the midlands and south (the north having proportionately more schools in metropolitan areas). This overlap between region and location will be of relevance when considering the regional and location performance estimates discussed later.

Another feature of the school population which readers should be aware of when reflecting on the description of the survey schools which follows is the uneven distribution of different types of school between the three regions.

It was thought that, for the purpose of reporting the science performances of 13 year old pupils, it would be useful to sub-divide the very large comprehensive school sector by age of transfer. We have, then, two types of comprehensive school considered in this report: 'junior' comprehensives which include middle schools and all comprehensive schools with a leaving age of 12/13/14 years; and 'senior' comprehensives which include all comprehensives with a leaving age of 16 or over. In addition, in this chapter we consider resource findings for the modern and independent schools contained in the survey sample, and

Figure 7.1 *The three geographical regions and their counties*

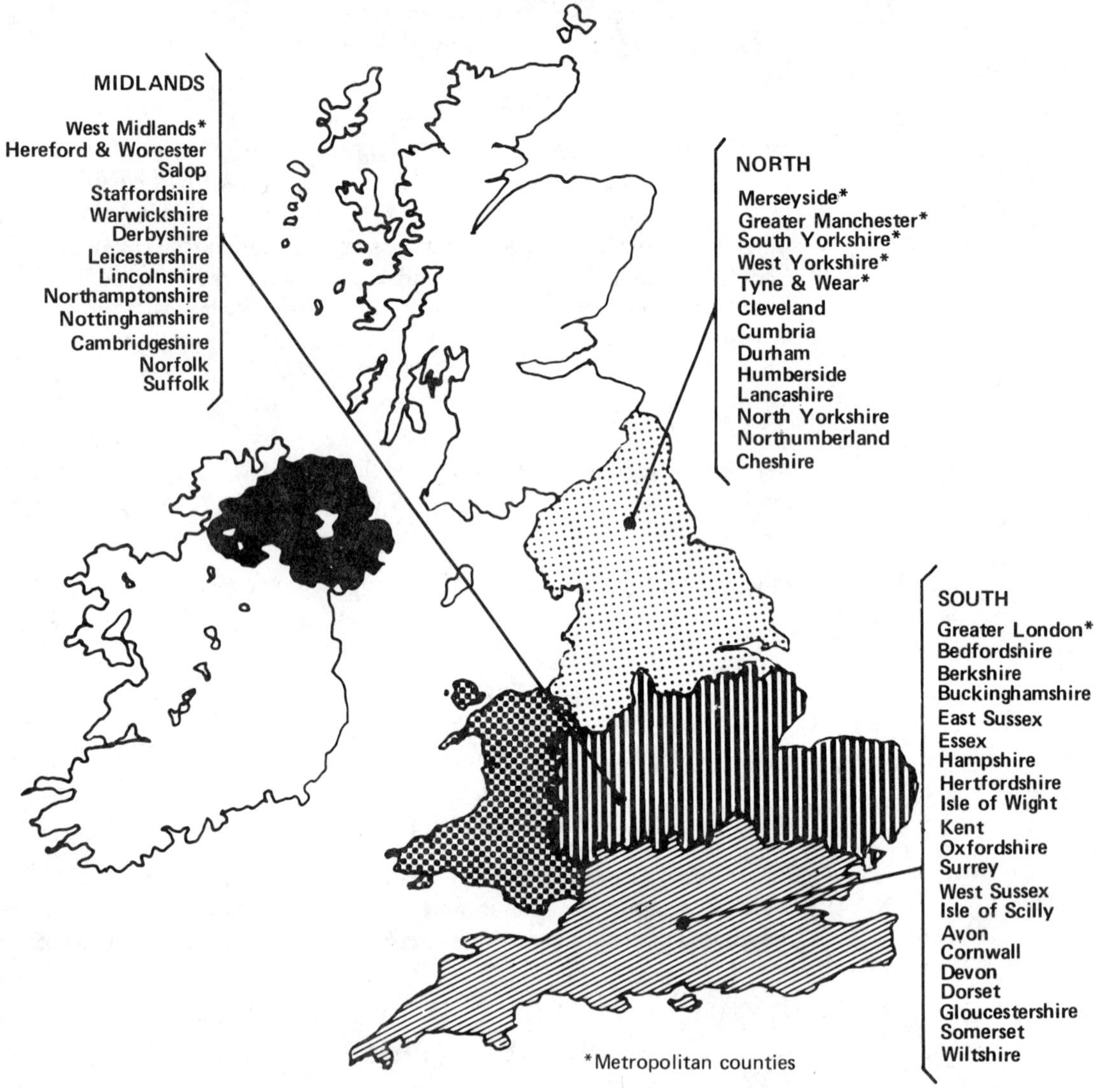

MIDLANDS

West Midlands*
Hereford & Worcester
Salop
Staffordshire
Warwickshire
Derbyshire
Leicestershire
Lincolnshire
Northamptonshire
Nottinghamshire
Cambridgeshire
Norfolk
Suffolk

NORTH

Merseyside*
Greater Manchester*
South Yorkshire*
West Yorkshire*
Tyne & Wear*
Cleveland
Cumbria
Durham
Humberside
Lancashire
North Yorkshire
Northumberland
Cheshire

SOUTH

Greater London*
Bedfordshire
Berkshire
Buckinghamshire
East Sussex
Essex
Hampshire
Hertfordshire
Isle of Wight
Kent
Oxfordshire
Surrey
West Sussex
Isle of Scilly
Avon
Cornwall
Devon
Dorset
Gloucestershire
Somerset
Wiltshire

*Metropolitan counties

occasionally comment on the resource features of the 20 survey grammar schools. (The regional findings refer to *all* these different kinds of school).

The main differences in regional composition in terms of these school types are that there are proportionally more independent schools and proportionally fewer comprehensive schools in the southern region than in either of the other two regions.

7.2 School stability

Having completed the questionnaire, schools were invited to comment on any major restructuring they had recently experienced which might explain unusual capitation figures, and it is of interest to note that just over one in ten of the sample schools were undergoing — or had undergone in the last six years —

reorganisation of one kind or another. Of these 51 schools, 32 were in the process of becoming comprehensive (either by changing the composition of their pupil intake or by merger with other existing schools), six were in the process of becoming middle schools, and five were new schools. The rest were losing or gaining sixth forms, experiencing rising or falling rolls for one reason or another, becoming co-educational, and so on.

In addition, 15 schools were receiving or had received new laboratories, or were having existing laboratories re-furbished, and a number of schools were changing the nature of the science courses taught (mainly schools introducing 'A' level or middle schools introducing Nuffield Science).

The degree of instability in the survey sample (and therefore presumably in the school population as a whole) is a factor which perhaps should be borne in mind when the pupils' performance levels assessed in this and following surveys are considered.

7.3 Policy and organisation

Curriculum choice   The curriculum information provided for each of their tested pupils by 93 per cent of the survey schools revealed little curriculum choice within schools in terms of science courses. With few exceptions schools adopted a single curriculum approach for all pupils in the 13 year old age group.

In the vast majority of schools, 13 year old pupils took a general science course (70 per cent of the schools which provided curriculum information), the next most common option being separate-subject courses in physics, chemistry and biology (18 per cent of the schools). About two per cent of the schools provided a choice of separate-subject or general science courses at this age. Each of the remaining schools offered some predetermined combination of physics, chemistry, biology and general science, the particular combination depending on the school.

On the basis of this information schools were classified into those offering only general science, those offering separate-subject courses (physics, chemistry and biology), and others. Figure 7.2 presents regional comparisons, and we see from this table that proportionally fewer of the sample schools in the south offered a general science course compared with those in the north and midlands.

Figure 7.2   *Science courses offered to 13 year old pupils (% schools within region)*

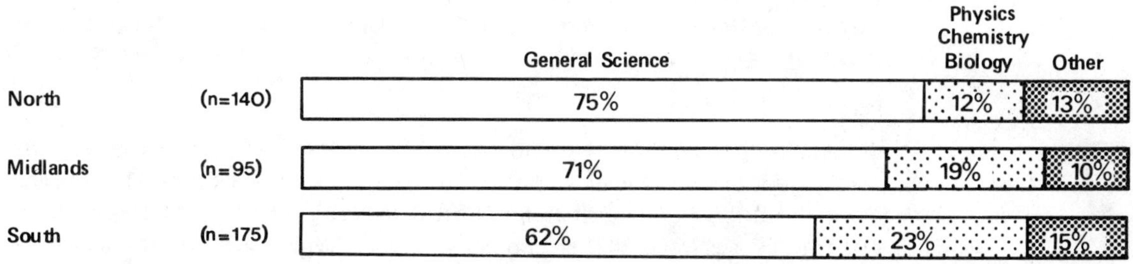

Figure 7.3 provides this same kind of curriculum information for each of the four different types of school in the survey sample.

Figure 7.3   *Science courses offered to 13 year old pupils (% schools within type)*

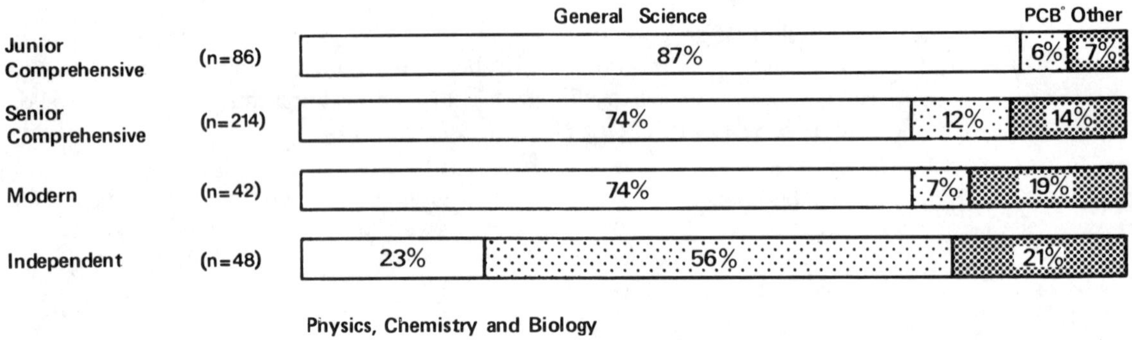

One point to note from Figure 7.3 must be the similarity between the 'senior' comprehensives and the modern schools in this respect. Also these 'senior' comprehensives differ from the 'junior' comprehensives, with proportionally more of the latter offering a general science course only. The independent schools differ markedly from these other groups, with a much higher emphasis here on separate-subject courses. (It may be of interest to note that the 20 grammar schools in the sample showed a similarly high proportion offering separate-subject courses in physics, chemistry and biology).

Time spent on science   With few exceptions, schools either had a 35-period timetable cycle with each period lasting 40 minutes, or a 40-period cycle with each teaching period lasting 35 minutes. On the evidence of the questionnaire information, most 13 year olds took between three and six periods of science in a timetable cycle (usually a week). About half of the schools in fact allocated four periods to science, 16 per cent allocated five and 19 per cent allocated six.

Figure 7.4, which provides regional comparisons, shows a high degree of similarity between the regional profiles for this variable.

Figure 7.5 reveals that proportionally more independent schools devote more time to science than other types of school — perhaps related to the fact already noted that proportionally more independent schools offer separate-subject courses to their 13 year old pupils than do other school types.

Group size for science work   The school questionnaire asked for the number of teaching groups into which the whole 12/13 age group was divided for science work, the purpose of this question being to provide an indication of average group size for science work in the schools concerned. This figure was obtained by

Figure 7.4   *Number of teaching periods allocated to science (% schools within region)*

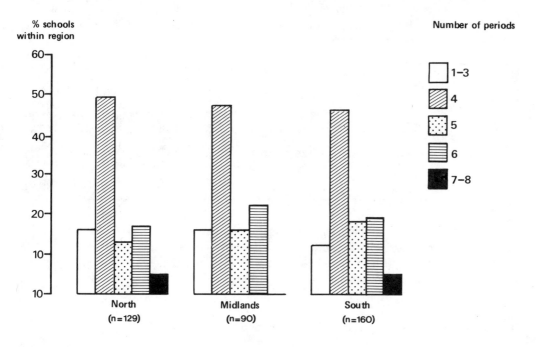

Figure 7.5   *Number of teaching periods allocated to science (% schools within type)*

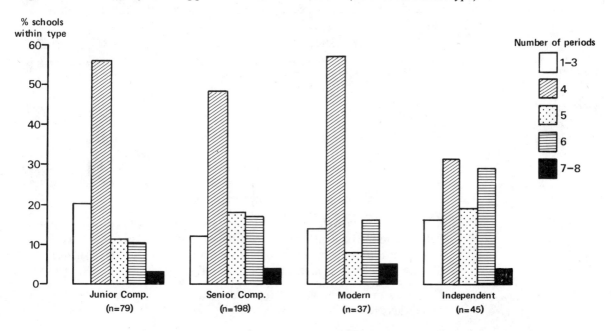

dividing the number of pupils in the year group by the number of teaching groups, and it should be borne in mind that it need not be the case that all the pupils in a particular school were actually taught science in groups of the size indicated.

Figure 7.6 presents the regional findings in terms of average size of group for science work, and it is clear that regional variation is slight, with the south having a marginally higher proportion of schools with smaller teaching groups than the other two regions.

Figure 7.6   *Average group size for science work (% schools within region)*

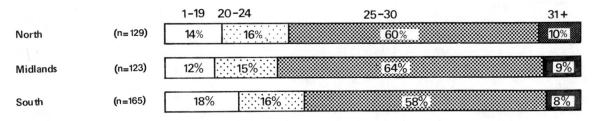

The clearest point emerging from the school type comparisons shown in Figure 7.7 is the difference between the independent schools and all others in terms of this variable, with about three-quarters of the independent schools having the smallest group size for science work.

Figure 7.7   *Average group size for science work (% schools within type)*

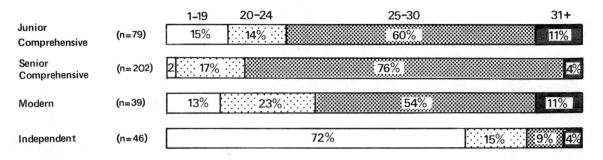

Outside visits   Schools were asked whether or not they had link courses with colleges of further education and whether their pupils visited field centres or industrial sites as part of their science learning.

About 45 per cent of the schools had used field centres, and a similar proportion had made industrial visits. There was similar regional variation in each case, with the proportions rising from the midlands at about 40 per cent, through the north at about 45 per cent, to the south at 50 per cent.

The proportion of schools sharing link courses with FE colleges was under a fifth, with little regional variation.

Comparing different types of school, about 60 per cent of the 'senior' comprehensives and the modern schools had used field centres or made industrial visits, compared with 20–30 per cent of the 'junior' comprehensives and the independent schools.

A low four per cent of the 'junior' comprehensives and of the independent schools shared link courses with FE colleges, the proportion rising to 17 per cent for the 'senior' comprehensives and one-third for the modern schools.

7.4 Staffing and physical resources

Overall pupil/teacher ratio statistics were available for all of the sample schools from official sources.

In addition, each school was asked to indicate the number of teachers who were currently involved in teaching science in the school, and, of these, the number holding a science qualification. Information was also sought on laboratory availability and technician help.

Pupil/teacher ratio   LEAs are known to vary in the ways in which they compute pupil/teacher ratios for their schools, and it cannot anyway be assumed that such ratios bear any direct relation to the sizes of teaching groups within schools. It was nevertheless felt that some information about levels on this index could be of interest.

In order to maintain comparability with previous reports of APU surveys in the areas of mathematics and language, schools were classified into three ranges in terms of their pupil/teacher ratios. The ranges are 1–14.9, 15–17.4 and 17.5 plus.

There was little regional variation in terms of this variable, with about 30 per cent of schools in each of the two lower categories, a higher 40 per cent falling into the category of 17.5 plus.

Figure 7.8   *Pupil/teacher ratio (% distribution of schools within type)*

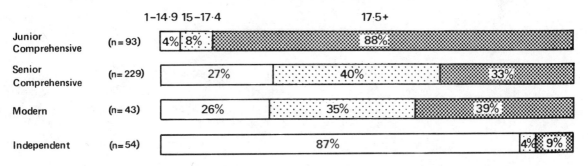

Figure 7.8 shows the distributions in terms of this ratio for the four types of school, and perhaps the most notable feature of Figure 7.8 is the very high proportion of independent schools having the lowest pupil/teacher ratio with a similarly high proportion of the 'junior' comprehensives experiencing the least favourable ratio.

Science teachers   A science qualification was here defined as either a science or applied science degree or a teaching certificate covering a main course in a science subject.

Figure 7.9 *Proportions of science teachers holding a science qualification (by region)*

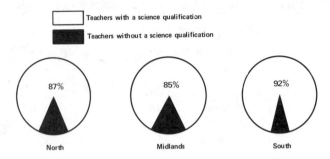

As Figure 7.9 shows, a higher proportion of the teachers who were teaching science in the survey schools of the south held one of these science qualifications compared with those in schools in the midlands and north.

Figure 7.10 *Proportions of science teachers holding a science qualification (by school type)*

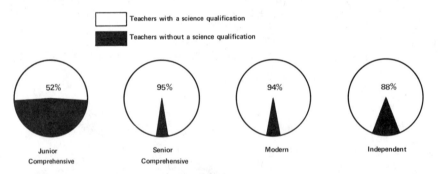

If we look at the different *types* of school, we see from Figure 7.10 that the 'senior' comprehensives, the modern schools and the independent schools in the sample all had very high proportions of science-qualified teachers teaching science. In the 'junior' comprehensives (which include middle schools) the proportion was low at 52 per cent.

Laboratories and technicians   The survey schools were asked to record both the number of science laboratories they each possessed and the number of technicians they employed to service these laboratories.

HMI in their recent secondary survey (DES 1979) produced rough, though useful, criteria for judging the adequacy of a school's laboratory accommodation. They assumed that science is practically based from the age of 11, and that it occupies about one-sixth of curriculum time (six teaching periods in a 35-period week) for pupils between the ages of 11 and 16. An n-form entry school with y year-groups would, then, require 6ny teaching periods per week of laboratory time. With, say,

30 teaching periods available per laboratory, such a school would need 6ny/30 laboratories for its science courses to be practically-based. For the purposes of this present survey, schools with ages of intake below 11 were considered to need laboratory accommodation only for the science courses taken by pupils of 11 and over.

HMI considered that schools offering sixth-form science would need one extra laboratory over the number required for pupils up to 16.

According to these criteria, a three-form entry 11−16 school would need three laboratories to be judged adequately accommodated, a two-form entry 10−14 school would need one laboratory only, and a four-form entry 11−18 school would need five laboratories.

On this basis, about three-quarters of the survey schools can be considered to have had adequate laboratory accommodation, with little variation in this overall proportion from one region to another.

Figure 7.11   *Adequacy of laboratory accommodation (% schools within type)*

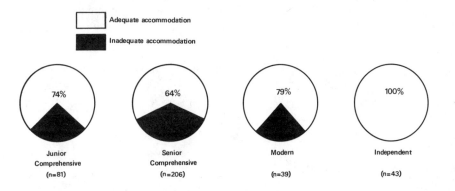

All of the independent schools (and, incidentally, all of the grammar schools) in the sample had enough laboratories for their needs. As Figure 7.11 shows, the senior comprehensives were less adequately accommodated in general; just over one-third of them did not have enough laboratories.

The questionnaire revealed that about nine out of ten of the technicians employed in the survey schools worked 40 or more weeks per year. The number of hours worked per week ranged widely from 13 to 37, though the majority of technicians were employed in a full-time capacity.

Although a very rough indicator of adequacy of technician support given the variety of employment conditions adopted by the schools, the HMI criterion of no more than three laboratories to each full-time technician was applied here. On this basis, about 40 per cent of the survey schools were without enough technicians to service their laboratories adequately. This proportion agrees with that reported by HMI (DES 1979).

There was a clear regional difference in levels of technician support, as Figure 7.12 reveals. About half of the survey schools in the north and midlands regions had enough technicians for their needs, the proportion rising to almost three-quarters for those survey schools in the south.

Figure 7.12 *Adequacy of technician support (% schools within region)*

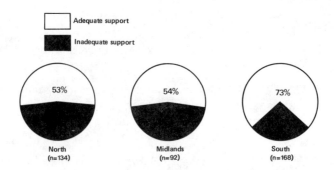

Figure 7.13 suggests that the independent and the junior comprehensive schools in the sample were the least well-supported in this respect.

Figure 7.13 *Adequacy of technician support (% schools within type)*

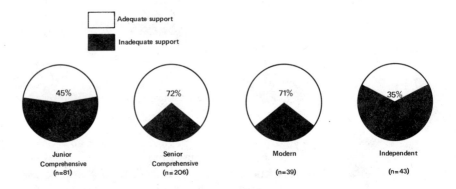

Overall, about one in ten of the survey schools had insufficient numbers of laboratories for their needs and also too few technicians to service the laboratories that they had. About four in ten of the survey schools had adequate provision in both respects.

7.5 Financial resources

The questionnaire asked schools in the maintained sector to indicate the amount of money spent by them from their LEA capitation allowances in each of the three years 1977/78, 1978/79 and 1979/80, and for the amount of money spent by their science departments in these years. They were also asked to indicate any additional grant received by their science departments from any source (LEA, industry, PTA, etc.).

Capitation allowance   The capitation figures proved difficult for a number of schools to provide for all three years, 16 per cent of the maintained sample schools failing to provide the full information. An average capitation figure (£ per pupil per year) was computed for each school with complete data, and the schools were then classified into three ranges depending on the average amount spent per pupil per year: under £16, £16–£20, and over £20.

Figure 7.14   *Capitation allowance (£ per pupil per year — % schools within region)*

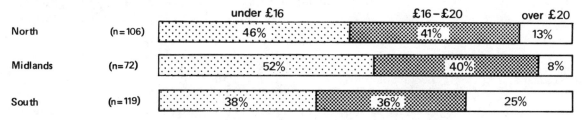

The regional results are shown in Figure 7.14, with proportionally more of the survey schools in the south receiving the higher levels of capitation allowance than those in either the north or the midlands.

Figure 7.15   *Capitation allowance (£ per pupil per year — % schools within type)*

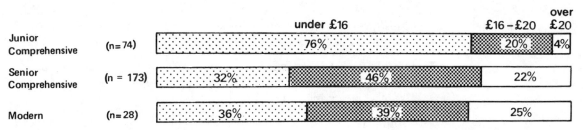

Figure 7.15 presents the findings for the three types of maintained school and it would appear from this figure that, in general, 'junior' comprehensives received lower per pupil capitation incomes than did the 'senior' comprehensives or the modern schools.

Science expenditure   A similar computation was carried out on the schools' information concerning the amounts of money spent by their science departments. However, a very high proportion of the schools (30 per cent) failed to provide this information, so that the figures presented here should be treated with some caution. Schools which did provide the information were classified into three ranges on the basis of the average amount spent per pupil per year: under £2, £2–£2.99, £3 or more.

There was little regional variation in terms of the amount spent on science with three out of five schools spending under £2 per pupil per year on science work, and a further quarter spending between £2 and £3.

Given that three-fifths of the 'junior' comprehensive schools failed to supply full information, it would not be wise to present any detailed school type figures for this index. The general picture which did emerge was of proportionally more of the 'senior' comprehensives spending at least £2 per pupil per year on science than either the 'junior' comprehensive or the modern schools.

Other income for science   About half of the schools in the maintained sector indicated that they had received money for their science departments in the form of special grants, PTA donations, and so on. Separate amounts ranged from £10 to £8,000 (most being in the hundreds), many of the larger figures being connected with the kinds of organisational changes referred to previously.

7.6 Summary

The state of transition in which many of the sample schools were found to exist at this time was also noted by HMI (DES 1979) to apply to *their* national sample of secondary schools, and by Rutter *et al* (1979) in relation to their London-region sample. An indication of the extent of change in the secondary school population over the last ten years is to be found in a comparison of this science school sample and that which was the focus of the language survey conducted for the Bullock Committee in 1973 (DES 1975). Both were selected by a random sampling process to reflect the school population from which they were drawn. In the maintained school sector of the sample described in *this* report we find a high 84 per cent of comprehensive schools, five per cent of grammar schools and 11 per cent of modern and other schools, while in the 'Bullock' sample we see quite a different mix with 36 per cent comprehensive, 19 per cent grammar and a high 46 per cent of modern and other schools.

The secondary school population has, then, been in a state of transition for some years, and this is a fact which may usefully be kept in mind when secondary pupils' performances are considered.

It was found to be almost universally the case that 13 year old pupils within any one school were offered a uniform science curriculum (whether a general science course or separate-subject physics, chemistry and biology), that timetable cycles lasted a week and consisted of 35 or 40 teaching periods of 40 or 35 minutes each respectively, and that science was allocated between three and six of these teaching periods. Average group size for science work was most commonly 25–30 pupils, and, overall, about one in ten of the teachers teaching science were without qualification in the subject. It was further noted that many schools were without adequate laboratory accommodation, and that many had a low level of technician support in their laboratories.

Many of the features outlined here in relation to *this* sample of schools were also noted by HMI in describing the schools involved in their recent secondary survey (DES 1979). For example, HMI commented on the uniformity of the curriculum for the first three years in secondary school, on the generally universal use of seven or eight teaching periods per day in a cycle lasting a week, and on the fact that science accounted for three to six of these teaching periods per week. They also remarked on what they saw as inadequate laboratory provision and technician support in many schools.

There were few regional differences in terms of the schools' policies for, and organisation of, science work, or in terms of their resources for this work. Where any difference did occur it was usually in favour of the schools in the south. For example, science was undertaken in smaller groups in proportionally more southern schools than schools in the midlands or north and the schools in the south had a generally higher level of technician support and of capitation income.

It is between the different *types* of school that major differences appear. The independent schools, for example, more often offered their 13 year old pupils separate-subject courses in physics, chemistry and biology than did the comprehensive and modern schools, and, perhaps as a consequence of this, they also in general allocated more time to science work. Further, proportionally more of the independent schools had lower pupil group sizes for such work.

If we consider comprehensive schools only, we find marked differences between our two categories of 'junior' and 'senior' in a number of respects. The 'junior' comprehensives had less favourable pupil/teacher ratios in general, a lower level of technician support and a much lower proportion of science-qualified teachers teaching science than did the 'senior' comprehensives, and they were also less well favoured in terms of capitation income.

8   Pupils' science performances

In this chapter pupils' performances in certain sub-categories of the assessment framework are to be considered in relation to each of a number of pupil/school characteristics drawn from those discussed in the previous chapter.

Although the assessment framework includes 17 sub-categories altogether, as explained in the introduction it was considered appropriate to compute test scores for only 13 of these, and they are:

1α	Reading information from graphs, tables and charts
1β	Expressing information as graphs, tables and charts
1γ	Using scientific symbols and conventions
2α	Using measuring instruments
2β	Estimating quantities
3β	Observing similarities and differences
3γ	Interpreting observations
4α	Describing and using patterns in information
4δ	Making sense of information using science concepts
5α	Identifying or proposing testable statements
5β	Assessing experimental procedures

Of these sub-categories, 1α and 1β essentially assess skills involved in the communication of information, with 4α also relying to some extent on these kinds of skill. Sub-categories 2α and 2β involve *measuring and estimation skills* of value in practical science work, with 3β and 3γ assessing *observation skills* in a practical context. Sub-category 4δ is concerned with the processes involved in *interpretation and application* using science concepts. In Chapter 6 it was pointed out that there are, in fact, three 4δ sub-categories broadly distinguished by the nature of the concepts involved — $4\delta_{AB}$ is concerned with *biological* concepts, $4\delta_{CD}$ with *physics* concepts, and $4\delta_{EF}$ with *chemical* concepts. Finally, the category 5 sub-categories of 5α and 5β relate to *skills of experimental design*.

Performance on all these sub-categories will be considered in relation to a number of *general* background variables (including pupil sex, region, location, school type, and pupil/teacher ratio), and also in relation to one or two science-specific school characteristics (for example, curriculum background and time spent on science).

The peformance figures presented throughout this chapter are *estimates* of those to be expected of the pupils in the various sub-groups defined by the characteristics under consideration. These estimates were produced by appropriately weighting the actual performance levels of the relevant pupils in the sample to take account of the clustering of pupils in their schools and of general imbalances in the representation of the pupil population in the sample. Appendix 5 provides further details of the estimation procedure, and includes a table summarising some of the main survey results.

The accuracy of any estimated performance level depends both on the size of the sample on which it was based and on the variability of performance among the sample pupils and schools. Included in every graphical presentation are the standard errors and 95 per cent confidence intervals associated with each performance estimate. Comments are often made about the statistical significance (at the five per cent level) of differences between the estimated performance levels of different pupil groups. (Where confidence levels do not overlap the difference in the performance levels concerned is likely to be statistically significant). Readers unfamiliar with the concepts of standard error, confidence intervals and statistical significance are referred to Appendix 6 for an explanation of these terms.

8.2 Overall performance levels

The general profile of performance, estimated for the whole population of 13 year old pupils across all 13 sub-categories, is illustrated in Figure 8.1. The *educational* significance of differences in levels from one sub-category to another is considered in Chapter 9.

Figure 8.1 *The profile of overall performance levels.*

	mean	*s.e.*
1α	58.2	1.1
1β	53.3	1.5
1γ	42.8	1.3
2α	51.3	1.8
2β	27.7	1.3
3β	53.4	0.7
3γ	51.0	0.9
4α	40.5	0.8
$4\delta_{AB}$	37.2	0.7
$4\delta_{CD}$	32.5	0.7
$4\delta_{EF}$	33.7	0.7
5α	48.4	0.9
5β	45.4	0.7

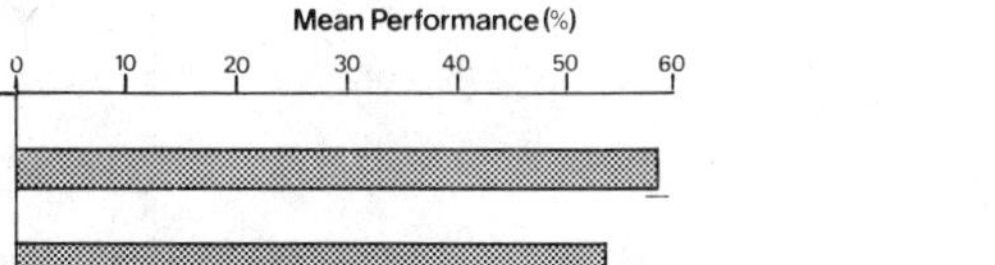

The horizontal lines on the figure (the 95 per cent confidence intervals) indicate the extent to which the estimated levels are in doubt. There is a 95 per cent probability that the true level lies within the range indicated. The fact that some confidence intervals are wider than others reflects the fact that pupils'

performances were more variable or that the sample size was smaller for some sub-categories than others. In particular the confidence intervals associated with sub-categories, 1α, 1β, 1γ, 2α and 2β are about twice as wide as those for all others. Hence larger differences in performance between sub-groups will be needed for these sub-categories than for others if similar levels of statistical significance are to be reached. Readers are advised to bear this in mind when viewing the graphical representations which follow.

8.3 Sex differences   Figure 8.2 illustrates the profiles of performance for boys and for girls across these 13 sub-categories.

Figure 8.2 *Estimated profiles of performance for boys and girls*

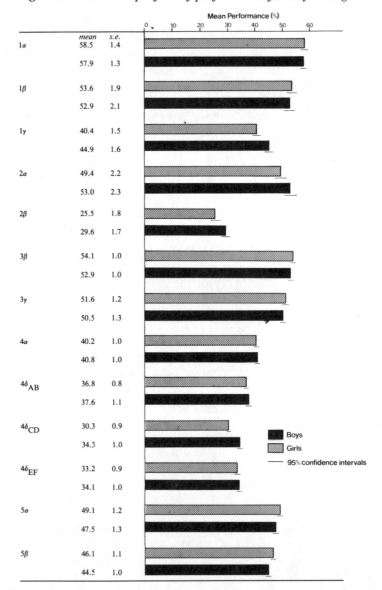

The only statistically significant difference between the performance levels of boys and girls appears for the sub-category concerned with the application of physics concepts. This finding is in line with the results of other major science surveys — the IEA Survey (Comber and Keeves 1973), the United States NAEP Surveys (see, for example, NAEP 1978a, 1978b) and the British Columbia Science Assessment (Hobbs *et al* 1978).

All of these surveys found consistent sex differences in performance in favour of boys at this age on tests involving physics concepts. Further, the British Columbia Science Assessment discovered no evidence of sex difference in performance on tests involving communication, observation (these two being a different division of our *combined* categories 1 and 3) or combined skills (our category 5).

Another notable feature of the sex difference in performance on tests involving the knowledge and application of physics concepts is that the gap between the performance of boys and girls has already appeared by the age of 11. This was shown both by the surveys referred to above, and also by the first APU survey at this lower age (DES 1981a).

8.4 General school variables

Sub-category performances were explored against each of seven general school descriptive variables — region, location, school type, school size, capitation allowance, pupil−teacher ratio and percentage uptake of free school meals. Each of the 16 different test packages used in this survey was administered in a sub-sample only of those schools described in the previous chapter (see Appendix 5 for details of the administration). Consequently, because of the small numbers of schools involved, there was no scope for the investigation of relationships between performance on any one sub-category and *combinations* of the school variables outlined above, and often restricted scope for the exploration of relationships with even these single variables. This being so, the findings which *did* emerge from this aspect of the survey investigation are presented below.

Performance estimates against particular school background variables are often given only for pupils in comprehensive schools. This restriction to one type of school was considered necessary in those cases where there were known to be large differences between types in terms of the background variable under consideration; otherwise such wide differences might tend to mask any relationship which did exist between pupil performance and the different levels of that variable. For example, the fact that independent schools mostly fall into the group with the lowest pupil-teacher ratio might mask any relationship between performance and this ratio.

Region   The pattern of regional performance is illustrated in Figure 8.3 (these performance estimates are based on regional samples which include all kinds of schools). The clearest feature of these results is perhaps the consistency with which the lowest performances are produced for the North region.

Figure 8.3 *Profiles of estimated regional performance*

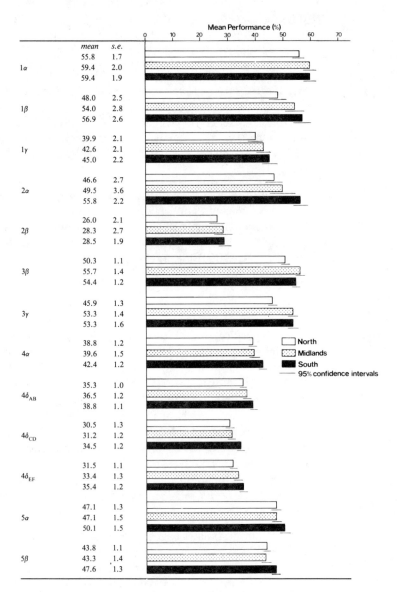

	mean	s.e.
1α	55.8	1.7
	59.4	2.0
	59.4	1.9
1β	48.0	2.5
	54.0	2.8
	56.9	2.6
1γ	39.9	2.1
	42.6	2.1
	45.0	2.2
2α	46.6	2.7
	49.5	3.6
	55.8	2.2
2β	26.0	2.1
	28.3	2.7
	28.5	1.9
3β	50.3	1.1
	55.7	1.4
	54.4	1.2
3γ	45.9	1.3
	53.3	1.4
	53.3	1.6
4α	38.8	1.2
	39.6	1.5
	42.4	1.2
4δ$_{AB}$	35.3	1.0
	36.5	1.2
	38.8	1.1
4δ$_{CD}$	30.5	1.3
	31.2	1.2
	34.5	1.2
4δ$_{EF}$	31.5	1.1
	33.4	1.3
	35.4	1.2
5α	47.1	1.3
	47.1	1.5
	50.1	1.5
5β	43.8	1.1
	43.3	1.4
	47.6	1.3

Differences between the performance levels of the Northern and Southern regions are statistically significant for ten of the 13 sub-categories, and, even if not large enough to reach statistical significance at the five per cent level, are clearly apparent in the remaining three cases (1α, 1γ, 5α).

An explanation for this phenomenon may perhaps lie in the social class distribution across England as a whole. It has been shown that academic achievement is often related to social class and that the compositions of these three geographical regions are unequal in terms of this variable, with proportionally more middle class people living in the south than in the midlands and more in the midlands than in the north (Davie *et al* 1972).

Figure 8.4   *School location performance profiles (comprehensive schools only)*

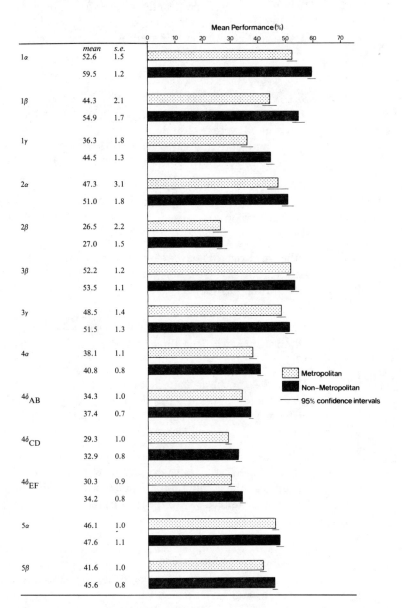

Location   Figure 8.4 provides the location results for comprehensive schools only, with a clearly consistent pattern emerging of pupils in non-metropolitan schools performing at higher levels than pupils in metropolitan schools. The performance differences are statistically significant for all but one (5α) of the paper and pencil tested sub-categories, and in the same direction also for the practical sub-categories.

Type of school   Performance estimates were produced for both kinds of comprehensive school described in the previous chapter, ie for comprehensive schools with an age of transfer of 12/13/14 years and those with a leaving age of 16 or above. Given the clear differences found between these two kinds of school in terms of their resources for science work, it is of interest that there were no statistically significant differences between them in terms of their pupils' performance on any of the sub-categories considered here.

Size of school   A sampling variable which had been used in selecting the total school sample was size of year-group for comprehensive schools only. The size ranges used were 5–180 pupils and 181 plus pupils (corresponding roughly to below and above a six-form entry). Performance estimates were produced, where possible, for these two ranges for the 'senior' comprehensives only.

There were too few schools in each size-range in the practical science sub-samples for this variable to be investigated in these cases, and there was no evidence of a general relationship between size of school and pupil performance on the written tests.

Other investigators have searched for a connection between pupil performance and school size (see, for example, Rutter *et al*. 1979, DES 1981b) but no relationship has yet been established.

Pupil/teacher ratio   This variable was investigated for the comprehensive schools only, with the three ranges previously defined: 1–14.9, 15–17.4 and 17.5+.

There was no clear pattern of relationship between this variable and pupil performance across the profile of sub-categories, and none of the sub-group differences which did appear was statistically significant — a result found also for mathematics performance in secondary schools (DES 1981b).

There are, of course, variations in the way in which different LEA's compute pupil/teacher ratio statistics, and headteachers and their deputies are usually included in the computation. Pupil/teacher ratios cannot, then, be assumed to relate in any direct way to the sizes of teaching groups in the schools concerned.

Uptake of free school meals   It was decided to collect information from the participating schools about the numbers of pupils who took a free school meal on a particular day around the time of testing, so that the percentage of pupils (on roll) who had taken a free school meal would be available as an index of the relative affluence of each school's catchment area.

Schools were found to divide roughly equally into the following three ranges of percentage uptake of free school meals: under four per cent, four to six per cent and over six per cent. Performance results for these ranges (for comprehensive schools only) are shown in Figure 8.5.

The picture revealed by Figure 8.5 is clear, with a strong relationship existing between pupil performance and this index across all sub-categories, increasing uptake of free school meals being associated with decreasing pupil performance. A similar phenomenon was found in the primary school sector in the age 11

Figure 8.5 *Percentage free school meal uptake and sub-category performance (comprehensive schools only)*

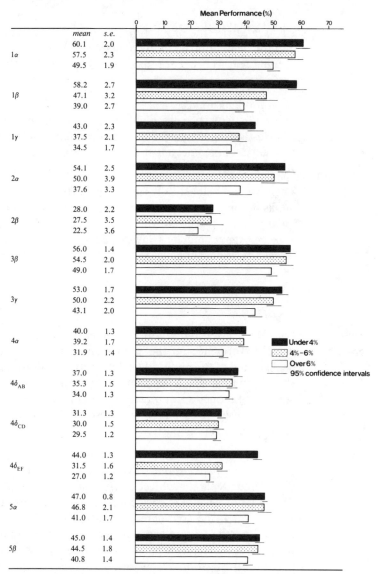

science survey (DES 1981a), and also in all the APU mathematics and language surveys (See, for example, DES 1980, 1981...)

Earlier in this chapter it was suggested that the differences found in the performance levels of pupils in the different regions could be linked to known differences in the social class compositions of these regions.

This is supported by the free school meals result, if the percentage uptake of free school meals can indeed be considered as a socioeconomic indicator. More than half of the survey schools in the north were found to fall into the group with more than six per cent uptake of free school meals, compared with about a quarter of the survey schools in the midlands and 15 per cent of those in the south.

Similarly, twice the proportion of survey schools in metropolitan locations fell into this high uptake group compared with those in non-metropolitan areas (46 per cent and 23 per cent respectively).

Capitation allowance   Very few schools appeared in the two extreme ranges of capitation allowance described in the previous chapter, so that, for the purpose of investigating this variable, the comprehensive schools were reclassified into *two* ranges of income: under £16 per pupil per year, and £16 or more per pupil per year.

There were no statistically significant differences between the performances of pupils in these two groups for any of the sub-categories involved, and, further, there was no suggestion of any consistency in the slight differences that did appear. Again, previous investigators in other areas have similarly failed to reveal a relationship between capitation and pupil performance (cf. Rutter *et al* 1979).

8.5 Science-specific school characteristics

Four science-specific school characteristics were explored for association with pupil performance on the science sub-categories. These were the curriculum background of the pupils, the number of periods of science taken each week, the size of group in which the pupils undertook their science work, and, finally, the amount of money spent on science per pupil per year by the schools concerned. In each case, investigation was restricted to comprehensive schools for the reason outlined previously.

Curriculum background   Two kinds of curriculum background were considered: separate-subject courses in physics, chemistry and biology, and a combined or general science course. There were too few schools offering other alternatives to be considered. In fact, the number of comprehensive schools falling into the first category of separate-subject courses was small, and there were too few offering separate-subject courses in the practical test sub-samples to allow investigation of this variable in these cases. The pattern of performance for the written test sub-categories is shown in Figure 8.6.

Figure 8.6 shows a consistent performance difference in favour of pupils whose schools offer them separate-subject courses in physics, chemistry and biology rather than a single course in general science.

The performance difference for $4\delta_{EF}$ (interpretation and application using chemical concepts) is statistically significant. While not reaching our particular specified level of statistical significance, there nevertheless appears to be a relatively large performance difference on $4\delta_{CD}$ (interpretation and application using concepts of physics) compared with 4α (interpretation) and $4\delta_{AB}$ (interpretation and application using biological concepts).

Figure 8.6 *Curriculum background performance profiles (comprehensive schools only)*

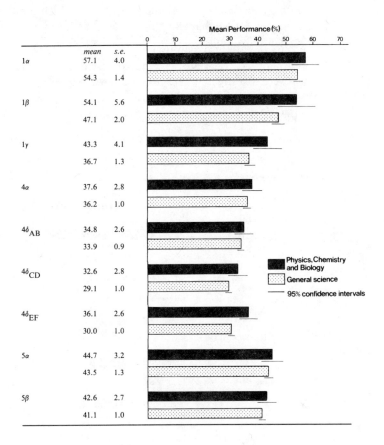

This would seem to suggest that the content emphases of the two kinds of curriculum have an effect on performance on some sub-categories and not on others. In other words, it is possible that a general science course has a less balanced emphasis on the three science subjects (greater emphasis perhaps being placed on *biological science*?) than does a curriculum diet of separate-subject courses.

Time spent on science   It was not possible to investigate this variable for the practical sub-categories as there were too few schools in these sub-samples offering pupils any alternative to four periods of science per week.

For the written tests, schools were classified into three groups: under four periods, four periods and over four periods. The resulting data provided no evidence of an association between pupil performance and time spent on science, although it must be said that the great preponderance of four-period science allocations meant that there was little school discrimination to investigate in this respect.

Group size for science work   'Group size' is the *average* size of science classes in the year group, computed by dividing the total number of pupils in the year group by the number of science classes into which they were divided. It does not necessarily follow that all or indeed any of the survey pupils in a particular school were actually taught in a group of that size.

Although four ranges of group size were described in the previous chapter, only two were investigated here because few comprehensive schools fell into either of the extreme ranges. The two sizes taken were under 25 pupils and 25 or more pupils, and the estimated performance profiles are shown in Figure 8.7.

Figure 8.7 *Average group-size for science work: performance profiles (comprehensive schools only)*

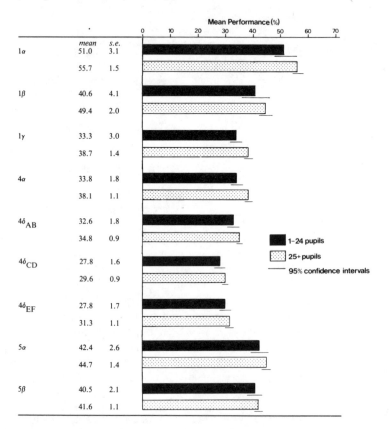

Figure 8.7 shows a clearly consistent pattern in which a *larger* average group size for the school is associated with *higher* pupil performance levels.

Science expenditure   There was little difference between schools in the amount of money spent per pupil per year on science, schools here being grouped into those which spent under £2 per pupil per year and those which spent £2 or more per pupil per year.

There was no emerging pattern of association between pupil performance and this variable, and no statistically significant differences between the two groups for any sub-category.

8.6 Summary

There was a statistically significant sex difference in performance in favour of boys on sub-category $4\delta_{CD}$ (interpretation and application using physics concepts).

Regional variation was consistent, with the performance of northern pupils being below that of pupils in the south in all cases, and below the midlands also for most sub-categories. Similarly, the location differences were consistent with pupils in non-metropolitan schools achieving higher performance levels than pupils in metropolitan schools on every sub-category. Given the location-region overlap mentioned in Chapter 7, these location and regional patterns are to some extent reflections of each other.

Despite the different levels of resource allocation found for the two kinds of comprehensive school (those with an age of transfer of 12/13/14 years and others), no differences were found between the performance levels of pupils in these two kinds of school.

No evidence was found of an association between pupil performance and school size, pupil-teacher ratio, or capitation allowance, but a strongly consistent association *was* found with the socioeconomic index (ie with the percentage uptake of free school meals — the higher the level of uptake the lower the level of pupil performance).

As far as more science-specific school variables are concerned, no association was found between pupil performance and either time or money spent on science — although the great uniformity shown by schools in these respects should be borne in mind.

Average group size for science work appeared to be *positively* related to performance on the written tests, with *larger* group size being associated with *higher* pupil performance levels.

The science curriculum studied by the pupils seemed to be relevant, performances being consistently higher for pupils studying physics, chemistry and biology as three separate subjects than for those taking a single general science course — particularly so on the sub-categories requiring some knowledge of symbolic conventions and the use of physics and chemistry concepts.

9   Interpreting the results

The sub-categories of the assessment framework relate to the skills and techniques often referred to as the processes of science. Demands on pupils are different from those commonly made in public examinations, for these often emphasise a view of science as a body of knowledge. The range of contexts in which questions are set is also wider than is usual. A lack of familiarity with the style of the questions used in the survey makes it difficult for the reader to interpret the results on the basis of past experience and this is why the categories have been so fully discussed in Chapter 6 and illustrated by so many questions in earlier chapters.

In Chapter 8, reference is made to overall performance levels in many of the sub-categories tested, and this gives rise to a number of questions. How is a sub-category level of, say, 25 per cent to be interpreted? Is the test too hard, or the population of 13 year olds badly prepared, or is the activity in question inherently difficult? What is the educational significance of differences in performance levels between one sub-category and another?

No sub-category performance level has any automatic value in absolute terms: it has to be read not only in conjunction with the definition of the sub-category but also in the light of questions and mark schemes that have been used to illuminate that definition. This is not something peculiar to the tests used in this survey. A mark or grade in, say, a public examination has meaning largely because of experience with past examinations of a similar nature. Teachers in particular have a fair idea of the standards of performance necessary for a candidate to achieve a given grade; they can associate past pupils with each grade so that the grades themselves have come, through familiarity, to have meaning. The assessment methods used in this survey are breaking new ground, and so results are difficult to interpret. Readers must bear in mind that the tests are at once more contained and more wide-ranging than their traditional science counterparts: contained by the tight definition of the types of demands made by the questions used in them; wide-ranging in the novelty of the contexts in which some of them are set. However, performance levels of stated values will become more meaningful as the types of question used become more familiar.

9.2 Sub-category differences

The performance levels reported in Chapter 8 for various sub-categories can be grouped, in terms of mean sub-category scores, as in Table 9.1.

Is it sensible to compare one category with another in terms of performance level —to say, for example, on the basis of these results, that estimation (in 2β) is harder than the use of measuring instruments (as in 2α)? The question is in the same category as one which asks whether 'O' level chemistry is harder than 'O' level French: the difference in the nature of the subject matter makes it hard to answer. It can also be argued that the mean score for any sub-category could easily have been raised, simply by using an easier set of questions. On the other hand, it must be borne in mind that the selection was made on a random basis

Table 9.1 *Sub-category performance levels*

Approximate ranges of scores:			
50% – 60%	45% – 50%	35% – 45%	25% – 35%
1α	5α	1γ	2β
1β	5β	4α	4δ$_{CD}$
2α		4δ$_{AB}$	4δ$_{EF}$
3β			
3γ			

from a bank containing many questions with as wide a range of difficulty, and as evenly spread across this range, as the writers could arrange for, within the constraints of the question descriptors and with an upper limit appropriate to 13 year old pupils.

It might also be said that the mean score for an individual question could have been raised by the use of an easier mark scheme. But this often cannot sensibly be done. Suppose that an attempt were to be made to raise the performance level of 2β (which has a mean score of 28 per cent) by this method. It would become necessary to accept estimates very wide of the mark. For example, pupils were awarded full marks for estimating the temperature of water actually at 40°C to be between 35°C and 45°C, and given some credit for an estimate as low as 20°C or as high as 60°C. On this basis the mean score for the question was 30 per cent. To raise it to 60 per cent it would have been necessary to give full marks for any estimate between 20°C and 60°C. Since one of these corresponds to the temperature of water from the cold tap and the other to that of water suitable for washing dinner plates, this would clearly be defeating the purpose of the question. Similar arguments can be advanced with respect to other types of question in other categories.

In these circumstances it seems reasonable to say not only that the particular 2β test was harder than the 2α test, but that the estimation of quantities is in general harder than the use of measuring instruments. It does seem to be the case that pupils find some skills, some processes, harder than others. In fact, the results match common-sense expectations.

Questions in category 4 (interpretation of information) really are more demanding, in general, than those in category 3 (using observation); abstract generalisation is more difficult than noting similarities and differences. However it is also clear from the table above that not only do different processes make demands of different difficulty: the concepts that pupils are required to use also have a big effect. The contrast in performance levels across sections of category 1 are of interest here. The first two sub-categories taken together involve the transfer of information to and from symbolic form in a general context; the performance level is over 50 per cent. The third involves the same two transfers but to and from symbolic forms in which the conventions are specific to science; here the mean score dropped to about 40 per cent. In category 4, as soon as the need to use science concepts is superimposed on the process of interpretation, the performance level drops. This is perhaps hardly surprising. The effect is much more obvious in $4\delta_{CD}$ and $4\delta_{EF}$ (which relate to the physical and chemical concept regions) than it is in $4\delta_{AB}$. This could be because biology is better taught, or more widely taught, than physical science at age 13. But alternatively it may be because at this level the concepts met in biology are much more closely related to everyday life than those met in physics and chemistry; they are also less abstract, and much more likely to be discussed outside science lessons, so that through familiarity they become easier to use.

9.3 Sub-group differences

Sex differences   The performances of boys and girls in the survey were very similar. Any differences have been mentioned sub-category by sub-category as they became evident, and again in a more general way in Chapter 8.

The performance of boys appears to be higher than that of girls in four of the 13 sub-categories for which mean scores were computed: 1γ, 2α, 2β, and $4\delta_{CD}$, but it is only in the last of these that the difference reaches the five per cent level of statistical significance. Two of them, 2β and $4\delta_{CD}$, though making quite different demands in terms of process (estimation of physical quantities as opposed to interpretation and application) are heavily loaded with concepts and contexts associated with physics. 1γ, on the other hand, is only partly oriented towards physics. However there appears to be another factor involved which might be associated with a sex difference. 1γ is concerned with the use of symbolic representation in science: at age 13, questions usually involve the translation of information to or from diagrams — either section diagrams of general laboratory apparatus or circuit diagrams. The second type of diagram is clearly associated with physics and the sex bias in this area occurs in whichever direction the translation process is required. In the first type, however, where the physics association is not so strong, there was a consistent sex bias when the task required pupils to translate a 3-D drawing into a conventional section diagram, but not when the process was reversed. This effect may be related to the sex-linked difference in spatial ability which is consistently reported in research. But the question still remains — why do girls perform less well in these areas and in these areas alone?

It is interesting to compare these results with those obtained at age 11. The sub-category 1γ is not included in the framework of assessment for age 11 pupils for obvious reasons, and 2β and $4\delta_{CD}$ are not tested separately as they are at age 13; nevertheless the same bias in favour of boys was reported whenever questions required the use of physics concepts. It appears that the lower level of performance in physics is not something caused only by the treatment of the subject in secondary schools, but has its roots in very much earlier experiences.

Differences in performance associated with background variables   Differences in performance associated with region and location of schools are quite marked, but have already been discussed in Chapter 8.

No links were found, in this survey, between performance levels and certain of the variables investigated: overall capitation allowance, pupil-teacher ratio, size of school and type of school were among them. Because no links were found, it does not follow, of course, that none exist, and the results must be treated with some caution. The number of schools in some sub-groups was rather small, and the initial analysis has been made as though each variable were independent of all others, and this is clearly not so. This point was made in the discussion of the overlap of the regional and location variables in Chapter 8. In some cases also, there was little discrimination between schools in terms of the background variable in question. An example is science expenditure, where it was found that the vast majority of schools in the survey spent under £3 per pupil per year on all books, apparatus and other equipment. (This in itself is a remarkable item of information). If very few schools spend amounts above this range, it is clearly impossible to discover whether the extra expenditure might be effective or not.

It seems strange, perhaps, that 'type of comprehensive school' should not be associated with performance, in view of the different levels of resource (in terms of qualification of teachers, of laboratory and technician provision) reported for our 'junior' and 'senior' comprehensive schools. The 'senior' comprehensives among the survey schools seemed to be much better provided with qualified science teachers than were the 'junior' comprehensives. But it is the school as a whole which is well provided for, and not necessarily the 13 year old pupils within it. The qualified science teachers — especially the physical scientists — may have to devote all their time to examination classes. The same kind of argument may apply to laboratories and other resources. Conversely, in 'junior' comprehensive schools, of which middle schools form a proportion, 13 year old pupils may well benefit from a larger share of the science resources available in their school than their younger colleagues. The collection of information which relates directly to each of the survey pupils rather than to their schools as a whole would pose very considerable problems for members of staff in the sample schools; though clearly such information would help to illuminate the associations — or lack of association — found between performance and resource levels.

Many teachers will find it strange that the relationship between group size and level of performance which emerges from the survey is positive, a larger group being associated with higher performance levels. But it should not be assumed that such a link is directional — that is, that the relationship is one of cause and effect. The 'group size' in question is not necessarily the size of class in which the sample pupils were themselves taught — it is simply an average size for the year group in the sample schools. There are also a number of other factors to be taken into account: small classes may be the result of falling rolls, a circumstance often accompanied by loss of qualified science teachers; or they may occur more often in small schools in rural areas with inadequate facilities.

Why is high performance in all sub-categories associated with separate science courses as opposed to a combined or general course? Is it tied up with time spent, or qualifications of teachers, or the ability of the pupils to whom such courses are offered? It is true that within any one sample school, the curriculum tends to be uniform; but the initial decision to offer general or separate science courses may well have been influenced by knowledge of the ability range of the intake, or by the preferences of the teacher within the school. It does not follow from the results of the survey that a wholesale switch from general science to separate subjects would of itself give rise to a higher performance level.

There may be factors which tend to override all others of which it has not been possible to take account: teaching style, the general tone of the school, the amount of support a pupil can expect from parents, and general ability are some which would bear investigation. If they are thought to be important, there remains the problem of how to measure them in order to detect any association between them and performance levels.

The survey has raised a good many questions; it will be possible to answer some of them as data accumulated over the years becomes available for analysis. There are, however, other problems which may be better tackled by independent in-depth research methods.

9.4 Implications of the results

The report cannot give information about any individual pupil or school or local education authority, since anonymity was deliberately built into the programme. It does tell us something about the relationship of performance levels to certain background variables, although as already pointed out, there are limits to the interpretability of the results. There are, in addition, aspects of the work involved in the development of the monitoring framework, as well as some of the findings of the survey, which may be of immediate use.

There is general agreement that one of the more desirable outcomes of pupils' scientific education is that they should have developed the ability to apply the methods and concepts of science to problems arising in unfamiliar situations. Sometimes it happens that questions set to test scientific ability invite the kind of response that could be equalled by a well trained parrot: a response triggered by one word in the question. It is then difficult for the marker to discern whether a pupil has really understood either question or response. This is not to say that automatic recall of facts or relationships is of no value; it is often essential. However, it is important to be able to discover whether or not a pupil can put such recall to work to make sense of other information — and it is much harder to write questions which fulfil this aim. Members of the monitoring teams have spent considerable time in the attempt to design such questions in large numbers, and in the course of the exercise have written themselves guidelines in the form of the question descriptors listed in Chapter 6. Teachers engaged in the task of assessing their own pupils' performance may find that they can make use of ideas in that list.

Although recall does not figure in the assessment framework except as a prior requisite for some other activity, the report does describe the level and spread of performance on questions from seventeen different sub-categories. It may prove valuable to consider these performances in relation to the demands and assumptions of the school syllabus in current use, or to any that are being considered for adoption. For example, sometimes skills are assumed but never directly tested. The generally low level of performance on sub-category 2β (estimating quantities) suggests that pupils have little feeling for the concepts of mass, area or volume. Lack of confidence — perhaps just lack of familiarity — at this basic level may underlie difficulties which normally only become apparent during the assessment of more complex abilities. A further instance of this effect occurs in connection with the use of observation. In sub-category 3γ, pupils often seem unable to interpret observations because they have failed to notice relevant changes. In 3β, it is apparent that pupils are not systematic in taking notice of similarities and differences when left to themselves; for example they seldom make use of senses other than sight unless directed to do so. There seems to be a general absence of self-directed systematic observation. It is possible that if relatively simple failings such as the ones quoted were to be diagnosed at an early stage, the consequent difficulties could be reduced.

One clear pattern that emerged from the results is concerned with the interaction of process and content. The range of processes represented in the framework appears to be reasonable for the age group, and when tested in general contexts yields reasonable levels of performance. The range of concepts represented also appears to be reasonable — or at any rate it reflects a consensus of opinion. For some of the processes a reasonable level of performance is obtained using these concepts. But the framework allows questions to be set which demand the complete range of processes across all the concept areas, in novel situations. It seems that for some of these processes, the addition of a concept load, in a context not normally associated with the concept, causes the level of performance to drop dramatically. If this finding is substantiated, does it have implications for curriculum development? Must the range of concepts now included in a school science course be reduced in order to balance any shift in favour of process? Or could familiarity and practice so change the situation that the present spread of concepts could be maintained alongside a greater emphasis on process, without a corresponding drop in the average level of performance?

9.5 Concluding comments

This survey should be seen as the first of a series rather than a definitive study. In subsequent years it will be possible to add to the information available; the report for 1981, for example, will include an account of the individual practical assessment of performance of investigations. An investigation into the relationships between sub-category results is being undertaken. More comparison across ages, both at question and sub-category level, is being built into the monitoring programme. An increase in the number of questions may make it possible to identify more clearly patterns of performance arising as a consequence of the interaction between process and content.

As the data accumulates, further analyses will be carried out to investigate the effects of some of the background variables already discussed. However, the large number of sub-categories involved in the framework, with the consequently large variety of test packages to be administered to pupils, limits the amount of information which analysis can yield. As already pointed out, one function of the monitoring exercise has been to expose problems which can only be properly explored by separate research studies, specially designed for the job and conducted outside the monitoring framework. Apart from these, many questions remain to be answered. Some of the problems involved have conflicting requirements, so they cannot all be tackled. We are faced with a problem of optimisation: of choosing the most useful design for future monitoring programmes. This will need careful consideration of the possibilities, which we hope will be strongly influenced by public debate.

Appendix 1

Development and selection of the science questions

The categories and sub-categories of the assessment framework are outlined in Chapter 6. It is with this framework in mind that questions have been developed for use in the monitoring programme. Questions are subjected to a number of procedures in order to check that they are suitable.

Each question is first reviewed ('shredded') by a small group of people (usually including one or two team members and practising teachers) who comment on its suitability with regard to content, format, language and so on.

Once approved by such a group, a question is included with others in a 'test package' and administered to a small number of pupils (about 30) in two or three volunteer schools. On the basis of these pupils' responses the mark scheme is developed and finalised.

Questions belonging to the same sub-category should ideally share a common mark scale if they are to make equal contributions to the sub-category test score when they are chosen for use in a survey. However, it was decided that, given the variety of question types which could be written for some sub-categories, it would impose artificial constraints on question development if all questions were required to have a common maximum mark. The original ('raw', 'natural') mark allocation is therefore allowed to vary from one question to another, so that one question might, for example, carry a maximum mark of six, while another might carry a maximum of four or five or three. This means that if equal weight is to be given to each question in a test the natural scores achieved by individual pupils on individual questions have to be transformed on to a common mark scale. The way in which such transformations are to be carried out is decided question by question by a group of question writers in the team. In most cases, a common scale is used with marks ranging from 0–3. For some sub-categories, (4δ for example) two groups of questions have to be distinguished— those with a natural maximum mark of one whose scores are not transformed (usually multiple-choice questions), and those with natural maximum marks of three or above whose scores are transformed, when necessary, onto a 0–3 scale.

The validity of the questions is judged by a group of science educators. Each question is scrutinised by seven people, working independently, who either assign it to a specific sub-category or else indicate that such an assignment is not, in their opinion, possible. A question is considered validated if five out of seven 'validators' assign it to the same sub-category as that intended by the team. Questions can be rejected completely at this stage.

Questions are also trialled on a large scale, by administration in test packages to between 100 and 200 pupils for written tests and to about 90 pupils for practical tests. The criterion of suitability for use in a sub-category test for which a mean performance level is to be computed is that the correlation between pupils' transformed scores on an individual question and their total test scores for the relevant sub-category should reach 0.3. Questions failing this statistical criterion are rejected.

Finally, every suitable question has attached to it a series of descriptive 'labels', on which agreement has been reached by a group of question writers from the monitoring team. These labels indicate, for example, the relevant sub-category and question descriptor, the question's maximum raw and transformed marks, its transformation algorithm, required apparatus or other resources, and so on. In addition, a synopsis and a number of keywords are provided.

The Question Bank which contains all the available science questions is in two parts: the question texts, diagrams and mark schemes are manually filed, while the descriptive labels associated with the questions are computer-stored. These labels, in combination, describe the totality of questions available. Each question is given a unique identification number and this provides the link between the two sections of the bank.

The computer-storage of question labels serves a major function in the monitoring exercise in allowing the automatic production of random selections of questions. These selections form the sub-category tests to be used in the surveys.

An appropriate set of labels is used to identify all the questions which together form the 'pool' for a particular sub-category. From within this pool, questions are randomly selected to produce the collection of questions known as the 'sub-category test'. Such random selection is usually subject to a minimum, but necessary, number of constraints to avoid, for example, the chance production of a question selection which may carry too great a burden in terms of apparatus provision or testing time, or which may contain unsuitable emphasis on one kind of question or task at the expense of some other.

A complete sub-category test (one which contains a sufficient number of questions to represent it in a single survey) is usually sub-divided into two or more shorter tests, and any selected pupil will take only one of these within an hour-long test package. In 1980, the sub-tests within one sub-category were created separately and independently, and were of similar composition in terms of the number and variety of questions they contained.

Appendix 2

The organisation and logistics of testing

Written tests

<u>Testing.</u>   In each school taking part in the survey a group of 27 pupils took paper and pencil tests, although only nine received any one package of questions. Tests were administered by a teacher on the staff of the school, who had earlier received written instructions about the conduct of the test, of which the following is an extract.

"If different written tests have been sent to your school, they may be given at the same time. If some pupils have been designated to answer two tests, the order in which they do them is not important.

We should like every pupil to have sufficient time to do all of which he or she is capable, so there is no time limit for the tests. However, we expect most pupils to finish within one hour. Please provide for those finishing early by arranging some quiet work for them.

Before the pupils begin the test, help them fill in the boxes on the cover. Write the date on the board and give any assistance necessary to write their age.

When the cover has been completed, tell the pupils to turn to the next page and to read the instructions carefully. Please note that different tests have different instructions.

We are anxious that pupils' responses should not be unduly affected by poor reading ability. Therefore, if any pupil asks for help, please read the instructions or any of the questions to him or her privately, once slowly whilst pointing out words, and a second time at normal speed. For pupils who ask for individual words, these can be read without giving the whole question.

Emphasise that the pupils should try all the questions and thus if they are stuck on certain questions they should leave these, go on and possibly return to the difficult ones later."

Each test booklet had on its first page an indication of any special aspects of the questions inside and of the kind of responses required. Answers were written in spaces provided in the booklet.

Any given package of questions was distributed in two different versions: in one the order of the questions was the reverse of that in the other.

<u>Marking.</u>   Experienced teachers were recruited from all over the country to mark the scripts. They attended a training meeting at Chelsea College during which they each marked a number of scripts as a check on reliability. Most questions were marked using a numerical mark scheme, and for some an additional category marking scheme was used. Markers allocated different types

of response to different categories, each of which had been pre-defined and given a code letter. Both code letter and numerical score were entered on the marking sheets. Subsequently a proportion of the scripts was marked by three different markers in turn, so that the extent of variation for different types of question could later be assessed.

Practical tests

Organisation of the tests.   There were two different kinds of practical tests, one relating to category 2 and one to category 3. Though different in terms of the demands made on the pupil, they were similar in their method of organisation. Each test lasted about 1¼ hours and was organised as a 'circus'.

In a circus each pupil starts at a different station — a numbered bench space supplied with apparatus for a particular question (or questions)—and moves to the next after a given interval of time. The exercise continues until all pupils have had the chance to tackle all questions. The smooth running of the test depends on there being as many stations in the complete circuit as there are pupils to test, and on the task (or tasks) at each station taking a similar time. It had been found by trial and error that eight minutes was the optimum time per station for 13 year old pupils; this means that, if nine pupils are to be tested in a school, a circus can be completed in just over an hour. Compared with an arrangement in which all pupils progress through the tasks in the same sequence, the amount of apparatus needed is reduced by a factor of nine.

Provision of apparatus.   Consideration was given to the suggestion that schools themselves be asked to provide the equipment needed for the tests, as is the case in public examinations. However, this would have put a considerable burden on the schools, as well as raising difficulties of standardisation and it was decided instead to ask the science teachers who take on the administration (and of course the marking) to carry the apparatus with them from school to school. Once arrived in the laboratory, the administrator sets out the apparatus at the nine stations. This is made as easy as possible by the system of packaging used by the supplier, Messrs. Philip Harris Biological Limited. Materials for each task are packed in a custom-built cardboard box. Since each pupil in each school visited by the administrator must be equally well served, and since there is no opportunity for washing glassware between visits, provision must be made for the necessary replacements. Thus, if a pupil needs, for example, eight clean test-tubes for a particular task, the administrator will need a supply of 72 for each school visited, for that one question alone. Replacements are also needed for reagents, and for other consumables. It is easy to visualise the chaos that would result were the packaging arrangements not of a very high standard.

Administration in category 2 tests.   For some of the tasks, more was required of the administrator than the simple setting out of apparatus. The extent of the checking to be done before the pupils arrived is indicated on the summary which follows.

Summary of checks to be made

Before you begin, list pupil numbers on scripts with pupil letters on labels

Stations	Services needed	Checks needed		
		Before session	During session	After session
1. How and what	Gas point (for manometer — none used)	All readings after setting up the instruments — see check list		
2. Set up	Gas point — none used	Check apparatus is dismantled	Check apparatus dismantled. Mark each pupil — see check list	
3. Deliver	Water	Label filter papers A−J (exclude I)		Mark 'product'
4. LAG	Window — for microscope		Position slide B and *de*-focus for each pupil	
5. Kaleidoscope				
6. Guesstimate		Fill flask with water at 40°C		
7. Pink fizz	Sink (helpful — not essential)	Fill washbottles and dropping bottles		Tip contents of bottles away in case they leak *
8. Blackout				
9. Blue	Water Gas (teacher observed)	Brief teacher. Provide instructions and check lists	Teacher observes, records & replaces	Collect check lists from teacher

*This kit has litre bottles included in it; larger ones for replacement liquids are in a separate box & will not be needed every session.

An apparatus check-list was provided for each visit, on which administrators were to record the value of readings on some instruments, and to check the state of some other arrangements before the circus began. This check-list is reproduced opposite.

Recruitment of administrators. A pair of administrators was recruited from each of twelve local education authorities, suitably located with respect to the schools selected for the survey. One of each pair was equipped with apparatus for one category 2 test and one category 3 test, while the other was equipped for two

SAC2. Apparatus Check List (Please enclose with marked scripts)

Station 1 How and What	Standard value	Actual value	Mid-session check	Post session check
			(Tick if no change noticed)	
a Measuring cylinder 1201	42 cm³			
b Forcemeter 1202 (Stretch band between bosses)	27 N			
c Manometer 1204 (If no gas, tilt and cork)	? cm water			
d Thermometer 1205 (Fill flask, insert bung)	35°C			
e Stopclock 1206 (Label, wind up)	2 m 23 s			
f Ammeter 1207	0.38 A			
g Voltmeter 1208	3.8 V			

Other stations to be checked before circus starts	(Tick only needed)
2. Set up (apparatus dismantled)	
3. Deliver (filter papers labelled A−J)	
4. LAG ('B' in position & instrument defocussed)	
5. Guesstimate (flask filled with water at 40°C)	
7. Pink fizz (washbottles & dropping bottles full)	
9. Blue (teacher briefed & supplied with lists)	

different category 3 tests. Each administrator had sufficient materials to last for ten sessions of each test, because during the fortnight in which tests took place, up to ten different schools could be visited.

Some administrators had longer journeys than others and sometimes an overnight stay was necessary. In spite of this, and of the heavy traffic encountered by those visiting inner city schools, no administrator failed to arrive at the school at the appointed time.

Appendix 3

The selection of pupils for testing in this survey involved two stages of sampling. The first stage required the stratified random selection of a sample of schools with pupils in the 13 year old age group, the second the random selection of appropriate numbers of pupils from within each of these schools. In other words, the survey sample was selected by a two-stage stratified cluster sampling scheme.

At the school selection stage, the population of English schools was first stratified by reference to three descriptive variables: region, school type and school size.

The three regions of north, midlands and south were defined as indicated at the beginning of Chapter 7. The school type classifications used were: comprehensive, other maintained and independent. In addition, the comprehensive school sector was further sub-divided into two size-of-age-group categories: 5–180 pupils, and 181 plus pupils.

Schools were selected from within each of the resulting sub-groups in numbers which reflected sub-group size. In other words, the proportion of 'large midlands comprehensives' in the survey sample was intended to reflect the proportion of such schools existing in the population as a whole.

As Table A.3.1 shows, 580 schools were actually invited to participate in the survey, and 448 of these eventually formed the participating sample.

Table A.3.1 *School participation*

Invited to take part	580
Unable to take part	72
No reply	30
Initial agreement, but withdrew later	12
Tests not returned or returned not completed	18
Tests received	448

Figure A.3.1 illustrates the regional composition of both school sample and population: the composition of the sample reflecting very closely that of the school population from which it was drawn.

The compositions of school sample and population in terms of different types of school are shown in Figure A.3.2. As explained in Chapter 7, for reporting purposes the comprehensive school sector was divided into those schools with an age of transfer of 12/13/14 ('junior' comprehensives) and those with a higher

Figure A.3.1 *Comparison of school sample with population in terms of regional distribution.*

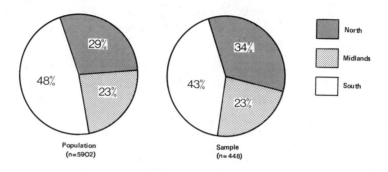

Figure A.3.2 *School type distribution with sample and population.*

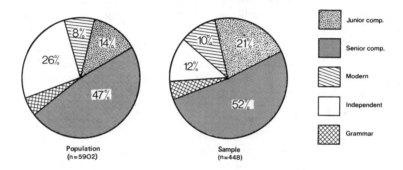

leaving age of 16 or over ('senior' comprehensives). Figure A.3.2 includes this distinction.

The most notable feature illustrated in Figure A.3.2 is the large preponderance of 'senior' comprehensives (mostly 11−16 and 11−18 comprehensives) in both the school sample and its population (about half of all schools).

Sixteen different test packages were administered for survey purposes (in addition to one or two packages which were to provide further sources of useful research data). Each sample school took at least three different packages, and occasionally more than three if some of their pupils were to take two tests (there was a proportion of double testing of pupils in order to provide data for the later exploration of relationships between, for example, practical and written test performances).

The number of pupils in any school who would attempt the same test package was fixed at nine by reference to the size used for practical circuses, so that a school would have provided 27 pupils in total for survey testing.

Within each participating school, pupils were randomly selected on the basis of specific birth dates from all of those of the appropriate age in the school (ie those born between 1 September 1966 and 31 August 1967 inclusive). To make the selection the school was asked to list all pupils of the relevant age who were born on the first day of any month, followed by all of those born on the second day of any month, then those born on the third day, and so on until the required number of pupils was reached. The names of the selected pupils remained known only to the school concerned, all other parties having access only to the pupils' unique identifying numbers.

The only pupils explicitly excluded from the survey were those in special schools or in units designated as 'special' within normal schools. However, the headteacher of each selected school was told that discretion could be used in withdrawing particular pupils from the testing sessions if it was felt that participation would cause undue distress.

One other procedural point which should be mentioned here is the method of handling pupil absentees. Pupils who were in the sample but were absent on the day on which the school undertook a written test session were given the relevant test if they attended school at any time within two weeks of the school's main test session. This was an attempt to avoid introducing an unnecessary bias into the pupil sample which would occur if, for example, persistent absentees happened also to be the lower performers in general. Economic reasons prevented such a procedure being adopted in the case of practical test sessions, which involved visits by trained administrators. For practical tests only, pupils absent on the day of a test session were replaced by reserve pupils who had previously been listed by the school.

11 078 pupils were tested in the survey, after the schools' withdrawal of 28 pupils and the absence of 322 others. 172 pupils were substituted for absentees in the practical test sessions. Clerical errors of one kind or another resulted in the overall loss of test results for about three per cent of the pupils at the final analysis state, the loss per test package varying between one per cent and five per cent (the most usual being three per cent to four per cent).

Table A.3.2 provides details of the actual numbers of scripts which were involved at the analysis stage for each of the 16 survey test packages.

Table A.3.2 *Pupil and school samples at the analysis stage*[1]

Category	Test Package	Pupils	Schools
1	1	469	54
	2	567	64
	3	573	64
2	1	459	50
3	1	430	48
	2	531	59
	3	486	53
4	1	756	83
	2	835	91
	3	693	83
	4	679	81
	5	772	87
	6	775	86
5	1	842	78
	2	637	89
	3	798	96

[1] The numbers of pupils and schools sum to more than the actual total survey sample sizes, because schools took three or more of the sixteen test packages and many pupils within these schools attempted more than one test.

208

Appendix 4

School number:

Assessment of Performance Unit, Department of Education and Science

ASSESSMENT OF PERFORMANCE IN SCIENCE

SCHOOL QUESTIONNAIRE

Age 13 survey

It is an essential part of the Science Monitoring exercise to relate the test results to information about the general provision for science in schools. This questionnaire is designed to gather such information.

If a question has a number of coded alternative responses none of which exactly describes your particular circumstances please select the one which is closest to the actual situation. If a particular question cannot be answered in the form required then please leave the appropriate box(es) blank and attach an explanatory note to the questionnaire.

We realise that completing the questionnaire is an extra burden imposed on you, but we hope that you will understand that it is only with such information that full use can be made of the survey results.

Thank you for your help.

APU SCIENCE: AGE 13 SURVEY 1980
SCHOOL QUESTIONNAIRE

1. Please provide the following general school information.
   - (a) *What is the age-range of your school?*
   - (b) *How many pupils are on your school roll?*
   - (c) *How many **teaching groups for science** is your age 12/13 year group divided into?*

Teachers and Science-Teaching Resources

2. For the purposes of this question, a formally qualified science teacher is defined as a science or applied science graduate *or* a teacher with a teaching certificate with a main course in a science subject.
   - (a) *How many "full time equivalent" teachers do you have on your staffing establishment?*
   - (b) *How many of these teachers are currently involved in teaching science?*
   - (c) *How many of the teachers in (b) hold formal science qualifications?*

3. For the purpose of this question, a laboratory is to be considered as a working space where pupils can do small-group and individual practical work with services (gas, water, electricity).
   - (a) *How many laboratories does your school have?*
   - (b) *How many of these laboratories can accommodate 20 or more pupils?*
   - (c) *How many technicians work in your science department?*

4. When answering this question, please count a double teaching period as two single periods.
   - (a) *How long, in minutes, is a single teaching period in your school?*
   - (b) *How many periods are there in your timetable cycle?*
   - (c) *What is the total number of science periods your 12/13 year-group **as a whole** receives during a full timetable cycle?*

5. Do any of your staff use one or more of the following out-of-school resources as part of science courses up to age 16? Use codes Y or N as appropriate in each case.
   - (a) *Field centres*
   - (b) *Industrial visits*
   - (c) *Link courses with colleges of F E*
     Other — please specify:

6. For each of the technicians indicated in 3(c), please provide the following information:
   - (a) *Total hours/week the technician is employed*
   - (b) *Total weeks/year the technician is employed*
   - (c) *Does the technician work during school holidays?*
   - (d) *Please estimate the hours/week spent by the technician in work for non-science departments.*

N.B. Use one set of boxes for each technician.

Financial Resources

If yours is an independent school, please provide the total amount of money received by your school for teaching resources as an answer to question 7 and ignore question 9.

7. Please indicate the total amount spent by the school in each year from the LEA allowance on teaching resources.

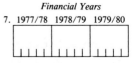

8. What was the amount spent by the science (or science subject) departments from this allowance?

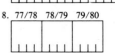

9. If any additional grant was received by the science department from any source (eg LEA, industry, parents' association) please indicate the total amount here.

10. Please estimate the amount spent by the science department on the following items:

(i)   Paper, stationery, and consumable reprographic materials

(ii)   Text books and resource books (excluding those in school library)

(iii)   Apparatus, equipment and consumable materials other than those in (i).

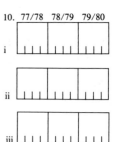

11. If your school has been involved in any kind of restructing (eg a merger with another school) which would explain major changes in your budget figures over the last three years, please describe the circumstances:

Comments

If you would like to comment on any difficulties you experienced in completing the questionnaire, or if you would like to provide information not asked for in the questionnaire but which you feel relevant, then please do so here:

Appendix 5

Notes on the survey analysis

The survey data is held on the Amdahl V/7 computer at the University of Leeds and all analyses were conducted on this machine.

Question detail   The individual question results reported in Chapters 1 to 5 are raw sample statistics and were produced with the aid of SPSS (Nie *et al.,* 1975) The function of this information in the report is principally to illustrate the nature and variety of task embraced by the titles of the various science sub-categories.

The school questionnaire   The school questionnaire data was also analysed using SPSS. As the school sample was produced by a simple random sampling procedure within each stratum it would be appropriate to apply the usual χ^2 and other significance tests to the data if the statistical significance of any of the sub-group differences is of interest.

The sub-category mean performance estimates   Population mean performance estimates and their associated estimated variances were produced test package by test package for the sub-categories contained in them. Where a sub-category was represented in two or more different test packages, the separate, independent performance estimates produced from these were combined.

When producing the population estimates for each science sub-category in each test package (after initially adjusting all question scores onto a common mark scale — as explained in Appendix 1) it was necessary to weight the raw sample data to take account of the stratified cluster-sampling scheme which was used in sample selection. The method adopted here to produce a population mean estimate for any particular sub-group ('north', 'junior comprehensive', etc.) was first to multiply each school mean by that school's size (ie by the number of pupils in that school of the appropriate age), to sum the resulting figures over all schools in that sub-group sample, and then to divide the whole by the total number of pupils of the appropriate age in those sample schools (technically termed a biased ratio estimate). Estimates were produced in this way for sample breakdowns by the stratifying variables, ie school location, school type and region. Weighted variance estimates were produced simultaneously — the relevant formula being found in any text on survey sampling (for example, Kish 1965, Cochran 1977, ch. 9; Hansen, Hurwitz and Madow 1953, Vol.2, ch.6; Deming 1960).

The overall population mean and variance estimates, and those for boys and girls separately, were produced by appropriately weighting the separate regional estimates before combining.

The sub-category mean estimates reported throughout Chapters 1 to 5, and particularly in Chapter 8, were produced by averaging the appropriate sub-test estimates, and the standard errors associated with these final mean scores were produced in the usual way for an average of independent variates by dividing the square root of the sum of the separate variance estimates by n (where n is the number of sub-tests involved).

Design effect   Kish (1965) first introduced the notion of the *design effect* of a survey sampling scheme. The design effect of a sampling scheme indicates the degree to which population estimates based on the resulting sample are more or less accurate than they would be had they been based on a simple random sample of similar overall size.

A stratified sampling scheme, for example, can often result in a more efficient sample in estimation terms than a simple random sampling procedure, while a cluster sampling scheme usually produces a less efficient sample in this sense. The design effect is defined as the ratio of the variance associated with a population estimate based on the sample produced by a particular sampling scheme to the variance which would have been associated with that estimate had it been based on a simple random sample of similar size.

The design effects for this survey vary from sub-category to sub-category, ranging from 3.6 to 4.4. This means that the standard errors quoted in Chapter 8 are about twice as large, and consequently the confidence limits twice as wide, as they would have been had the performance estimates concerned been based on similarly-sized simple random samples of pupils.

A design effect of 2 was applied to raw sample standard errors to produce estimated standard errors for the performance estimates of pupil sub-groups for which no population information was available (eg for pupils attending schools with average group-sizes for science work of *fewer than 25* or *25 or more*). In other words, the standard errors produced by treating the respective pupil sub-samples as though they were simple random samples were doubled in these cases.

Links between sub-category results and questionnaire data   Data resulting from a sample survey of this kind, involving the administration of many different test packages, has limited potential for the exploration of relationships between test performances and various pupil and school characteristics. In this particular survey the potential for this kind of work was rendered rather more limited by the need to incorporate a pilot survey element into the package administration design. Each test package was administered to about nine pupils in any school, and the total school sample for any one package was between 50 and 100 schools. The sub-sample of 'senior' comprehensive schools in each case was about one-half of the total sub-sample size. It will be appreciated that with these small numbers there were often insufficient numbers of schools in every cross-classification cell to allow any investigation of association between test performance and some of the school background variables. Also it was noted in Chapter 7 that there was often little variation across schools for certain of the potential background variables. In view of this, it should be said that the absence in this report of evidence of associations of one kind or another does *not* imply that no such association in fact exists. Where the statistical significance of a comparison is indicated, this is at the five per cent level.

Table A.5.1 *Summary of some survey results*

Sub-category		Sex			Regions			Location[1]		School size[2]		Pupil teacher ratio[1]			% uptake free school meals[1]		
		Overall	Boys	Girls	North	Midl	South	Met	Non-met	<180	181+	<15 17.4	15–	17.5+ 6%	<4%	4%–	>6%
1α	mean	58.2	58.5	57.9	55.8	59.4	59.4	52.6	59.5	54.3	55.2	55.2	53.3	55.2	60.1	57.5	49.5
	s.e.	1.1	1.4	1.3	1.7	2.0	1.9	1.5	1.2	1.6	2.0	2.7	2.4	1.9	2.0	2.3	1.9
1β	mean	53.3	53.6	52.9	48.0	54.0	56.9	44.3	54.9	45.3	50.6	45.9	45.9	48.8	58.2	47.1	39.0
	s.e.	1.5	1.9	2.1	2.5	2.8	2.6	2.1	1.7	2.1	2.8	3.4	3.0	2.5	2.7	3.2	2.7
1γ	mean	42.8	40.4	44.9	39.9	42.6	45.0	36.3	44.5	36.0	39.3	35.3	35.3	38.0	43.0	37.5	34.5
	s.e.	1.3	1.5	1.6	2.1	2.1	2.2	1.8	1.3	1.9	2.2	3.2	2.9	2.2	2.3	2.1	1.7
2α	mean	51.3	49.4	53.0	46.6	49.5	55.8	47.3	51.0			45.7	49.6	49.7	54.1	50.0	37.6
	s.e.	1.8	2.2	2.3	2.7	3.6	2.2	3.1	1.8			3.3	2.9	2.3	2.5	3.9	3.3
2β	mean	27.7	25.5	29.6	26.0	28.3	28.5	26.5	27.0			24.2	24.4	23.8	28.0	27.5	22.5
	s.e.	1.3	1.8	1.8	2.1	2.7	1.9	2.2	1.5			2.8	2.5	1.9	2.2	3.5	3.6
3β	mean	53.4	54.1	52.9	50.3	55.7	54.4	52.2	53.5			49.1	51.7	52.2	56.0	54.5	49.0
	s.e.	0.7	1.0	1.0	1.1	1.4	1.2	1.2	1.1			2.3	1.7	1.4	1.4	2.0	1.7
3γ	mean	51.0	51.6	50.5	45.9	53.3	53.3	48.5	51.5			44.0	48.0	48.0	53.0	50.0	43.1
	s.e.	0.9	1.2	1.3	1.3	1.4	1.6	1.4	1.3			2.6	2.2	1.6	1.7	2.2	2.0
4α	mean	40.5	40.2	40.8	38.8	39.6	42.4	38.1	40.8	34.8	38.6	33.3	37.1	38.6	40.0	39.2	31.9
	s.e.	0.8	1.0	1.0	1.2	1.5	1.2	1.1	0.8	1.1	1.5	2.0	1.6	1.3	1.3	1.7	1.4
$4b_{AB}$	mean	37.2	36.8	37.6	35.3	36.5	38.8	34.3	37.4	33.5	34.3	31.7	33.9	35.7	37.0	35.3	34.0
	s.e.	0.7	0.8	1.1	1.0	1.2	1.1	1.0	0.7	1.0	1.4	2.0	1.5	1.2	1.3	1.5	1.3
$4b_{CD}$	mean	32.5	30.3	34.5	30.5	31.2	34.5	29.3	32.9	27.8	30.4	27.4	29.6	30.0	31.3	30.0	29.5
	s.e.	0.7	0.9	1.0	1.3	1.2	1.2	1.0	0.8	0.9	1.3	1.9	1.6	1.2	1.3	1.5	1.2
$4b_{EF}$	mean	33.7	33.2	34.1	31.5	33.4	35.4	30.3	34.2	30.0	30.4	28.3	30.4	30.9	44.0	31.5	27.0
	s.e.	0.7	0.9	1.0	1.1	1.3	1.2	0.9	0.8	0.9	1.4	1.8	1.5	1.1	1.3	1.6	1.2
5α	mean	48.4	49.1	47.5	47.1	47.1	50.1	46.1	47.6	44.4	45.3	41.8	46.5	43.5	47.0	46.8	41.0
	s.e.	0.9	1.2	1.3	1.3	1.5	1.5	1.0	1.1	1.0	1.4	2.0	1.5	1.2	0.8	2.1	1.7
5β	mean	45.4	46.1	44.5	43.8	43.3	47.6	41.6	45.6	39.3	43.3	37.9	41.6	42.6	45.0	44.5	40.8
	s.e.	0.7	1.1	1.0	1.1	1.4	1.3	1.0	0.8	0.9	1.3	1.9	1.5	1.3	1.4	1.8	1.4

[1] Comprehensive schools only
[2] Senior comprehensives only; school size defined by size of year group. Insufficient sample sizes to produce figures for practical sub-categories.

Appendix 6

Standard errors, confidence limits and statistical significance

The mean performance figures presented in Chapter 8 are based on a sample of pupils, and therefore are estimates of the mean performance levels of the population of pupils in the various sub-groups discussed in that Chapter. The accuracy of a particular estimate will depend on the size of the pupil sample on which it is based, on the degree of 'clustering' of pupils in schools allowed in the sampling scheme and on the degree of variation of performance found among these pupils and schools.

The *standard error* associated with a particular performance estimate provides an indication of its accuracy. On the basis of statistical theory, there is a 95 per cent probability that the true mean performance level will be within a range of about two standard errors either side of the estimated value. Thus, if we have an estimated mean level of performance of 61 per cent with an associated standard error of 1.6, then we can be 95 per cent certain that the actual mean level of performance for that pupil sub-group lies within the range 61± 3.2, ie within the range 57.8 to 64.2. This range is called the 95 per cent *confidence interval* for the performance estimate, and these intervals have been shown in the graphical presentations of Chapter 8.

A difference in the estimated mean performance levels of two pupil sub-groups is said to be *statistically significant* at the five per cent level if such a difference could in theory occur by chance at most five times in a hundred. In order to establish whether or not a difference in estimated mean performance levels is statistically significant, we must first calculate the standard error associated with this difference. If a performance difference is larger than twice its standard error, then the difference is said to be statistically significant (at the five per cent level).

A useful visual indicator of statistical significance is provided by the confidence intervals of the performance estimates. Where the confidence intervals do not overlap, or overlap only very slightly, then the performance estimates concerned are likely to be significantly different from each other in the statistical sense.

A cautionary note to readers might be appropriate at this point.

Firstly, the criterial level of statistical significance applied throughout this report is a fairly arbitrary, though commonly used, one. If a more severe one had been adopted (the one per cent level, for example) then many of the performance differences identified as statistically significant in this report could lose this 'status'. Similarly, had a more lenient level been applied (the ten per cent level, say) then many performance differences which were not commented upon would become statistically significant.

Secondly, many of the performance differences which proved not to be statistically significant at the five per cent level had high standard errors associated with them. It could be that population differences in performance levels actually exist in some cases, but that the sample sizes available for performance estimation were too small for these differences to be detected. Sometimes, for example, despite the fact that few individual performance differences reach statistical significance, the consistency in the direction of performance differences across the profile of sub-categories can be taken to suggest an underlying population difference (see, for example, the findings for the two curriculum groups reported in Chapter 8).

Finally, it should be recognised that *statistical* significance is not synonymous with *educational* significance, and this has a bearing both on the interpretability of many of the findings and on their implications for science education.

Appendix 7

APU Steering Group on Science

Mr T A Burdett, HMI	Chairman
Professor P J Black	Director, Centre for Science Education, Chelsea College, University of London
Mr N B Evans, HMI	HM Inspectorate (Wales)
Mr A R Hall	Sir Joseph Williamson's School, Rochester
Sister M Hurst	Schools Council
Mr J Jeffery	Pocklington School, Pocklington
Professor D Layton	Director, Centre for Studies in Science Education, University of Leeds
Mr C Parsons, HMI	HM Inspectorate
Dr B Prestt	Manchester Polytechnic
Mr J C Taylor	Manchester LEA
Mr K Wild	Staffordshire LEA
Mr G D Williams	Wellesbourne County Primary School, Liverpool

Appendix 8

Monitoring Services Unit staff at the time of the survey

Mrs Barbara Bloomfield   Head of Unit
Mrs Anne Baker   Deputy
Miss Susan Darby
Mrs Mary Hall
Miss Elizabeth Evans   Secretary

Appendix 9

Members of the APU Consultative Committee

Professor J Dancy (Chairman)	School of Education, University of Exeter
Miss J E L Baird	Joint General Secretary, AMMA
Mr P Boulter	Director of Education, Cumbria (ACC)
Mrs J Bushby	Councillor, Bromsgrove District Council
Mr P J Casey	Deputy Director (Education and Training) CBI
Mr R G Cave	Former Senior Education Officer, Cambridgeshire
Mr L Cooper	Deputy Headmaster, Sherburn High School (NAS/UWT)
Mr H Dowson	Deputy Headmaster, Earl Marshal School, Sheffield (NUT)
Professor S J Eggleston	Department of Education, University of Keele
Mr P J P Eley	National Confederation of Parent-Teacher Associations
Mr A Evans	Education Department, NUT
Mr G S Foster	Headmaster, The Towers School, Ashford (NUT)
Mr G Hainsworth	Director of Education, Gateshead (AMA)
Mr K S Hopkins	Deputy Director of Education, Mid-Glamorgan (WJEC)
Councillor P Horton	Sheffield Metropolitan District Council (AMA)
Mr C Humphrey	Director of Education, Solihull (AMA)
Dr K Jones	Parent and Doctor, Sheffield
Mr T M Jones	Headmaster, Werneth Junior School, Oldham (NUT)
Mr J A Lawton	Kent County Council (ACC)
Mr G M Lee	Doncaster Metropolitan Institute of Higher Education (NATFHE)
Mr S Maclure	Editor, Times Educational Supplement
Mrs R Mills	Consultant Economist
Mr M J Pipes	Headmaster, City of Portsmouth School for Boys (NAHT)
Dr W Roy	Headmaster, The Hewett School, Norwich (NUT)
Professor M D Shipman	Department of Education, University of Warwick
Miss A C Shrubsole	Principal, Homerton College
Mr F A Smithies	Assistant General Secretary (Education) NAS/UWT
Mr T P Snape	Headmaster, King Edward VI School, Totnes (SHA)
Professor J Wrigley	School of Education, University of Reading
Mr A Yates	Director, National Foundation for Educational Research

Appendix 10

Note on the APU

The Assessment of Performance Unit (APU) was set up in 1975 within the Department of Education and Science. It aims to provide information about general levels of performance of children and young people at school and how these change over the years.

The terms of reference of the APU are:
'to promote the development of methods of assessing and monitoring the achievement of children at school, and to seek to identify the incidence of under-achievement'.

Associated with these terms of reference are the following tasks:

1. To identify and appraise existing instruments and methods of assessment which may be relevant for these purposes.

2. To sponsor the creation of new instruments and techniques for assessment having due regard to statistical and sampling methods.

3. To promote the conduct of assessment in co-operation with local education authorities and teachers.

4. To identify significant differences of achievement related to the circumstances in which children learn, including the incidence of underachievement, and to make the findings available to those concerned with resource allocation within government departments, local education authorities and schools.

The APU monitoring programme has been concerned to reflect the breadth of the curriculum in schools and to display the wide range of pupil performance. The assessment model adopted by the APU is based on a number of lines of development. At the present time, monitoring is proceeding in mathematics, language and science, and the first survey of children's performance in their first foreign modern language will take place in 1983. The assessment of pupils' aesthetic and physical development, and of their abilities in the field of design and technology is under consideration; but there is no commitment to monitoring in these areas.

The assessment procedures in science are developed by the Science Monitoring Teams based at Chelsea College, University of London and at the University of Leeds. The work is steered by a group consisting of teachers, advisers, teacher trainers, educational researchers and HMI. The work of all groups and the progress of the monitoring surveys is supervised by a small management team, which includes the administrative and professional heads of the Unit together with the chairman of each group. More generally, the APU is advised by a Consultative Committee, which is broadly representative of education, industry, commerce and parental concern.

In producing national pictures of aspects of pupil performance, the Unit does not report on the performance of individual pupils, schools or local education authorities. Survey results are published regularly, in the form of reports, by Her Majesty's Stationery Office. This is the first report to be published on the science performance of 13 year olds. The report of the first survey on the science performance of 11 year olds was published in December 1981. Publication of the first science survey report at age 15 is expected later this year.

Further information about the work of the APU is available from the Department of Education and Science, Information Division, Room 2/11, Elizabeth House, York road, London SE1 7PH.

References

Cochran, W G (1977). *Sampling techniques.* New York: Wiley.

Comber, L C and Keeves, J P (1973). *Science education in nineteen countries: an empirical study.* Stockholm: Almqvist and Wiksell, and New York: Wiley.

Davie, R, Butler, N and Goldstein, H (1972). *From birth to seven.* London: Longman.

Deming, W E (1960). *Sample design in business research.* New York: Wiley.

DES (1975) *A language for life.* The Bullock Report. London: HMSO.

DES (1979) *Aspects of secondary education in England.* A survey by HM Inspectors of Schools. London: HMSO.

DES (1981a) *APU Science in schools.* Age 11: Report No. 1. London: HMSO.

DES (1981b) *Mathematical development.* Secondary Survey Report No. 2. London: HMSO.

Hansen, M H, Hurwitz, W N and Madow, W G (1953). *Sample survey methods and theory.* New York: Wiley.

Hobbs, E D, Boldt, W B, Erickson, G L, Quelch, T P and Sieben, G A (1978). *British Columbia science assessment.* Summary Report to British Columbia Ministry of Education.

Kish, L (1965) *Survey sampling.* New York: Wiley.

NAEP (1977) *Science technical report: summary volume.* Washington Education Commission of the States.

Nie, N H, Hadlai Hull, C, Jenkins, J G, Steinbrenner, K and Bent, D H (1975). *Statistical package for the social sciences.* New York: McGraw Hill.

Rutter, M, Maughan, B, Mortimore, P and Ouston, J (1979). *Fifteen thousand hours.* London: Open Books.

Printed in England for Her Majesty's Stationery Office by Commercial Colour Press, London E.7.
Dd.717183 C30 6/82